Philosophical
Perspectives
on
Language

Philosophical Perspectives on Language

Robert J. Stainton

broadview press

Cataloguing in Publication Data

Stainton, Robert J., 1964-
   Philosophical perspectives on language

Includes bibliographical references and index.
ISBN 1-55111-086-5

I. Language and languages — Philosophy. I. Title.

P106.S73 1996   401   C96-930156-1

Broadview Press gratefully acknowledges the support of the Canada Council, the Ontario Arts Council, and the Ministry of Canadian Heritage.

Broadview Press Ltd. is an independent, international publishing house, incorporated in 1985.

North America:

PO Box 1243, Peterborough Ontario, Canada K9J 7H5

3576 California Road, Orchard Park NY USA 14127

phone, fax and e-mail addresses for North America: (705) 743-8990 (phone); (705) 743-8353 (fax); 75322.44@COMPUSERVE.COM

UK and Europe:

BRAD (Book Representation and Distribution Ltd.)

244a London Rd., Hadleigh, Essex ENGLAND   SS7 2DE (1702) 552912

Australia:

St. Clair Press, PO Box 287, Rozelle NSW 2039 (02)818 1942

elsewhere:

Please order through local wholesalers or direct from North America.

PRINTED IN CANADA

Contents

Acknowledgements

To begin with, I'm grateful to the following for comments on earlier drafts: Arshia Asudeh, Andrew Botterell, Andy Brook, Tim Kenyon, Robert Martin, Kate Talmage, Stephen Talmage, Daniel Stoljar and Todd Verge. Thanks also to two anonymous reviewers.

I'd also like to thank my various instructors for feeding my fascination with mind and language. In particular, I'm indebted to Richard Cartwright, Noam Chomsky, Lenny Clapp, Chris Collins, Lynd Forguson, Michael Gregory, Ken Hale, Irene Heim, James Higginbotham, Ann and Nollaig MacKenzie, Robert Stalnaker and Daniel Stoljar (again). Most of all, I would like once again to express my enormous intellectual debt to Sylvain Bromberger, teacher and friend.

Finally, I'd like to recognize Nada Khirdaji, for her enormous help in typing the first draft. Most of all, thanks to Anita Kothari, for unfailing support, and for keeping me human.

The writing of this book was supported by the Social Science and Humanities Research Council of Canada, and by an award from Carleton University's Research and Publication Fund.

Preface

Philosophical theorizing about language has evolved considerably in the last two decades. There has been an increasing emphasis on empirical work, multiple shifts in focus, and a renewed convergence with philosophy of mind, formal semantics and logic. This book reflects these changes. First, it contains a reasonable amount of linguistics proper, since it is my view that an adequate philosophical understanding of language requires some basic familiarity with the relevant empirical work. In particular, the book presents— at an introductory level—background material in syntax and formal semantics. Second, the book draws out connections between language and mind: language learning, the language of thought hypothesis, the psychological reality of grammars, and so on.

Its attention to what's current is one distinctive feature of this book. Another is that it is organized around one general theme: language as a system of symbols which is known and used. I have felt dissatisfied with some currently available texts precisely because they present philosophy of language as a collection of (at best) loosely related topics: speech acts, demonstratives, sense and reference, truth and meaning, etc. Pedagogically, this can be disastrous. Students become quickly mired in the details and soon lose their footing—and their interest. At the same time, I have tried to avoid the equally unhappy alternative of offering a coherent treatment, but one which is overly narrow or one-sided.

A third distinguishing mark: the book targets upper level undergraduates who have some background in philosophy, but not an extensive training. Other texts that I am familiar with are either too introductory for this level, or are better suited to advanced students.

Those are, I think, all positives. Now for the negatives: in trying to stick to my theme, I've found it impossible to offer a comprehensive treatment of the topics in this area. Despite their importance, many issues (e.g. proper names and rigid designation, externalism, analyticity, natural kind terms, situation semantics, presupposition) are discussed only briefly or not at all.

Also, where necessary to make things clearer and more concise, I have sometimes chosen to shape and mould views taken from a given author. (Some may say I've bent and broken them. I hope not.) Furthermore, in attempting to provide an overview of what is current in philosophy of language, I have regularly omitted issues which are now, for better or worse, principally of historical interest. For these reasons, the book should under no circumstances be read as intellectual history, let alone as strict philosophical exegesis.

To my teachers, friends and family

Chapter One:

Introduction

1. Three Perspectives on Language

Repeat after me: language is a system of symbols which we know and use. This is the theme of the book. Only eleven words long: you can't complain about that. Spinning out this theme, however, requires quite a bit more time. Indeed, it requires the whole book. But allow me to say a bit more about it now.

The theme has three parts: that language is a system, that it's known, and that it's used. These are, if you will, three different perspectives on language.

Perspective One: Language as a system of symbols
Perspective Two: Language as something we know
Perspective Three: Language as something we use

The book is organized around these three perspectives: one part for each. Following the Introduction, I turn immediately to the system perspective, then it's the knowledge perspective, beginning at Chapter Six. I end with the use perspective. My overall aim is to flesh out each perspective (fill in the details, consider problems and objections, etc.) and then try to indicate, at the end, how these various approaches can be combined into a comprehensive picture.

Along with the three perspectives on language, there are three corresponding **theories of meaning.** For many philosophers, meaning derives from a relationship between sounds (and punctuation marks and so on) and *things in the world*. 'Cat' means what it does because it picks out a particular kind of object. Namely, cats. Others think of meaning as deriving from a relationship between sounds and *things in the mind*. 'Cat' gets its meaning from catty thoughts or catty images. Both these views have been around for a long time. A more recent suggestion is that a sound's meaning comes from its *use*, not from its relationship to objects in the world, or to ideas in the mind. A lot of this book will be dedicated to spelling out these competing theories of meaning, and seeing whether they can be combined into a single coherent picture.

2. Who Cares?

Some have called philosophy of language dry. I disagree; I think it's deeply fascinating. In part because the material itself is rich and intellectually challenging, but also because an adequate view of language is so important. Still, arguments in philosophy of language can be difficult and technical. So, by way of motivating you, let me say a little about the centrality of language. What I'm going to suggest is that language is related to human action, thought, and culture. And it has an important role to play in philosophizing. This discussion really deserves a book to itself, so my treatment will be pretty sketchy.

First reason why language is important: it lies at the heart of human activity. Just look at all the things people *do* with language. Here's the most obvious language-based endeavour: people communicate in language. This includes idle chat—telling stories, jokes, commenting on daily happenings—as well as exchanging vital information, even across generations. But communicating information is just one of the things done with language. There are many others. People get married in language (I say 'I will' in the right circumstances, and thereby make myself wed), people organize themselves in language, buy and sell in language (Fran says 'Two bucks', Akira says 'Done'), and work in language. They insult, complain, threaten and promise in language. Indeed, it's hard to think of activities which *don't* involve language in some way.

Second reason why language is important: there's some kind of connection between language and thought. The exact nature of the connection is exceedingly controversial. But even those who deny that the connections are substantial or important need to explore the nature of language—if only to rebut the views of the other side. And the other side makes some startling claims: it is sometimes said, for example, that language is *the* "vehicle of thought": that all thought occurs in language. This seems too strong, at least at first glance. For one thing, it seems that animals and pre-linguistic infants exhibit some kind of thought, even though they lack language. For another thing, there are thought processes that just don't seem linguistic: people apparently think about stuff for which they have no words, many people claim to "think in pictures", and so on.

Nevertheless, the idea that there's *no* connection between thought and language seems equally implausible. First, there's plenty of introspective evidence of a connection. If you know at least two languages, you will be familiar with the phenomenon of "switching" the language in which you're thinking. But even unilinguals can be aware of "talking to themselves" silently—thinking things through in their native tongue. Second, that language at least *facilitates* thought seems obvious. Consider, for example, the thoughts that:

(1)
(a) If particle accelerators cost several million U.S. dollars, and Uruguay doesn't have that kind of money to spend, then Uruguay will not buy any particle accelerators
(b) Grunge was really hip until Kurt Cobain died

A person without language—or a person whose language lacked the phrase 'particle accelerator', the word 'million' and the word 'dollar'—simply could not have the first thought. It's just too complicated. (Imagine trying to explain this claim to someone who didn't know any terms dealing with physics or the U.S. monetary system. Imagine doing it without introducing such terms!) The second thought is at least as complex. But it also illustrates another problem. It is a thought *about Kurt Cobain*, not about (say) Jim Morrison. And it's about grunge, not about hip-hop. And too: a thinker who has no direct link to Kurt Cobain can nevertheless have this thought—presumably because she has a word which refers to Kurt Cobain. Put roughly, thoughts are about things, and you can't have a thought about a thing unless you have the right kind of "connection" with it. Language sometimes provides that connection.

This is all pretty vague. But it illustrates a line of argument that links thought to language. And some linguists and philosophers have been enormously impressed by these links. Here's why: it has just been claimed, in effect, that the language a person thinks in shapes the thoughts she does have and can have. If this is right, what people think about the world around them will depend upon what language they speak! Here's a famous example. It's often alleged that the Inuit have lots of different words for snow. As the story goes, they've got a word which means wet snow, and a word which means hard snow, and so on. So, the claim runs, when an Inuit sees what English speakers call 'snow', they see something different than English speakers do. The latter just see snow. But an Inuit sees either wet snow, or hard snow, or whatever. If this is right, the bonds between language and thought are very intimate indeed.

In fact, it turns out that Inuit languages have about as many words for snow as English does.[1] Moreover, it's a matter of considerable debate what would follow if a language *did* have many words for snow. In the end, I'm personally sceptical about these kinds of arguments. But, whether or not they're sound, they're certainly interesting. At the very least they deserve a rebuttal. Hence, they make the study of language of great interest.

I've said: language is important because it is related to thought and action. But it's not just individuals, it's also communities which speak languages. And this provides the third connection, between language and culture. It's tempting to suppose that a group's language reflects its collective history and learning. Looking again at the snow example, an anthropologist might conclude that a language which contains many words for snow does so for good reason: because snow plays an important part in the daily life of the language users. In general, one might think, the way a people lives (and has lived) indelibly shapes their language; just as, it's sometimes supposed, their language shapes the way they live. In which case, language and culture are closely connected. (Whether language and culture really *are* closely related, there's no question that people *believe* they are. It's because of this belief that nationalist politicians write language preservation laws, for instance.)

These are some of the reasons—some good, some rather dubious—why language has become central in the humanities, the social sciences, and elsewhere. But why should *philosophers* care about it? Well, on the one hand, they care about thought, action, and culture. Hence they may be concerned to explore—or deny—the various connections hinted at above. But there is another reason why philosophers in particular are interested in language: some of them think of language as providing, if not solutions, at least insights into traditional philosophical problems. Some—Michael Dummett (1991, 1994) for example—even suppose philosophy of language to be *first philosophy*: the ground on which everything else is built. Let me briefly explain.

Some philosophers claim that instead of asking about goodness, justice, the will, truth, or knowledge—all traditional philosophical issues—one should instead ask about the meaning of the word 'goodness', or the meaning of the word 'justice', or the meaning of the verb 'to know'. These questions are easier, it might be thought. Hence, pursuing them offers greater promise of new insight into hitherto resistant philosophical problems. Another leading idea is that studying language will allow philosophers to *dissolve*, rather than solve, philosophical problems. For, when you look at how words are actually used, it turns out that philosophically loaded words are seldom employed in the common tongue in the way traditional philosophy has used them. In which case, you might conclude, traditional philosophers have been *misusing* language. (An example: it's been suggested that to even *ask* 'How do I know that I exist?' is to misuse the verb 'know'. The question, therefore, is literally meaningless—and needs no reply.)

Here's a different sort of example of dissolving problems. Suppose I tell you that Santa Claus doesn't exist. Fair enough, right? Okay, but *who* is it that doesn't exist? Who is being talked about here? Well, Santa Claus. You mean *that guy*? The guy that supposedly doesn't exist? Maybe you see the problem. It looks like one is talking about an object, and attributing a property—namely, not existing—to that object. But if it's an *object*, an object which has properties, then it must exist! So, to say that Santa Claus doesn't exist is contradictory nonsense. A philosophical puzzle. But one that—it's been claimed—can be dissolved by linguistic analysis. The problem arises, it's been suggested, from taking (2) to be a sentence of **subject-predicate form**, on a par with (3):

(2) Santa Claus does not exist
(3) John is tall

That is, it's supposed that sentence (2) has as its subject the word 'Santa Claus' (which presumably denotes some individual) and has as its predicate 'does not exist' (which, you might think, picks out that property had by all the things which don't exist). Consequently, it's reasoned, the sentence as a whole says that this object Santa Claus has this special property. In which case, this object *must* exist—else it could have no properties. In which case, (2) cannot be true. A step towards a solution is to recognize that sentence (2) is not of subject-predicate form. That is, the sentence 'Santa Claus does not exist' doesn't correspond to the attribution of some property to some object. (I don't mean to suggest that this is a satisfactory solution to the problem. Here again, I want simply to illustrate how work on language can impinge upon philosophical debates.)

To sum up, then: language is important for a variety of reasons. It is related—somehow—to action, thought and culture; and it's a source of insights about philosophical puzzles. Nor are these the only sources of language's intellectual interest. It's my hope, however, that this brief list will whet your appetites for what is to come, and will furnish a context for some of the more technical issues that follow. Speaking of which, it's time to turn to the philosophy of language.

3. Some Terminology

So much for fun. I'll end this chapter with a bit of terminology. Throughout the book, you'll encounter the **type-token** distinction. It's not easy to define effectively, so let me introduce it by way of example. Notice that the word 'letter' is ambiguous. For instance, suppose I hold up a sign with 'AAA' on it. Now consider: how many letters appear on the sign? You might say that there are three: the one on the left, the one in the middle and the one on the right. On the other hand, you might equally correctly reply that there's only one letter on the sign: the first letter of the alphabet. The reason both answers are correct is that there isn't one question here. Rather, there are two: one for each meaning of the word 'letter'.

To mark the difference between these two meanings of 'letter', philosophers of language distinguish **letter tokens** from **letter types**. What appears on the sign is a single letter type—the letter type A. But three tokens of it. There aren't just tokens and types of *letters*, of course. There are also word types and word tokens, sentence types and sentence tokens. Examples follow:

(4)
(a) apple, apple, apple, apple, apple [Five tokens of a single word type]
(b) The apple is red. The apple is red. The apple is red. [Three tokens of a single sentence type]

Similarly, suppose a man owns three copies of *War and Peace*, and no other books. How many books does he have? Well, he has one book type, but three tokens of it.[2]

This distinction may not hit you right away. But, as it appears again and again, it will eventually become natural. For the moment, remember this: a language like English is made up of *types*, not of *tokens*. When people ask, for example, how many words there are in English, they are asking how many word *types* there are.[3] To get a good idea of how many word types English contains, one could consult a good dictionary. On the other hand—practically speaking, anyway—it's impossible to know how many English word *tokens* there are; we'd have to catalogue every English utterance, by any person, anywhere, at any time. Not to mention checking every copy of every book, film or computer disk in English. Besides, the class of English word tokens literally changes from one utterance to the next. Not so the class of English word types. That remains fairly constant.

So much for the type-token distinction. There's another essential distinction that will come up repeatedly. This one should be easier to keep in mind. The distinction is between expressions, symbols, signs, etc. and the **referents** of those expressions, symbols and signs. One must distinguish, for example, the word 'water' from water; similarly, there's a big difference between the name 'Kurt Cobain' and the bearer of that name. Water will make you wet; 'water' won't. Kurt Cobain died, but 'Kurt Cobain' didn't, and couldn't.

Here's a related notational convention. When an expression appears in quotation marks, it is **mentioned**, rather than **used**; that is, the thing being referred to is *the expression* (sign or symbol) inside the quotation marks. For instance, the expression in (5a) refers to *the name* of an ex-Prime Minister of Canada, whereas the expression in (5b) refers to the person, not the name.

(5)
(a) 'Kim Campbell'
(b) Kim Campbell

Here are three examples of mixing up the expression with the thing—all of which I've actually seen.

(6)
(a) John is spelled with an h

(b) 'Jesus' is lord

(c) No 'shirt', no 'shoes', no 'service'

I'm not sure whether it even makes sense to say that some guy is spelled with an h, but if it makes sense, it certainly isn't *true*. What is true is that:

(7) 'John' is spelled with an h

And, regardless of your religious preference, you surely don't believe that the *name* 'Jesus' is lord. What you might believe is sentence (8):

(8) Jesus is lord

Finally, I doubt whether, when going into a restaurant, you hope for 'service'. What you want is service. Nor does the restaurant management really want you to bring along the words 'shirt' and 'shoes'; instead, they expect you to have a shirt and shoes. (And, though the sign doesn't say as much, the management expects you to *wear*, rather than carry, the shirt and shoes!)

This is the use-mention distinction. One final complication, which you've probably clued into already: single quotation marks aren't the only way to mention an expression. An expression may also be mentioned, rather than used, by off-setting it in the text. So, for instance, I just mentioned the sentence 'Jesus is lord' by putting an example number beside it.

Notational Conventions

Where it might not be obvious that I refer only to the meaning of an expression, meanings appear all in capitals. As discussed above, expressions which are mentioned appear in single quotes. Thus 'cerebro' stands for a Spanish word, whose meaning is BRAIN. This meaning is shared by 'brain'. Double quotes are reserved for direct quotation and so-called scare quotes. Emphasis is indicated by italics, while bold face is used to introduce unfamiliar or technical terms, like **mention**. Speaking of which: it will sometimes happen that a word or phrase appears in the text *before* being explained. When this occurs, read ahead: don't retrace your steps, unless your confusion persists for several paragraphs.

Following standard practice in linguistics, ungrammatical sentences are marked with an asterisk, as in (9).

(9) *The child seems

Example expressions in languages other than English are glossed first, and then translated. For example:

(10) Está   lloviendo
     Is-*3rd-singular* raining
     It's   raining

Note, however, that none of these conventions are applied within material quoted from other sources: I prefer to preserve the cited author's notation. I also leave their examples untouched, even though some of them now have an antiquated ring (e.g. "I met a man" rather than "I met a person").

Suggested Readings

For more on language as activity, see J.L. Austin's (1961) paper "Performative Utterances". John Searle (1965) builds on Austin's work, dealing specifically with promising. In linguistics, try M.A.K. Halliday's (1978) *Language as Social Semiotic*. A brief introduction to his views can be found in Halliday 1984.

There is an enormous literature on language and thought. The view that they are intimately related is defended in Davidson 1975 and Harman 1970. For arguments that language actually *influences* thought, see Whorf 1956. Pinker's (1994) *The Language Instinct*—an introductory survey of things linguistic—goes in precisely the opposite direction, suggesting that thought and ordinary language are quite independent. See especially the chapter called 'Mentalese'. Gareth Evans (1982) argues that thought is importantly prior to language in many cases, and inveighs against moving too quickly from the nature of language to the nature of mind. (He also provides a fascinating discussion of the ability to think about unfamiliar individuals.) Related themes appear in Jerry Fodor's (1975) *The Language of Thought* and his (1987a) "Why there still has to be a language of thought".

There are a number of introductory books on language and philosophy. W.P. Alston's (1964) *Philosophy of Language* is a useful summary of language's role in metaphysics, logic, epistemology, and elsewhere. It's a bit dated, though. Ian Hacking's (1975) *Why Does Language Matter to Philosophy?* is also useful and readable. Michael Dummett's (1994) *Origins of Analytical Philosophy* is more difficult, but very worthwhile. A gem, in fact. As a general introduction, Blackburn 1984, Davis 1976, Devitt and Sterelny 1987, and Platts 1979 are difficult but quite good. They can also help with the terminology, as can the Introduction to Martinich 1990. Robert Martin's (1987) *The Meaning of Language* is a very fine, though elementary, introduction. This book owes a lot to it.

Part One:
The System Perspective

Chapter Two:

Syntax

1. Introduction

I said: language is a system of symbols which we know and use. Considered as a system of symbols, a language can be looked at from three points of view: the phonological, the syntactic, and the semantic. Phonology is that branch of linguistics concerned (very roughly) with how a language *sounds*. Syntax describes how sentences and other compound expressions are built up out of words and other simple terms; how sentences are *structured*. Semantics deals with what simple and compound expressions *mean*.

In the chapters to come, I'll spend a lot of time on semantics. But—by way of background, and as a point of reference that will come up repeatedly—I'll use this chapter to introduce some basic syntax. I've decided to skip phonology. Sorry.

2. Option One: Rule Systems

Painted very broadly, one way of describing a language's syntax is to provide a rule system. The rules in question are like the instructions for putting together parts of a bicycle. They tell you what the parts are, and how they fit together. For example:

(11) *Grossly Simplified Rule System*
(a) Noun Phrase → Article + Noun [Read: A noun phrase consists of an article followed by a noun]
(b) Article → 'the', 'a' [Read: 'the' and 'a' are articles]
(c) Noun → 'boat', 'apple' [Read: 'boat' and 'apple' are nouns]

Having these rules at your disposal, you can "build" Noun Phrases (NPs).[4] For instance: choose an article word, say 'the'; now select a noun, say 'boat'. Now put them together, using the rule in (11a), and you get 'the boat'.

This Grossly Simplified Rule System captures only an exceedingly tiny part of English. There are, self-evidently, other kinds of Noun Phrases (e.g. 'Queen Mary', 'Canada', 'Seven women'), not to mention other categories of phrases and words. For instance, English contains verbs ('run', 'smoke', and thousands of others). And verbs can combine together with adverbs ('quickly', 'foolishly' and many many more) to form Verb Phrases ('run quickly', 'smoke foolishly'). Notice too that these complexes can combine together yet again. One can, for example, build a sentence (abbreviated as S) out of the Noun Phrase 'The boy' and the Verb Phrase 'runs quickly'. The result—described in a **syntactic tree** that highlights the grammatical categories of the minimal elements, and how they combine—looks like this:

(12)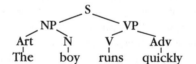

So, to fill out the Grossly Simplified Rule System, I have added rules for verbs, adverbs, verb phrases, and sentences. The result, still utterly inadequate, appears below (I have used abbreviations, as syntacticians are wont to do):

(13) *Somewhat Less Grossly Simplified Rule System*
(a) NP → Art + N
(b) VP → V + Adv
(c) S → NP + VP
(d) Art → 'the', 'a'
(e) N → 'boat', 'apple'
(f) V → 'run', 'smoke'
(g) Adv → 'quickly', 'foolishly'

This still isn't enough, of course. To construct a total rule-based grammar for English, I would have to complete the list of verbs, adverbs, nouns and articles. And account for the other categories of minimal expressions—including prepositions ('to', 'on', 'at', and dozens more), adjectives ('tall', 'quiet', and so on), and others. Furthermore, the rules of combination, as given, are far too simple. All these various minimal expressions can be combined and re-combined in very complex ways that, for the most part, aren't important for present purposes.

Nevertheless, I do want to introduce one complication. It will be very important in what follows. The rule system as it stands is **compositional**. That is, complex expressions are "composed of" (i.e. "built up from") minimal parts, and the nature of a complex linguistic expression is exhaustively determined by what its parts are, and how they're arranged. Compositionality is important. But the system also has to be **recursive**. In this context, that means that the outputs of a rule can also serve as inputs to it. So, for example, here is a recursive rule:

(14) S → S + 'and' + S

This rule says that you can form a sentence by placing the word 'and' between two sentences. And this is certainly the case. Consider sentence (15), whose tree is given in (16).

(15) John smokes and Ann drinks

(16)

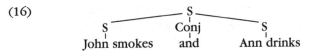

But now the sentence 'John smokes and Ann drinks' can serve as an *input* to the rule in (14). It can be combined with another sentence, and end up as a part in a larger whole, as in 'John smokes and Ann drinks and Rover barks'. The tree for that mouthful appears below:

(17)

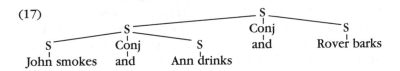

This, then, is how a rule system works. There are specific rules which introduce minimal elements. And specific rules which say how to combine those elements—rules which typically take as inputs their very own outputs. Importantly, rule systems with a finite number of minimal elements and a finite number of rules can generate an unlimited number of outputs—if the rules are compositional and recursive. That's because, in such a system, each output can serve as a source of a still-more-complex structure. Which means that knowledge of this finite rule set suffices for understanding an unlimited number of sentences! (Crude comparison: imagine a body-shop that can both build cars, and add gadgets to any existing car. Is there, in principle, a maximum number of gadgets that this shop's car-creations could have? No. Because any car which comes out of the shop can be re-introduced at will—and have yet another gadget attached. Such a body-shop would be "recursive" in some sense.) Rule systems are one way of doing syntax. Maybe even the most popular way. But they're not the only way.

3. Option Two: Principles and Parameters

In the 1970's, many linguists became dissatisfied with the just-described way of doing syntax. The reason: even if one could write rules which generate every complex expression of English, "we would always want to know why we have these kinds of rules and not others" (Chomsky 1990, 520). That is, linguists want an *explanation* of why a language is the way it is—why it contains certain rules, and not others. They don't just want a mere *description* of the language, however accurate. And that's what rule systems basically are: descriptions. (Compare: it's not enough to know, of a series of liquids, what their boiling points are. One also wants to know the underlying generalization—a generalization about molecular bonds, kinetic energy, and who-knows-what—which *explains* these facts. Rule systems miss the corresponding deeper generalizations about languages.) This dissatisfaction with the rule system approach led some linguists to adopt a **principles and parameters approach**. (For some interesting historical background, see Harris 1993.)

A syntax for a language, on this approach, doesn't focus on specific rules, but rather on general principles. To borrow a phrase from Pinker 1994, principles are "super rules", general guidelines rather than exact blueprints, very sweeping laws that apply to *all* human languages. The specific rules are supposed to flow out of these principles; the principles thus explain why the language has certain rules, rather than any others.

An example might help. There are lots of principles that linguists have proposed, but most of them require too much background to describe in a book like this. Here's one which isn't too technical.

(18) *The Structure Dependence Principle*: All grammatical rules are structure dependent.

What this means is, there aren't any rules of combination which ignore structure. All rules of syntax, in all languages, refer to at least one of the following:

(19)
(a) modification relations
(b) phrase structure
(c) syntactic categories (e.g. Noun vs. Verb)
(d) c-command, etc.[5]

No language yet studied violates this principle.

Isn't this principle vacuous? No. It disallows rules that apply solely on the basis of word order, for example. And this is more than a little surprising. To take specific cases, the structure dependence principle disallows rules like (20 a-b), favouring instead the rules (21 a-b).

(20) *Rules not observed*
(a) *Fake Rule 1*: Invert the first and second word in a declarative sentence to form a question.
(b) *Fake Rule 2*: Delete every third word, if its meaning can be recovered.

(21) *Rules actually observed*
(a) *Actual Rule 1* (Sub/aux inversion): Invert the subject and the auxiliary verb of a declarative sentence to form a question.
(b) *Actual Rule 2* (VP Ellipsis): Delete the Verb Phrase, leaving the auxiliary verb, if the meaning can be recovered.

The Fake Rules are simple. It's easy enough to understand how these rules would work. Fake Rule 1 would allow you to take (22a) and convert it into (22b) by inverting 'this' and 'guy'. The resulting sentence would, in the imagined language, be interrogative.

(22)
(a) This guy doesn't smoke
(b) Guy this doesn't smoke?

Fake Rule 2 would permit the deletion of the third and sixth words of (23a), since the meaning of the whole sentence would be fully recoverable. The result is given in (23b).

(23)
(a) He lives at the corner of Bank and Glebe streets
(b) He lives the corner Bank and Glebe streets

Using these rules wouldn't impede communication. But no known language displays these rules—or even anything like them— because they disobey the structure dependence principle: they make reference only to word order, not to modification relations, phrase structure, c-command or any other structural relation. (Facts of this kind will loom large when I turn to arguments for innateness.) In sum: a principle is a very general law that applies to all languages, the structure dependence principle being one example. Principles are universal, common to every human language.

But, obviously, languages differ. For one thing, they have different minimal parts—different words. (English has 'cheese', French has 'fromage', Spanish has 'queso'.) Which means that, to get the syntax of a particular language, a **lexicon** for that language must be included, a kind of dictionary or list of words (though one which notes the words' syntactic categories). You already saw an example of that:

(24)
(a) N → 'boat', 'apple'
(b) V →'run', 'smoke'
(c) Adv →'quickly', 'foolishly'

And lexical differences—variation in the minimal elements—aren't the only differences between languages: the means of combination aren't wholly uniform either. Hence, linguists must allow for some variation here as well. They do so by introducing **parameters**: basically, principles with some minimal amount of optionality. To give a simple analogy: in every country, there is a law to the effect that one must drive on only one side of the road. This is a principle. But there is some variation from country to country as to *which side that is*. In some places you drive on the left, in some you drive on the right. The choice of side is a parameter.

One example of a linguistic parameter is the so-called **pro-drop parameter**. You may know that in Latin, Italian, and Spanish (among other languages), speakers can optionally delete the grammatical subject of a sentence. The following Spanish sentences, for instance, are perfectly okay—even though they have no grammatical subjects.[6]

(25)
(a) Está   lloviendo
    Is-*3rd-singular* raining
    It's   raining

(b) ¿Estás   loco?
    Are-*2nd-singular* crazy
    Are you   crazy?

Leaving out the subject in English, however, results in ill-formed sentences. Compare the Spanish (25a) and (25b) to the following English counterparts:

(26)
(a) *Is raining
(b) *Are crazy?

This is a parameter: *can* versus *cannot* optionally delete the subject phrase. Spanish sets this "switch" to *can*; English sets it to *cannot*. Taking a principles and parameters approach, one describes a language by noting which way it sets each of the (rather small) bank of switches—not by giving a whole host of construction-specific rules, exhibited only by the language in question.

To sum up, then: a syntax of a language describes how minimal units combine together into larger wholes. There are two ways of doing this. One is to give quite specific rules. The other is to give very general principles, some parameters, and a lexicon—from these three, specific rules may be derived.[7] Syntax is one component of the system perspective. Another—one I put aside—is phonology. The final component, semantics, will occupy the next two chapters.

Rules or Sets?

I pause to introduce an important contrast. You've just seen two conceptions of what a *description* of a language will look like: specific rules or general parameters. These are options for syntactic *theories*. I now want to contrast two conceptions of language, rather than two conceptions of language theory.

Let me begin by putting one conception aside, for the moment. Chomsky (1990) labels it the **common sense conception**. To retell an old joke: a language, on this conception, is just a dialect plus an army. Authority and class structure, norms of correct usage and language academies all play a part in this picture of language. But, Chomsky says, this concept "is not designed for inquiry into the nature of language" (1990, 509). Common sense may hold that, for example, the Southern U.S. pronunciation of 'anti' is wrong. (They say 'ant-*eye*'. What's "right" is 'ant-*e*'). It may urge that 'livid' means PALE—rather than FLUSHED, or RED—even though few English speakers recognize this. It may say that a sentence cannot begin with 'and'. But, as will shortly emerge in the discussion of prescriptive grammar, scientifically-minded linguists don't have much time for these folk views. As Chomsky puts it, "whatever all this might mean, it plainly has nothing to do with an eventual science of language..." (1990, 509. See also Chomsky 1986, Ch. 2.)

Having eschewed the common sense conception, Chomsky suggests adopting instead some technical notion, just as one does in theoretical inquiry generally. (E.g. in evolutionary biology, what one means by 'fitness' has little to do with what ordinary speakers mean by this word. Ditto for 'force' and 'spin' in physics.) Chomsky considers, as candidate technical notions of language, the **E-language** and **I-language** conceptions. For present purposes, the E-language conception has it that a language is **extensional**, in the sense that a language is a *set* of some kind. Treating a language as extensional, one might take it to be a set of well-formed utterances, as Bloomfield (1926) did. Or one might think of a language as a set of sound-meaning pairs, as David Lewis (1975) does. According to the I-language conception, on the other hand, a language is **intensional** in the sense that, instead of being a set of elements, a language is a series of specific rules or general principles and parameters. These rules determine (i.e. **generate**) sets. But the set of expressions which a language generates is not, Chomsky says, the same as the language itself.

A comparison may help. You can imagine someone saying that the game of chess is defined by all the legal board positions. And someone else responding: no, chess is defined by its rules of play. These rules of play do indeed *determine* which board positions are possible and which are not, but this is a by-product. The first is an E-chess view: chess is a set of elements (here, board positions); while the second is an I-chess view: chess is a collection of rules which *determine* this set of elements. Chomsky thinks the I-language conception, not the E-language conception, is the most promising candidate for the technical notion of "language"—at least for work in syntax. Allow me to explain why.

According to the E-language picture, a language is a set. This strikes Chomsky as a weakness. Consider **semi-grammatical sentences** such as (27)—where '?' indicates the oddness of the sentence.

(27) ?The child seems sleeping

Chomsky asks: is this sentence in the language or outside it? The right answer seems to be neither unequivocally 'yes' nor unequivocally 'no': this linguistic string seems to be "inside the language", because it has a definite meaning; however, it seems also to be "outside the language", because it is not entirely well-formed. In effect, (27) obeys certain rules, but not others. Chomsky says that this statement, though correct, isn't one which the E-language conception of language allows. Talk of being slightly ill-formed versus completely ungrammatical is natural enough—assuming perfect grammaticality amounts to violating no rules, minor ungrammaticality amounts to violating one inessential rule, and complete ungrammaticality amounts to disobeying one or more very central rules. But only the I-language perspective allows mention of rules in the characterization of grammaticality—the E-language conception only permits talk of one set (i.e. "the language") and its complement. For this reason, Chomsky favours the I-language conception.

A related point: in the science of language, one wants to mark *grades* of well-formedness. Saying which symbols are perfectly well-formed—i.e. in the set—and which are not is insufficient. An example: (28a) and (28b) are both ill-formed. But (28a) is significantly better than (28b).

(28)
(a) *John wants that himself leave
(b) **John the at

Here too, the E-language conception is impoverished, because it can say exactly one thing—and the very same thing—about both (28a) and (28b): that they are not in the set called 'English'. Once again, the I-language approach fares better. An I-language will determine, for each ill-formed expression, whether it violates a single rule or several rules, and whether it violates an important and central principle, or some inessential "surface rule". Which means that, unlike the E-language conception, the I-language construct permits, in a quite natural way, talk of graded ill-formedness.

Here's another case where the set approach proves descriptively impoverished. Speakers of English and Japanese differ about how they hear sentences of unfamiliar languages. They may even differ in how they hear mere noises. But the E-language conception has no resources for distinguishing between Japanese and English speakers on these fronts. All an E-language proponent can say is: "The set called 'English' contains neither sentences of (say) Hindi, nor noises of type N; similarly, the set called 'Japanese' also fails to contain these things". The I-language conception fares significantly better here. Since it equates a language with a bunch of *rules*, which apply blindly to any input, the language can

> assign a status to a vast range of physical events, including the utterance "John seems to be sleeping", the utterance "John seems sleeping", a sentence of Hindi, and probably the squeaking of a door, if we could do careful enough experiments to show how speakers of English and Japanese might differ in the way they "hear" this noise (Chomsky 1990, 513).

In short: taking language to be a series of rules (i.e. an I-language) allows one to describe a speaker's propensities in a way that adopting the set-of-expressions (i.e. the E-language) approach cannot. Hence the I-language conception is superior.

Here's a deeper problem for the E-language conception: the problem of **extensionally equivalent grammars**. Any set of linguistic items (utterances or expressions) can be characterized in many different ways. This is merely the application of a fact about sets generally: for *any* set, there are lots of distinct ways of describing it. Take, as an example, the set in (29).

(29) {1,2,3}

There are very many ways of delineating this set. Here are three.

(30)
(a) The set consisting of the first three whole numbers
(b) The set consisting of 1^2, 1x2, and (1x2)+1
(c) The three-membered set of whole numbers whose sum is six

Just as (29) can be described in many different ways, so can any set. In which case, if a language is a set, then there exist any number of correct descriptions of each language. I will call a correct description of a language *L* a **descriptively adequate grammar** of *L*. And here comes the problem: if there are any number of descriptively adequate grammars which all capture a language *L*, which of these grammars is *the* right one? None of them looks like "*the* right one", since they're all right. Some are simpler, or more elegant, but none is more correct. In which case, linguistics becomes "weird science": unlike biology, physics and so on—where it makes sense to seek the unique right answer—in linguistics, pursuing a single right answer seems pointless. (See Quine 1972 for discussion.) A problem. And one which arises from taking languages to be sets of expressions, rather than rule systems. Here again, Chomsky thinks the I-language conception is preferable to the E-language alternative. He writes:

> The I-language L may be the one used by a speaker but not the I-language L', even if the two generate the same class of expressions...
> (Chomsky 1986, 23)

Chomsky concludes: "The source of all of these problems resides in an inappropriate choice of the basic concept..." (1990, 512). Instead of E-language, or the common sense concept of language, what's needed is I-language.[8] Chomsky's conclusion is controversial. It's not my intention to defend it. Instead, I simply wish to draw your attention to two ways of understanding the claim that language is a system of symbols. This claim may easily be construed as equating a language with a *set* of symbols. Language, so conceived, is extensional: an E-language. Alternatively, as I've just stressed, the system can be thought of as a system of *rules* for generating symbols. Taken as a body of rules, the system is intensional: an I-language. So, the slogan works either way.

4. Epilogue: Prescriptive and Descriptive Syntax

I want to end by stressing an important distinction—between **prescriptive** and **descriptive** syntax. This will also highlight some of the reasons why scientifically-minded linguists sometimes exhibit little patience for the common sense conception of language. To put it roughly: a prescriptive syntax for a language (or, as it's more commonly called, a prescriptive *grammar*) tells you how its users *ought* to speak, according to who-knows-what authoritative body; a descriptive grammar, on the other hand, details how people *actually* speak. In the view of most linguists, descriptive grammar isn't just a different topic—it's a better-motivated topic. Let me explain.

I start off with some examples of so-called "incorrect speech", just so you know what prescriptivists and descriptivists disagree about. (My discussion follows Pinker 1994.)

(31) *Examples of Incorrect Speech*

(SUPPOSEDLY) INCORRECT	(SUPPOSEDLY) CORRECT
(a) Hopefully, this talk will go well	It is hoped that this talk will go well
(b) Who did you meet?	Whom did you meet?
(c) I can't get no satisfaction	I can't get any satisfaction
(d) And Johnny came in	Johnny came in
(e) Me and Johnny love the movies	Johnny and I love the movies
(f) That's the song I'm tired of	That's the song of which I'm tired
(g) They want to boldly go	They want to go boldly

A *descriptive* grammar would simply state that the dialects actually spoken by typical North American Anglos include the expressions on the left-hand side. It would not judge as to the inherent quality of this dialect, nor try to impose a "better" dialect.

Moreover, descriptive linguists typically believe that attempts to impose "correct speech" are misguided: the rationale for such campaigns is, they insist, largely ill-founded. Some examples. You have, in all likelihood, heard the following complaints about "incorrect speech". A descriptive linguist might well call them "the usual suspects".

(32) *The Usual Suspects*

(a) *Suspect One*: Incorrect speech impedes clear thought and effective communication.

(b) *Suspect Two*: Incorrect speech is illogical.

(c) *Suspect Three*: Incorrect speech represents the decline of English and of standards generally.

In fact, says the descriptivist, each of these claims is dubious.

Suspect One presupposes a rather intimate link between language and thought. But there are good reasons to doubt that there is such a close connection. Animals and pre-linguistic infants don't have language, but they have thoughts; moreover, everyone is familiar with the sensation of looking for *le mot juste*—that is, having a thought but not having the words to capture it; and, there may even be ineffable thoughts, thoughts we simply *can't* put into words. So, insofar as language and thought are separate, using "incorrect" language may not affect thinking. Whether it does is certainly an open question.

As for achieving effective communication: in the first place, even if (31a) through (31g) are truly incorrect, they are perfectly understandable. What's more, even flatly ungrammatical sentences can be understood and used in effective communication. Consider, as examples, the sentences in (33). These are unquestionably incorrect in English. But they are fairly easy to understand.

(33) *Ungrammatical (But Interpretable) Sentences*

INCORRECT	CORRECT
(a) *The child seems sleeping	The child seems to be sleeping
(b) *Dats stoopid	That's stupid
(c) *Don't take your mother for granite	Don't take your mother for granted

In sum: the link between effective communication and so-called correct speech cannot be as tight as prescriptivists make it out to be.[9]

Suspect Two, that incorrect speech is illogical, is based on examples like (31c). Supposedly, this sentence is self-contradictory. But this claim is premised upon a misunderstanding of how language—particularly certain dialects of English—actually works. In many languages, including Middle English (the language of Chaucer) negation is expressed by *a pair of words*. French is like this. One says,

(34) Je *ne* t'aime *pas*

There are also, I'm told, languages in which negation is always expressed by a single word. And, obviously, there are languages which mix the two systems: Spanish is one such language; contemporary English is another. Some examples:

(35)
(a) <u>No</u> fumo [Single word negation in Spanish]
    Not smoke-*1st-singular*
    I don't smoke
(b) <u>No</u> tengo   <u>ningun</u> amigo
    [Pair of words negation in Spanish]
    Not have-*1st-singular*   none   friend
    I don't have any   friends

(36)

(a) I do*n't* smoke [Single word negation in English]

(b) I do*n't* have *any* friends [Pair of words negation in English]

French speakers and Middle English speakers are not less logical just because they use the pair-of-words system of negation. Nor are Spanish speakers and contemporary English speakers any less logical for using the mixed system. So, Suspect Two is implausible as well.

I turn, at last, to Suspect Three: the claim that incorrect speech represents the decline of English and of standards generally. Nobody can deny that English is changing. But is it *decaying*? Oddly, the people who think it is do not generally agree that their own usage is degenerate. And yet the English of the early twentieth century—the standard against which current English is often judged—is different from that of the 1800's. And even more different from the English of the 1700's and 1600's. English has been evolving rapidly since it was first spoken in the fourteenth century. And it will continue to change. But that's not necessarily a bad thing. Indeed, a language which remained perfectly static would cease to serve the needs of its speakers. How could speakers get along without new words like:

(37)

(a) Computer

(b) Download

(c) Microwave

Besides, many of the rules which speakers purportedly "break" aren't really part of English anyway. A little history is in order here. In the eighteenth century, London's dialect of English became a dominant language. Being a powerful person came to be associated with speaking this particular dialect. (Being stylish and cultivated required it, too.) This created a desire to learn London's dialect, which in turn created a demand for handbooks, style manuals, and grammar books. These were often written by grammarians who, until that time, had studied Latin. These grammarians found, to their displeasure, that English violated some of the rules of Latin. It became their sacred task to amend this "defect". Here are some examples:

In Latin, infinitives are single words. 'Amare', for example, means TO LOVE. Evidently, you can't put a modifier in the middle of a Latin infinitive—precisely because it's not a phrase, but a single word. In English, on the other hand, infinitives are made up of two items: 'to' and the verb stem. Now, the English rabble had the natural habit of "splitting" infinitives by interposing a modifier between these two words. Sentence (31g) is a contemporary example. And now for the historical curiosity: the folks who were writing the influential style manuals made it a new rule of English not to split infinitives. They imposed a totally artificial restriction on the grounds that some other language (namely Latin) had this rule. Another example. In Latin, you can't end a sentence with a preposition. But the placement of prepositions *in Latin* is irrelevant to English. Nevertheless, the handbook writers decided to outlaw preposition stranding in English. All of a sudden, by fiat, (31f) became ungrammatical. Given this, it's just perverse to insist that speaking English *as it was before this artificial imposition* represents a decline!

To sum up: so-called "improper speech" is not illogical, does not impede clear thought or communication, and does not threaten the language. For this reason, most empirical linguists think prescriptive grammar isn't just a different topic: it's a pretty shaky enterprise. In their view, lexicographers and grammarians should *report* the facts about what words mean and how words are combined together into sentences—they should not try to dictate these facts.[10] Whatever the merits of this conclusion, two lessons can be drawn. Lesson one: there's an important distinction between descriptive and prescriptive grammar. Very roughly, the former recounts what speakers do; the latter describes what, by some authority's lights, they *ought* to do. Lesson two: failing to follow the prescriptive rules won't make you an illogical or unclear thinker; nor will it render you unable to express yourself; still less will it bring down Western civilization. So, if prescriptive grammar is important, it's not for these reasons.

Suggested Readings

For a general overview of linguistics, see Fromkin and Rodman 1993. In addition, Pinker's (1994) *The Language Instinct* is a very lively and entertaining discussion of issues in and around linguistics. Classics in the "rule system" tradition include Chomsky 1957 and Lees 1960. Chomsky's (1965) *Aspects of the Theory of Syntax* may well be the high-water mark of this tradition. His enormous written corpus also includes two quite accessible book-length discussions of the principles and parameters approach. The first, Chomsky 1986, addresses issues in both linguistics and philosophy of language. The second, his (1988) *Language and Problems of Knowledge: The Managua Lectures*, is a thoroughly introductory discussion of generative linguistics. It explicitly introduces the pro-drop parameter. Chomsky's ideas are constantly evolving. Quite difficult but rewarding discussions of his more recent views appear in Chomsky 1993a, 1995 and Marantz 1995. For more on rules of phrase structure, see especially Jackendoff 1977, and Pinker 1994, Ch. 4. Andrew Radford's (1981) *Transformational Syntax* is a nice, elementary introduction to rule systems. His (1988) *Transformational Grammar* is an equally good elementary introduction to principles and parameters. There are several more advanced texts which adopt the principles and parameters framework, though they offer a corresponding increase in difficulty. They include Haegeman 1991 and Lasnik and Uriagereka 1988. My source for the discussion of prescriptive/descriptive syntax is Pinker 1994. It contains a much more complete treatment of the issues.

Chapter Three:

Direct Reference

1. Three Approaches to Meaning

Looked at from the system perspective, a well-formed linguistic expression combines (at least) a syntactic structure and a **meaning**. In the last chapter, I introduced the former. But what are meanings? Where do meanings "come from"? And what makes certain syntactic forms—or, for that matter, certain sound combinations, or letter combinations—meaningful in English (e.g. 'feeble', 'anxiety', 'Jane is sleeping') while others are meaningless (e.g. 'dersta', 'anbup', 'Jane-ing is')? Finally, given that a syntactic form is meaningful, why does it have the particular meaning it does, and not some other? (E.g. why doesn't the English word 'feeble' apply to things which are corpulent and healthy? Surely it might have.) These are the kinds of questions which a philosophical **theory of meaning** is meant to address.

There are, by my count, three classes of meaning theories. The one I'll examine first is the Thing Theory of Meaning. According to this line, meaningfulness lies (roughly) in the relations between symbols and external objects of various kinds. To take a simplified example: the French 'Platon', the Spanish 'Platón' and the English 'Plato' might be said to correspond to the guy, Plato. And, the story would go, it's because of this "correspondence" that

'Platon', 'Platón' and 'Plato' are meaningful; moreover, it's because all three correspond to *the same guy* that they are synonymous.

Beyond the Thing Theory, the remaining approaches are the Idea Theory of Meaning and the Use Theory of Meaning. According to the Idea Theory, the meaning of a symbol is what one mentally grasps in understanding it. This leads naturally to the supposition that meaning comes, initially, from "inside the mind" — rather than directly from objects "in the world". For example, the French 'rouge', on this view, might correspond to the internal sensation of redness, rather than to external red things. According to the Use Theory, on the other hand, meaningfulness lies neither in the mind nor in relations to worldly entities, but rather in the way people *exploit* symbols; i.e. in the actions performed in speaking these symbols. Thus, to give the meaning of 'I'm sorry' is to say, among other things, how it's employed, for what purpose, and in what circumstances. I'll consider these two alternative theories in later chapters.

A Constraint: Semantic Productivity

Before starting, however, let me note an important constraint on *any* satisfactory theory of meaning. There exist, in any natural language, indefinitely many well-formed, fully meaningful expressions. For example, (38a-c) through (40a-c) are all meaningful sentences of English.

(38)
(a) Phil is sleeping
(b) John thinks that Phil is sleeping
(c) Alex surmises that John thinks that Phil is sleeping
(d) Rudolf fears that Alex surmises that John thinks that Phil is sleeping
(e) Phil thinks that Rudolf fears that Alex surmises that John thinks that Phil is sleeping

(39)
(a) It's cold in Ottawa
(b) It's really cold in Ottawa
(c) It's really, really cold in Ottawa

(40)
(a) Alice won't be happy until she's earning two million dollars a year

(b) Alice won't be happy until she's earning three million dollars a year
(c) Alice won't be happy until she's earning four million dollars a year

Each list can be extended indefinitely. The first list is extended by recursively embedding the last sentence on the list in something of the form ⌜A φ is that S⌝, where φ is replaced by a propositional attitude verb (e.g. 'love', 'like', 'believe', 'hope', etc.) and A is replaced by a name. (Note: the unfamiliar marks are called **corner quotes**. Regular quotes are employed when you want to mention *a particular sentence*. Given this usage, 'A φ is that S' would refer to a *particular* formula. But that isn't what is intended in the example at hand. What's wanted, instead, is to talk about any expression sharing this *form*, treating A and φ as variables. So, in place of single quotes, one writes ⌜A φ is that S⌝. In general, corner quotes may be read as 'any expression got by replacing the variables in ___ with appropriate linguistic expressions'.) The first list can be extended *indefinitely* because the same names and verbs can be re-used; notice, for example, that 'think' and 'Phil' appear twice in (38e). The second list is extended by placing another 'really' after the last 'really'. Again, this can be repeated forever—admittedly without much point—with every resulting formula being a meaningful sentence of English. Finally, the third list is extended by substituting the numeral in the previous sentence with the next highest numeral. And, as everyone knows, there is no highest numeral.

This fact about languages is sometimes called **semantic productivity**. It imposes an important constraint on meaning theories. Any successful theory of meaning for a natural language must answer the $64,000 Question, "What makes an expression meaningful, and what makes it have the meaning it does?"—for an unlimited number of expressions, most of which no one has ever encountered. It must, therefore, incorporate a **compositional semantics** which determines the interpretation of complex expressions, given the interpretation of their parts.[11]

The only alternative to introducing a compositional semantics would seem to be a meaning theory in the form of a phrase book: a list of expressions followed by an explanation of why they are meaningful and why they have the meanings they do. But phrase books are finite. And no finite list will do. (In effect, this follows from the fact that—as I explained in Chapter Two—natural language syntax is recursive.) So this option is ruled out.

If that doesn't move you, here's another way of making more or less the same point, without appealing to *unlimited* productivity. Giving a theory of meaning in the form of a phrase book might go like this: the semanticist would catalogue all the meaningful expressions—list them all—and then say why they were meaningful, and why they had their particular meanings. There's a problem, though. What is meant by 'all the meaningful expressions'? It could only be something like 'all the expressions people have encountered, plus all the ones they've thought of'. But everyone can understand expressions that they have never encountered, including expressions they've never even previously thought of. Indeed, there are surely expressions which *no one* has ever encountered or thought of, but which *would be* understood on first hearing. Consider an example:

(41) In my dream I saw, in the dim light of dawn, six off-white whales in the Carleton University parking lot!

I take it that every English speaker immediately understands this sentence. So the theory of meaning needs to include it. But the phrase book model would, in all likelihood, leave it off its list: chances are, none of the book's compilers would have encountered this sentence before, or even have thought of it. The compositional semantics model, on the other hand, could naturally capture this sentence. Its lexicon would give the meaning of the single words in (41). And its compositional rules, being perfectly general, would supply a meaning for the whole sentence, given (a) the meaning of the parts and (b) the way they are put together. (The meaning of the parts alone isn't enough because, in many languages, *order counts*. 'Man bites dog' and 'Dog bites man' aren't synonymous, though they share the same meaningful parts.) So, once again, the phrase book model looks unpromising.

2. Direct Reference Theories

So much for the constraint. It's time to survey the various Thing Theories of meaning. According to the Thing Theory, meaning comes from the relation between sounds and syntactic structures (and marks, though I'll leave these out of the present discussion) on the one hand, and "external objects" on the other. Now, there are a number of options for understanding this relation to 'external objects'. This chapter and the next will be devoted to surveying those options, some of which are rather complex. This chapter will introduce the most straightforward version of the Thing

Theory, which may be called the **extensional** or **direct reference** theory.

According to the direct reference theory, a word corresponds to an external object, *and nothing mediates between the word and the thing referred to*. (The importance of this lack of mediation will emerge in the next chapter.) Each theory of meaning has a paradigm case for which it works well. For the direct reference theory, the case is proper names. According to this theory, the meaning of 'Plato' just is the famous philosopher. Similarly, the meaning of the Spanish 'Julio César' is the guy who ruled Rome, and conquered the known world; while the meaning of 'Bruto' is the man Brutus, one of the senators who stabbed said ruler. This is the paradigm for the direct reference theory because, evidently, these proper names are all meaningful solely in virtue of referring—in virtue of having a **denotation**. (Roughly, the denotation of an expression is the thing named—i.e. the thing which the expression stands for.)[12]

What one might call "complex names" also pose no immediate problem for the direct reference theory. I'm thinking of phrases like:

(42)
(a) The Prime Minister of Canada in 1995
(b) The Queen of England in 1995
(c) The guy who invented the telephone

These expressions, like 'Plato', denote an individual. Respectively, they refer to Jean Chrétien, Elizabeth II, and Alexander Graham Bell. That, according to the direct reference theory, is why they are meaningful and why they mean what they do.

So far so good. But, as you saw in the chapter on syntax, there are lots of expressions beyond names, be they proper or "complex". For instance, to list just a few:

(43)
(a) Verbs ('run', 'talk', 'enjoy', 'kiss')
(b) Sentences ('Tim kissed Phil at the airport')
(c) Conjunctions ('and', 'or', 'but')
(d) Quantifier Phrases ('everyone', 'somebody', 'several girls')
(e) Articles ('the', 'a')

To make the direct reference theory work, it's necessary to assign to *every* meaningful expression some "thing". Some external object. To satisfy the constraint noted above—that the theory handle an unlimited number of expressions, including unfamiliar ones—the theory must compute the denotation of non-primitive expressions from (a) the denotations of their minimal parts and (b) the way these are combined.

Verbs and Functions

What are verb meanings? For instance, what would be the meaning of 'smokes'? As a first approximation, I will treat 'smokes' as denoting a *function*. A function, in the mathematician's sense, is like a simple rule. Give it an input, apply the rule, and out comes...the output. The inputs are called the **arguments** of the function. ('Argument' here is a technical term. It has nothing to do with disputes.) The outputs are called its **values**. I'm sure you're acquainted with the following example:

(44) x^2

'x^2' denotes a function from numbers to numbers. (Note: the function is the thing *denoted*, not the expression which has the denotation. Functions are meanings—external objects of a peculiar kind. They are *not* symbols. If you don't see this yet, read on anyway: it should become clear in what follows.) Give this function TWO as an argument, and it will output FOUR as value. Give it FIVE as an argument, and it will output TWENTY FIVE as a value. In fact, give it any number as an argument and it will output, as the value, that number multiplied by itself.

A function is "incomplete, in need of supplementation, or 'unsaturated'" (Frege 1891, 140) in the sense that it cries out for inputs. But the inputs don't have to be numbers. What (45) denotes is a function from countries to languages:

(45) Most commonly spoken language in x

Give this function HOLLAND as argument, and it yields DUTCH as value; give it URUGUAY as argument, it yields SPANISH as value. And so on. Here's another kind of function: one from numbers to **truth values**. (For present purposes, assume there are exactly two truth values: TRUE and FALSE.)

(46) $x^2=4$

This function yields the value TRUE, given the number TWO as argument. That's because two times two is, indeed, four. (Ditto for MINUS TWO.) But this function yields FALSE for every integer other than two and minus two. THREE yields FALSE. As does SIXTEEN, MINUS FIVE, ZERO, and so on.

There are functions whose outputs/values are truth values (e.g. $x^2=4$) and functions whose inputs/arguments aren't numbers (e.g. Most commonly spoken language in x). So there's no reason one can't have functions from non-numbers to truth values. And— here comes the proposal—the meaning of 'smokes' is just such a function. It outputs TRUE when given a smoker as input; and it outputs FALSE for every other input. This treatment is easily extended from verbs to **predicates** generally. Adjectives—'hungry', or 'foolish' for example—also denote so-called **propositional functions**: functions from individuals to truth values. In the case of 'hungry', the propositional function it denotes yields TRUE for all and only the hungry things. Ditto for Verb Phrases: 'is tall', 'snores incessantly', and so on. These also denote propositional functions.

So, to sum up the results so far: according to the direct reference theory, names denote individuals—where this means not just persons, but any particular item: Canada, my cat Weeble, the cup on my desk, the blue chair in my office, and so on. Predicates, on the other hand, denote propositional functions: functions from individuals to truth values.[13]

Importantly, this theory explains, in part, why a verb like 'snores' is meaningful: it corresponds to an extra-linguistic something—in this case a function. In the same way, the theory says why a made-up verb like 'koovs' isn't meaningful. 'Koovs' is meaningless because it doesn't denote anything at all. The theory also provides a story about why a word means what it does, rather than meaning something else. Why, for instance, 'snores' doesn't mean WHISTLE. The reason: what 'snores' denotes (namely, the function SNORES) doesn't yield TRUE for all and only arguments which whistle.

Detour: Semantics and Metasemantics

I pause to stress that the direct reference theory doesn't answer *all* the questions a philosopher would have about meaning. For instance, though it articulates what the meaningfulness of 'snores' consists in—it consists in "corresponding directly" to the SNORES-function—it doesn't say anything about *how* 'snores' came to be paired with this function. The theory leaves open what historical, causal, or other processes ground this "correspondence". In short, the proposal doesn't say "where meaning comes from".

I call **semantic facts** truths such as: that a certain form is meaningful, that a particular meaning attaches to an expression, and so on. The direct reference theory entails lots of these. It says, for example, that the meaning of 'smokes' is the function which yields TRUE for all and only the smokers. But semantic facts aren't basic, irreducible features of the world. Something must explain why certain semantic facts obtain, while others don't. (Compare: by-law facts aren't basic. Something must explain why a town has the by-laws it does. In the case of by-laws, the explanation appeals to past votes in the town's council.) The attempt to explain semantic facts, to discover that in virtue of which they obtain, is sometimes called **metasemantics**. Using this terminology, one can say that the direct reference theory of meaning isn't, by itself, a metasemantic theory: it does not reveal *in virtue of what* semantic facts obtain. At best, it explains—via a recursive compositional mechanism—semantic facts about complex expressions in terms of semantic facts about primitive expressions. But the direct reference theory doesn't explain the semantic facts about these minimal expressions. In this sense it is not, by itself, a philosophically satisfying theory of meaning. Nevertheless, though philosophically incomplete, the direct reference theory contributes to an understanding of what meaningfulness amounts to. (It amounts to non-mediated reference.) So, I suggest pressing on.

Sentences

Even putting aside for the moment such esoterica as conjunctions (e.g. 'and', 'or'), articles (e.g. 'the', 'a') and quantifier phrases (e.g. 'somebody', 'everything', 'several squirrels'), there is a central class of expressions still unaccounted for: sentences. I've been simplifying up until now, but I'll be simplifying even more in what follows. (Do not despair. It will get complicated soon enough.) The simplification I'm going to make is to treat sentences as denoting truth values. This is provisional, and it will change.[14] At this point, though, the reason for this move should be evident: given the compositionality constraint, the meaning of 'Andy smokes' must be determined by the meaning of its parts.[15] And what exactly *is* determined by the meaning of 'Andy' and 'smokes'? Well, according to the direct reference theory as presented above, 'Andy' denotes Andy, while 'smokes' denotes a function from individuals to truth values, such that it yields TRUE for x if and only if x smokes. What do these two meanings "determine"? Suppose Andy smokes. Then the meaning of 'smokes' (i.e. the function SMOKES) outputs TRUE for the meaning of 'Andy'. Suppose Andy doesn't smoke. Then the meaning of 'smokes' (i.e. the function SMOKES) outputs FALSE for the meaning of 'Andy'. In short,

(47)
(a) [The meaning of 'Andy smokes'] is [what is determined by the meaning of 'Andy' and 'smokes']
(b) [What is determined by the meaning of 'Andy' and 'smokes'] is [a truth value—either TRUE or FALSE]

This is the reason for saying that the meaning of 'Andy smokes' is a truth value—either TRUE or FALSE. *Which* truth value ends up being the meaning of 'Andy smokes' depends, of course, on whether Andy smokes.

I've now presented expressions of four **semantic types**, where an expression's semantic type is determined by the kind of thing it directly denotes.

(48) *Four Semantic Types*
(a) *Names* (proper and "complex"), which denote individuals (e.g. 'Plato' and 'Rob's aunt from Toronto')
(b) *"Incomplete names"* (if you will), which denote functions from individuals to individuals (e.g. 'x^2' and 'Most commonly spoken language in x')
(c) *Predicates,* which denote functions from individuals to truth values (e.g. 'snores' and 'smokes')
(d) *Sentences,* which denote truth values (e.g. 'Andy smokes')

These various denotation types are built out of three basic elements: individuals, truth values, and functions. This can be captured in the following table. (Read '*Ind*' as 'individual', '*TV*' as 'truth value' and '$X{\rightarrow}Y$' as 'a function from Xs to Ys'.)

Expression Type	Names	Incomplete Names	Predicates	Sentences
Semantic Type	Ind	Ind → Ind	Ind → TV	TV

To avoid possible confusion: giving the *semantic type* of an expression isn't yet to give its *meaning*. If I tell you that 'La Reina

Isabel' denotes an individual, I tell you its semantic type, but I haven't yet told you its meaning—because I haven't said *which* individual the name refers to. Similarly, telling you that the Spanish word 'roncar' denotes a propositional function informs you of the semantic type of the word, but not of its meaning. True, you need to know what semantic type the word belongs to in order to know its meaning, but you also need to know *what particular thing*, of that type, it corresponds to. Returning to the examples, what a meaning specification must say about 'La Reina Isabel' and 'roncar' is:

(49)
(a) 'La Reina Isabel' denotes an individual, namely Queen Elizabeth
(b) 'Roncar' denotes a function from individuals to truth values, namely the one which yields TRUE for all and only things which snore

Logical Connectives

The growing inventory of semantic types is still missing a few key elements. For one thing, it must eventually include **logical connectives** like the ones below.

(50)
(a) and
(b) if and only if
(c) or
(d) implies

Evidently, these fall into none of the four previously discussed semantic types. So what is their meaning?

Methodological principle, owing to Gottlob Frege (1848-1925): the meaning of any word is what it contributes to whole expressions in which it appears. So, to find the meaning of a connective—'and', for example—requires discovering "what it adds". Now, the meaning of 'and' combines with the meaning of the remaining parts of the sentence to give the meaning of the whole. What are "the remaining parts"? Two sentences, as you can see in (51).

(51) [Snow is white] and [grass is green]

Each "remaining part" has a truth value as its meaning. Similarly for the whole: it too is a sentence, denoting a truth value. Hence, what 'and' contributes combines with two truth values to produce one truth value. In short, 'and' contributes a function! A function from two truth values to one truth value. That is its semantic type.

But, as I said, specifying the semantic type of an expression isn't sufficient for specifying its meaning. To give the meaning of 'and', one needs to say not only what *kind* of function it denotes, but also which one. Once again, what does 'and' contribute to the sentences in which it appears? To answer this, the example must be fleshed out. The meaning of (51) is TRUE. Ditto for (52a) and (52b).

(52)
(a) Snow is white
(b) Grass is green

So the meaning of 'and' takes two TRUEs as argument and gives TRUE as value. Next step: the meaning of (53) is FALSE. Similarly, both (54a) and (54b) mean FALSE. But 'Grass is green' means TRUE.

(53) Snow is purple

(54)
(a) Snow is purple and grass is green
(b) Grass is green and snow is purple

So, what 'and' means takes the **ordered pair** <FALSE, TRUE> as argument and gives FALSE as value. Similarly, if you input the ordered pair <TRUE, FALSE> into the meaning of 'and', it outputs FALSE. (Note: An ordered pair is simply a two-membered set, in an ordering relation. In the angle brackets notation used here, the ordering relation is indicated by the element's place inside the brackets. For example: <*a*, *b*> refers to the set of elements {*a*, *b*}, with *a* coming first, whereas <*b*, *a*> refers to the same set {*a*, *b*}, but with *b* coming first.) Finally, (55) also denotes FALSE.

(55) [Snow is purple and grass is green] and snow is purple

It is composed of 'Snow is purple and grass is green' on the one hand and 'Snow is purple' on the other. The former, you've just seen, denotes FALSE. Ditto for the latter. So 'and' takes <FALSE, FALSE> to FALSE. I summarize all of this with the following **truth table** for 'and'.

P	*Q*	*P and Q*
T	T	T
T	F	F
F	T	F
F	F	F

In brief: 'and' expresses a function from two truth values to one truth value. In the notation of the table: $<TV, TV> \rightarrow TV$. The specific function it denotes is:

(56) The function f such that $f(<T, T>)=T$, $f(<T, F>)= F$, $f(<F, T>)=F$, and $f(<F, F>)=F$

Many other logical connectives are of this same semantic type: 'or', 'unless', 'implies', 'if-then'. They all denote some function from two truth values to one truth value. I won't burden you with their truth tables. What I *do* want to draw to your attention is that sentential connectives—like all the other expressions I've introduced so far—have meanings composed out of (at most) the three basic elements: individuals, truth values and functions thereof.[16]

Before going on, let me remind you of the game plan. I have been discussing language as a system of symbols, focussing in particular on the semantic part of the system. I've just sketched one story about what it is to be meaningful—about what meaning consists in: the direct reference theory. I'm in the process of extending the direct reference account beyond names, to cover meaningful expressions generally.

Semantic Trees

A notational aside before I complete the direct reference theory's catalogue of semantic types. In the chapter on syntax, I introduced **syntactic trees**, which highlighted pictorially how words combine together. I now introduce **semantic trees**; these indicate visually how *meanings* combine. (See Martin 1987, Ch.11 for an introduction to semantic trees.) For instance, a semantic tree for (57) is given in (58).

(57) Andy smokes

(58)

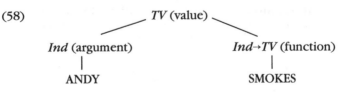

At the bottom of the tree are word-meanings: the minimal parts. The type of each word-meaning is indicated directly above. In this case, ANDY is of type *Ind*; that is, 'Andy' denotes an individual. And

SMOKES is of type *Ind→TV*; that is, 'smokes' denotes a function from individuals to truth values. In this tree, the two **sister nodes** *Ind* and *Ind→TV* combine together as function and argument. The value of this function gets "passed up the tree". So, in this example, the denotation of the **mother node**—the node which dominates the two sisters—is determined by what the SMOKES-function outputs for ANDY as argument. If Andy smokes, then the function outputs TRUE. In which case, the mother node will denote TRUE. If Andy doesn't smoke, the function outputs FALSE. In which case, the mother mode will denote FALSE.

To take a more complex example: the tree for 'The most commonly spoken language in Uruguay sounds beautiful' is given below. (I simplify by treating 'sounds beautiful' and 'the most commonly spoken language in' as if they were minimal parts.)

(59)

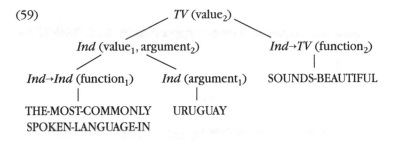

The value of the function THE-MOST-COMMONLY-SPOKEN-LAN-GUAGE-IN, given URUGUAY as argument, is SPANISH. This meaning is "passed up the tree" to the intermediate mother node *Ind* (value$_1$, argument$_2$). This mother node also has a sister, namely *Ind→TV* (function$_2$) and they share a mother: *TV* (value$_2$). The intermediate mother node *Ind* (value$_1$, argument$_2$), which in this case is SPAN-ISH, serves as the argument to the function SOUNDS-BEAUTIFUL. This function in turn, given SPANISH as argument, outputs TRUE. (Spanish—i.e. the most commonly spoken language in Uruguay—does indeed sound beautiful.) So that is the meaning which is "passed up" to the top-most node; it is what the sentence as a whole means.

Quantifier Phrases

So much for notation. It's time to get back to the direct reference theory of meaning. The semantic types introduced so far are still not sufficient. One important missing element is an account of what expressions like those in (60) mean:

(60) *Quantifier Phrases*
(a) Something
(b) Everything
(c) Nothing
(d) Some doctors
(e) All women
(f) Six cats
(g) No children

One might have thought that these quantifier phrases were another variety of complex names. But that can't be right, because of the logical puzzles that would arise. Here are some illustrations from Martin 1987, Ch.12:

(61)
(a) 'Something is tall' is certainly true, and so is 'Something is not tall'. But how can these sentences both be true? For 'Fred is tall' and 'Fred is not tall' cannot both be true.
(b) Nothing is better than steak; but hamburger is better than nothing; therefore, hamburger is better than steak.
(c) No cat has two tails. Every cat has one more tail than no cat. Therefore every cat has three tails.

These puzzles present themselves only if 'something', 'nothing', and 'no cat' are taken to name individuals—in the same way I've supposed 'Plato', 'Fred' and 'The Prime Minister' do. That this is a mistake can equally be shown by asking yourself what *object* 'nothing' or 'no cat' would refer to. Would it not seem, for instance, that if 'nothing' refers to some object, then the meaning of 'Nothing lives forever' is that *this object* lives forever?

(62) Nothing lives forever

But surely (62) would be false if there were an object, *any object*, that lived forever! You might say: 'nothing' is a name all right, but it refers to the empty set; similarly, 'everything' refers to the set of all things. But this won't work either. There can be no doubt: the null set doesn't live forever. That is, (63) is false. (unless it's nonsense.)

(63) The null set lives forever

But (62) certainly isn't nonsense. In fact, I expect it's true. So (62) and (63) can't be synonymous. Hence, 'nothing' cannot refer to the null set. Similarly for 'everything'. Sentence (64) doesn't say that the *universal set* is beautiful in its own way, does it?

(64) Everything is beautiful in its own way

Again, such puzzles arise by taking quantifier phrases—expressions like 'something', 'nothing', etc.—to be names of objects. Hence, one should not treat them as names. What is the alternative? Recall Frege's methodological principle, used in the case of 'and': the meaning of any word is what it contributes to whole expressions in which it appears. So, to find the meaning of quantifier phrases, find what they "add". Take 'something' as an example. As in the case of 'and', the meaning of 'something' must combine with its fellow sentence-part meanings to yield sentence meanings. What is "the remaining part" in this case? A predicate, as the following example from Martin 1987 illustrates. (The symbol ⌢ means 'is concatenated with'. It simply represents the fact that the symbols on either side of it combine into a complex symbol.)

(65) 'Something' ⌢ 'is purple'

Whatever 'something' contributes, it combines with a predicate meaning (i.e. a function from individuals to truth values) and yields a sentence meaning (i.e. a truth value—or so I've been provisionally assuming). That's one constraint. The other is that quantifier phrases, including 'something', do not denote individuals. Making the point pictorially: (66) has been ruled out.

(66)

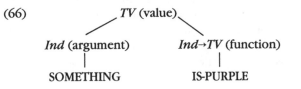

This looks like an impasse. The whole—the sentence—denotes a truth value; one of the two parts—the predicate—denotes a propositional function. And the two parts must "add up to" the whole. But how can this work, if 'something' doesn't denote an individual? The solution isn't far to seek. SOMETHING should not be taken as the *argument* of the propositional function IS-PURPLE. Instead, the propositional function IS-PURPLE should be taken as the argument of the function SOMETHING! 'Something' combines with a predicate, and together they denote a truth value. This is right. But SOME-

THING applies to what the predicate denotes, and not vice versa. (As Russell (1919) would put it: 'something' is not the **logical subject** of (65). Instead 'something' is the "logical predicate"—though Russell himself wouldn't use the latter term.) In which case, the semantic type of 'something' is:

(67) $<Ind{\rightarrow}TV>{\rightarrow}TV$

Hence the tree for 'Something is purple' is not (66), but rather (68).

(68)

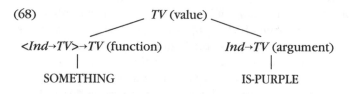

TV (value)

$<Ind{\rightarrow}TV>{\rightarrow}TV$ (function) $Ind{\rightarrow}TV$ (argument)

SOMETHING   IS-PURPLE

Progress. But, I repeat, specifying the semantic type of an expression isn't sufficient for specifying its meaning. To give the meaning of 'and' required saying not only what kind of function it denoted, but also which such function. Similarly for 'something'. Here again, one needs to ask what 'something' contributes to whole sentences. I'll start with this: when is sentence (65) true?

(65) Something is purple

It is true when there is at least one thing which is purple. In "function talk", 'something is purple' is true if (and only if) some argument to the function IS-PURPLE yields the value TRUE. Again: SOMETHING outputs TRUE for propositional functions that themselves output TRUE, and SOMETHING outputs FALSE for propositional functions that never output TRUE. Hence the meaning of 'something' is that function of type $<Ind{\rightarrow}TV>{\rightarrow}TV$ which outputs TRUE for propositional functions that themselves output TRUE.[17] (Notice: IS-PURPLE sometimes outputs TRUE. So SOMETHING outputs TRUE when given IS-PURPLE as argument. Hence, the sentence 'Something is purple' comes out true, as it should.) The same core meaning is shared by all **existential quantifier** phrases: 'at least one cat', 'there exists a doctor', 'one or more books', etc. Big conclusion: quantifier phrases like these don't denote objects; rather, they denote complex functions.

And what about sentence (69a)? Well, what it says can be captured by (69b).

(69)

(a) Everything is purple

(b) Every argument of the function IS-PURPLE yields TRUE as value

Indeed, these are just two ways of saying the same thing. Notice the pattern: the propositional function IS-PURPLE is the argument; the value of the function is a truth value. So, what is the semantic type of the quantifier 'everything'? It too is a function from propositional functions to truth values.

That completes the initial catalogue of semantic types, according to the direct reference theory of meaning. I sum up with another table, omitting "complex names", to save space.

Expression Type	Names	Predicates	Sentences	Sentential Connectives	Quantifier Phrases
Semantic Type	Ind	$Ind{\rightarrow}TV$	TV	$<TV,TV>{\rightarrow}TV$	$<Ind{\rightarrow}TV>{\rightarrow}TV$

Of course, there's much more to natural language semantics than this. There are many kinds of expression which I haven't considered: non-declarative sentences (e.g. 'Is it raining?', 'Turn that damn radio off!', 'Why does it rain all the time?'), mass terms (e.g. 'gold', 'water'), prepositions ('of', 'at', 'for'), adverbs ('quickly', 'foolishly'), and so on. But what I've provided here should be enough for present purposes. (For more developments see Bach 1989 and Chierchia and McConnell-Ginet 1990.)

3. Bertrand Russell on Descriptions

Near the beginning of this chapter, I considered "complex names" like those in (42):

(42)

(a) The Prime Minister of Canada in 1995

(b) The Queen of England in 1995

(c) The guy who invented the telephone

At that point, I imagined that these expressions denoted individuals. And, for many purposes, treating so-called **definite descriptions** like proper names works fine. However, there are problems when the resulting description describes nothing. Suppose, for instance, that Tracy lives alone. What would (70) refer to?

(70) The person that Tracy lives with

The answer is that, because Tracy lives alone, (70) has no reference. Yet, despite this, (70) isn't meaningless. For instance, it makes a meaningful contribution to sentence (71):

(71) 'Kim wrongly supposes that Silvia is' ⌒ 'the person that Tracy lives with'

That (70) makes a semantic contribution can be shown by substituting 'the President of Canada' for 'the person that Tracy lives with' in (71). According to the direct reference theory, neither of these can contribute an object, since neither of them refers. Yet the post-substitution sentence—'Kim wrongly supposes that Silvia is the President of Canada'—is clearly not synonymous with (71). And the only change from sentence (71) is in the part in question. So this part must be "doing something" semantically.

It appears, then, that (70) is meaningful. But what does it mean? And—of particular interest in the context of the direct reference theory—how can it be meaningful if its meaning is supposed to be "the individual it denotes"? After all, there is no such individual! Bertrand Russell (1872-1970) struggled mightily with this problem. (See Russell 1905, 1919, 1957.) I propose, as a way of exploring it, to scout Russell's views at some length.

First Preliminary: Propositions

I begin by making two preliminary moves. First, I hereby disabuse myself of the assumption, made earlier, that the whole meaning of a sentence is its truth value. This cannot be right, since not all true sentences are synonymous, nor are all false sentences synonymous. Instead, I now follow Russell and suppose that the denotation of a declarative sentence is a **proposition**.

Propositions are the things which people believe or disbelieve, assert or deny; they are answers to questions; they're the things one can give evidence for, and justify with arguments; the things which people judge true or false. Examples include: the proposition that philosophy is easy, the proposition that Mary is incredibly smart, the proposition that Canada is a federal state, and so on. I stress: propositions are not symbols; they are the *meanings* of certain symbols. Thus, as I will use the term, the very same proposition can correspond to distinct symbols. For instance, all of the

46

formulae in (72) denote the very same mathematical proposition.

(72)
(a) 2 + 2 = 4
(b) Dos más dos son cuatro
(c) Two plus two equals four

Taking sentences to denote propositions rather than truth values, all the sentences in (72) designate not TRUE but THE PROPOSITION THAT TWO PLUS TWO EQUALS FOUR. Similarly, 'snow is white' stands not for TRUE but THE PROPOSITION THAT SNOW IS WHITE. (You can now see the rationale for calling the meaning of predicates 'propositional functions' since, now that we have made this revision, predicates denote functions from individuals to *propositions*.) The following table summarizes the changes resulting from this revision:

Expression Type	Names	Predicates	Sentences	Sentential Connectives	Quantifier Phrases
Semantic Type	Ind	Ind→Prop	Prop	<Prop,Prop>→Prop	<Ind→Prop>→Prop

That's the first preliminary move in understanding Russell's analysis. The second is to explore his views on **indefinite descriptions**: expressions of the form 'a so-and-so'. This, I'm afraid, will be a rather lengthy preliminary.

Second Preliminary: Indefinite Descriptions

Russell begins with a sentential example, sentence (73), which contains an indefinite description.

(73) I met a man

He then asks: what do I really assert when I assert 'I met a man'? He considers two Wrong Answers, before offering his own answer (Russell 1919, 212).

(74)
(a) *Wrong Answer 1*: My assertion is about the individual who makes my statement true.
(b) *Wrong Answer 2*: My assertion is about some actual man or other.

The problem with Wrong Answer 1 is this: suppose it is Jones whom I met, and hence Jones who "makes true" my assertion that I met a man. Still, I may assert 'I met a man, but it was not Jones' without contradicting myself. So 'I met a man' isn't synonymous with 'I met Jones'—even when it was Jones I met. (Missing premise: 'I met Jones, but it was not Jones' *is* contradictory.) Another difficulty: suppose it is Jones who makes my statement true. Suppose further that the person I'm addressing has never heard of Jones. Nevertheless, the person I'm talking to can fully understand me (i.e. can recover the proposition which I assert). So again: 'I met a man' isn't synonymous with 'I met Jones', even when it was Jones I met. (Missing premise: a person who has never heard of Jones couldn't fully understand 'I met Jones'. To completely understand that sentence, the hearer must know who Jones is.)

Russell rejects Wrong Answer 2, that my assertion is about some actual man or other, for two reasons. First, the negation of 'I met a man' is 'I didn't meet a man'. Now surely *it* isn't about any particular man. (It's crazy to respond, 'Oh really, which particular man was it that you didn't meet?') But if the denial isn't about any particular man, the assertion isn't either. Second, sentence (73) could be significant even if there were no men, just as 'I met a unicorn' is a perfectly significant—though obviously false—sentence. (See Russell 1919, 212.) Hence, 'I met a man' cannot be about an individual. (Missing premise: a statement about *an individual* is significant only if that individual exists. I'll come back to this claim.)

So much for mistaken views about indefinite descriptions like 'a man'. Russell's own views can be captured by the following three claims:

(75) *Russell's Claims about Indefinite Descriptions*
(a) *First Claim*: Indefinite descriptions do not contribute **constituents** to propositions.[18] That is, there is no part of the proposition denoted by the indefinite description (1919, 212).
(b) *Second Claim*: Sentences containing indefinite descriptions do not have the same form as sentences containing names (1919, 213). In particular, sentences containing indefinite descriptions are not of subject-predicate form (1919, 214).
(c) *Third Claim*: Sentences containing names are such that the bearer of the name—the person named—is part of the sentence-meaning. Not so sentences containing indefinite descriptions. 'I met a man', for example, doesn't say that the individual named 'a man'— if you can imagine such a thing!—has the property of having been met by me.

To understand these claims, and to see how intimately connected they are to one another, it's useful to contrast **syntactic form** and **semantic form**. I call syntactic form the way words are put together to form sentences: the blueprint of the *symbols*, not of their meanings. Semantic form, on the other hand, is the blueprint at the level of meanings; it is, if you like, the form of the "stuff" denoted by the expression.

To illustrate the difference between syntactic form and semantic form, consider an example. The syntactic and semantic forms of 'Lisa is sleeping' are given in the syntactic tree (77a) and the semantic tree (77b) respectively. (Recall that, earlier on, I suggested treating sentences as denoting not truth values, but propositions. This is what 'prop' stands for in (77b).)

(76) Lisa is sleeping

(77)
(a) *Syntactic Tree of 'Lisa is sleeping'*

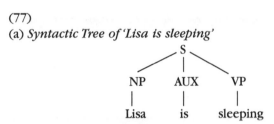

(b) *Semantic Tree of 'Lisa is sleeping'*

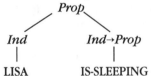

Notice that the bottom nodes of (77a) are *words*—elements from the lexicon—and the intermediate nodes are all syntactic categories: Noun Phrase, Verb Phrase, Sentence. In contrast, the bottom nodes of (77b) are *word meanings*: LISA on the one hand, and the propositional function IS-SLEEPING on the other.

Given the contrast between syntactic forms and semantic forms, one can illustrate Russell's three claims as follows: though (79a) might be the correct *syntactic form* for (78), (79b) is definitely not its *semantic form*.[19]

(78) A little girl is sleeping

(79)

(a)

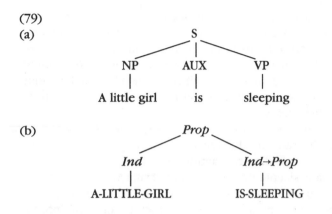

(b)

Prop
Ind → Ind→Prop
A-LITTLE-GIRL   IS-SLEEPING

Instead, on the Russellian analysis, the semantic tree for (78) looks something like this:

(80) *Russellian Semantic Tree for 'A little girl is sleeping'*

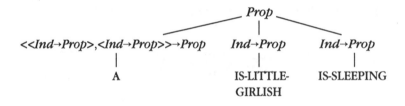

Spelling out the tree in prose: the propositional functions IS-LIT-TLE-GIRLISH and IS-SLEEPING serve as joint inputs to the function A. The latter, given these two propositional functions as arguments, yields a single proposition which is true if and only if at least one entity outputs TRUE for *both* the input propositional functions. And this effectively captures the meaning of the whole sentence: that there is something which is a little girl and which is sleeping.

This analysis strikes Russell as superior for the following reasons. First, according to (79b), the phrase 'A little girl' contributes a constituent to the whole proposition. That is, there is a part of the proposition denoted by the indefinite description 'A little girl'. This, as I've said, is a mistake according to Russell's First Claim. In (80), however, there is no "chunk", no "piece of the proposition", corresponding to the words 'a little girl'. Second, according to the tree in (79b) the sentence 'A little girl is sleeping' has the same semantic form as sentences containing names. In particular, the semantic tree suggests that 'A little girl is sleeping' is of subject-predicate form. Again, Russell insists that indefinite descriptions aren't name-like

50

semantically speaking. The tree in (80), on the other hand, is faithful to Russell's Second Claim, since it makes explicit that, at the level of semantic form, 'A little girl is sleeping' is of **quantificational**, rather than subject-predicate form. Finally, in (79b) there is an individual contributed by 'A little girl', and this individual is part of the sentence-meaning. Whereas, by Russell's Third Claim, sentence (78) should involve propositional functions, rather than individuals. This too is captured by the semantic tree in (80).

Definite Descriptions

Finally, the end of the preliminaries. It's time to apply all of this to definite descriptions. Recall the problem: in the context of the direct reference theory of meaning, it's puzzling how non-referring definite descriptions like 'The person that Tracy lives with' manage to be meaningful. After all, meaning is supposed to *be* reference. Russell has an answer. It hinges on an analogy he spots between indefinite descriptions (e.g. 'a little girl') and definite descriptions. Russell says about *the latter* that they don't contribute individuals as constituents, that they're not name-like, and that the sentences in which they appear are not of subject-predicate form. Instead, sentences that contain definite descriptions are of quantificational form. (Sound familiar?)

Remember, I had treated (42a-c) as complex names, each denoting an object. But it was hard to do the same for (70).

(42)
(a) The Prime Minister of Canada in 1995
(b) The Queen of England in 1995
(c) The guy who invented the telephone

(70) The person that Tracy lives with

Russell thinks this type of analysis is a mistake, both for definite descriptions that *don't* denote—like (70)—and for definite descriptions that *do* denote. It's true that the *syntactic* role of names and definite descriptions are very similar. But, an updated version of Russell would say, they have enormously different semantic roles.

Here's an example. Simplified syntactic trees for (81a) and (81b) are given in (82a) and (82b) respectively. As you can see, they are very similar:

(81)
(a) Jean is tall
(b) The P.M. of Canada is tall

(82)
(a)
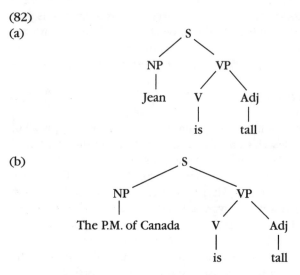

(b)

By contrast, adopting the Russellian analysis for (81a) and (81b), the *semantic* trees for these sentences prove to be *very* different. The semantic tree for 'Jean is tall' appears in (83a). A first pass at a semantic tree for 'The P.M. of Canada is tall' is given immediately below (consider yourself warned that this latter tree will need to be revised):

(83)
(a) *Semantic Tree for 'Jean is tall'*
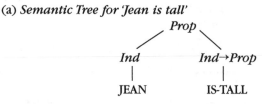

(b) *Simplified Russellian Semantic Tree for 'The P.M. of Canada is tall'*
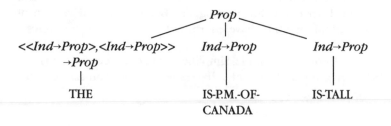

I stress: these two trees look strikingly different. In particular, 'the P.M. of Canada' is not being treated like a name in (83b). Instead, 'The P.M. of Canada is tall' ends up having quantificational form. This is exactly what Russell wants.

The Meaning of 'The'

A central issue remains unresolved: what exactly is the meaning of 'the', according to Russell's version of the direct reference theory? As should be clear, the semantic form of 'The P.M. of Canada is tall' is the same as the semantic form of 'Something is tall', 'Everything is tall' and 'Nothing is tall'. More generally, every expression of the form $\ulcorner$The F is $G\urcorner$ will have the same semantic form as every expression of the form $\ulcorner$Every F is $G\urcorner$, $\ulcorner$Some F is $G\urcorner$ and $\ulcorner$No F is $G\urcorner$. In these latter sentence types, a quantifier takes two propositional functions as input—namely those corresponding to F and G—and yields a proposition as output. Which means that 'the', on its own, must also denote a function which makes two propositional functions into a single proposition. But which such function? After all, every **bare quantifier** (e.g. 'some', 'every' and 'no'—as opposed to 'some*thing*', 'every*body*', 'no*where*') has this semantic type. What distinguishes 'the'?

Finding the specific meaning of 'the' requires asking what 'the' contributes to the meaning of whole expressions in which it appears. As usual, one starts with the whole and "subtracts" the remaining parts. The resulting "sediment" is the meaning of 'the'. Back to examples. Simplifying somewhat, Russell maintains that the meaning of (81b), 'The P.M. of Canada is tall', is captured by conjoining sentence (84a) with sentence (84b).

(84)
(a) There is exactly one P.M. of Canada
(b) Every P.M. of Canada is tall[20]

And these sentences, in turn, have the meanings shown in (85a) and (85b) respectively.

(85)
(a) IS P.M. OF CANADA is true of exactly one argument
(b) IS P.M. OF CANADA IMPLIES IS TALL is true of every argument

Putting this all together, the meaning of 'the' is a function from two propositional functions, PF_1 and PF_2, to a single proposition. This function yields a proposition which is true if and only if *exactly one thing* yields a true proposition for PF_1, and every argument which yields a true proposition for PF_1 also yields a true proposition when input into PF_2. (Since, by the first conjunct, there is only one such thing, this amounts to saying that *this very thing* also satisfies PF_2.) This can be illustrated with the following revised version of the semantic tree for 'The P.M. of Canada is tall':

(86) *Revised Russellian Semantic Tree for 'The P.M. of Canada is tall'*

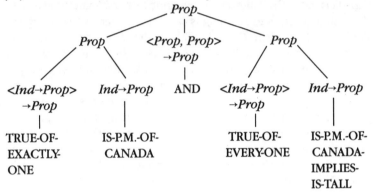

This is Russell's theory of definite descriptions as applied to 'The P.M. of Canada is tall'.

Evidence from an Ambiguity

Russell gives an interesting piece of semantic evidence for his analysis. He claims that his theory automatically captures an ambiguity which the "complex name" theory does not. Notice that (87), for example, has two readings.

(87) The King of France is not bald

One can understand 'The King of France is not bald' as being equivalent to (88)—a reading on which it is *false*.

(88) The King of France is non-bald

Sentence (87) is false on this reading because, given Russell's analysis, it entails that there is a King of France. Which there isn't. However, Russell notes, this sentence can also be understood as a synonym of (89):

(89) It's not the case that the King of France is bald

On this reading, (87) is *true* because it's the negation of a falsehood: that the King of France is bald. (As before, it's false that the King of France is bald because there is no King of France.) This ambiguity is predicted because, on Russell's theory, (87) contains a quantifier-like item: 'the'. And, generally speaking, quantifiers interact with negation to yield **scope ambiguities**. Take (90) for instance:

(90) All men are not bald

It exhibits both a **wide scope** and a **narrow scope** interpretation, paraphrasable as:

(91)
(a) It's not the case that all men are bald [Negation is given wide scope]
(b) All men are non-bald [Negation is given narrow scope]

So, the observed ambiguity of 'The King of France is not bald' is automatically explained, given the Russellian analysis of definite descriptions as quantificational. It remains unexplained on the alternative "complex name" account.

Philosophical Implications

Before leaving Russell's theory of descriptions—and with it the direct reference theory of meaning—I want to consider some of the philosophy that lies behind the semantics. The text I've been discussing—Russell 1919—is actually a chapter from Russell's book *Introduction to Mathematical Philosophy*. Written while Russell was in jail for protesting World War I, the book lays out (in a semi-popular fashion) some of Russell's mathematical findings, and some of his philosophy. Knowing this illuminates what Russell is doing in this text—and what he's *not* doing. Like Frege, whose work I'll introduce next, Russell is propounding a semantic doctrine to address logical, mathematical, and metaphysical worries. As you'll see, Russell is out to avoid nasty ontological commitments, and to solve logical puzzles. It's worth noting that neither Russell nor Frege took themselves to be doing linguistics.

The Ontological Advantage

As you saw above, Russell considers two Wrong Answers to

the question: what do I really assert when I assert 'I met a man'?

(74)
(a) *Wrong Answer 1*: My assertion is about the individual who makes my statement true.
(b) *Wrong Answer 2*: My assertion is about some actual man or other.

These answers may be wrong, but they have an advantage in Russell's eyes: they make the referent of 'a man' some concrete, actual individual. To understand Russell's philosophical achievement, consider a third Wrong Answer, which I have yet to discuss:

(92) *Wrong Answer 3*: My assertion is about some indefinite man.

Russell greatly dislikes this answer because of its peculiar ontological commitments. In deference to "a robust sense of reality", Russell insists on banishing so-called "non-existent" objects. Philosophers are not to countenance unicorns, sea-monsters or other phantasms: "In obedience to the feeling of reality, we shall insist that, in the analysis of propositions, nothing "unreal" is to be admitted" (Russell 1919, 213).

More to the point for present purposes, Russell insists that one should not posit "indefinite objects" either. For example, the object corresponding to 'a man'—not any particular man, mind you, but the indefinite man. Russell (1919, 215) writes:

> ...when we have enumerated all the men in the world, there is nothing left of which we can say, "This is a man, and not only so, but it is the 'a man', the quintessential entity that is just an indefinite man without being anybody in particular." It is of course quite clear that whatever there is in the world is definite: if it is a man it is one definite man and not any other. Thus there cannot be such an entity as "a man" to be found in the world, as opposed to specific men.

Russell is surely right to reject "unreal" and "indefinite" objects. And that is why he rejects Wrong Answer 3: because he thinks Wrong Answer 3 commits one to indefinite objects. But to effectively and convincingly reject Wrong Answer 3 requires an alternative analysis. And *this* is where the theory of descriptions comes in. For, instead of Wrong Answer 3, Russell maintains the view I've just surveyed:

(93) *The Right Answer*: 'I met a man' expresses the proposition that the propositional function I MET X AND X IS HUMAN is sometimes true.[21]

The Right Answer leaves no reference to "a man". Hence, no ontological commitment to the indefinite man. That is the ontological advantage of the Russellian approach.

Here's another way of making the same point. Russell wanted to avoid the following sort of argument, which he attributes to Meinong. (See Russell 1919, 213. I've reconstructed the argument to fit the present context.)

(94) *The Meinongian Argument*
Premise 1: Sentences which contain 'the golden mountain', 'the round square', and so on are meaningful.
Premise 2: 'The golden mountain', 'the round square', and so on are the logical subjects of such sentences.
Premise 3: If an expression is the logical subject of a meaningful sentence then what it denotes has "some kind of being".

From Premise 1 and Premise 2 it follows that 'the golden mountain', 'the round square' and so on are logical subjects of meaningful sentences. From Premise 3 one can safely infer that whatever 'the golden mountain', 'the round square' and so on denote has "some kind of being". This argument is logically valid. That is, if all the premises are true, the conclusion must be true. Yet Russell wants—rightly—to reject its conclusion. His way out of the argument is to deny Premise 2: Russell avoids ontological commitment to unicorns, the indefinite man, round squares, and such precisely by introducing the theory of descriptions. This theory has the advantage that descriptions—including 'a unicorn', 'a man', 'the present King of France' and so on—simply are not logical subjects. Using the recently introduced terminology: they are not subjects *at the level of semantic form*.

What's initially surprising—and very worthy of note—is that Russell accepts Premise 3. Why move so quickly from facts about meaningful sentences and their structure to facts about what there is? The reason is that, according to the direct reference theory Russell is working within, what logical subjects contribute to sentence-meanings is their *reference*. Hence, if they're meaningful, they must *have* a referent. In sum: because Russell accepts the direct reference theory, he must accept Premise 3.

Of course, Premise 3 holds only for expressions that are name-like. In which case, as long as descriptions like 'the unicorn' and 'a man' are *not* name-like, one cannot move from the meaningfulness of sentences in which they appear to the reality of what they denote—because their semantic contribution isn't the object which they designate. Indeed, there is no object which they denote! (Look again at (86): there is no single thing corresponding to 'the P.M. of Canada'.) And that is the grand ontological advantage of Russell's theory of descriptions.

Solving Puzzles

Russell, as I read him, presents a sustained argument against the "complex name" account of definite descriptions. His text, so conceived, goes like this: he presents his theory of indefinite descriptions; he uses this to elaborate a theory of definite descriptions; he argues that this theory is superior on the grounds that (a) it avoids some nasty ontological commitments and (b) it solves some puzzles. Let me end by introducing the puzzles.

As you'll shortly see, Frege (1892a) offers an explanation of why (95a) and (95b) (apparently) differ in content.

(95)
(a) The morning star is the morning star
(b) The morning star is the evening star

Very roughly, on Frege's view, both sentences pick out the same objects, in the same relation—at the level of what's referred to. At this level, they both denote the relation of identity between Venus and itself. But—Frege says—there is a difference in the way the single object is presented. Reference is **mediated** in different ways in the two cases. In (95a), the planet Venus is presented the same way twice. In (95b), it is presented in two different ways. This accounts for the divergence in meaning. (Much more on this shortly.)

According to Russell, reference is direct. So he cannot take this way out. However, given the theory of descriptions, the question of what relation sentences (95a) and (95b) express, such that there's a difference between them, simply does not arise. According to Russell, neither sentence expresses a relation at all. They both express complex existential claims. In short, because 'the morning star' and 'the evening star' are quantificational, neither is name-like. So, Russell gets the appropriate difference, without complicating things by introducing "mediations" between words and their referents.[22]

Another advantage of Russell's view over the "complex name" theory: it provides insight into the fact that sentences of the form ⌜x is unreal⌝ or ⌜x does not exist⌝ can sometimes be true. (See Russell 1919, 214.) Here's the problem: if meaning is simply reference, it looks like any instance of ⌜x does not exist⌝ which has the variable replaced by a meaningful expression N says of the referent of N that it does not exist. But, given that N is meaningful, the referent of N must exist. So any instance of ⌜x does not exist⌝ which has x replaced by a meaningful expression must be false! In short: a statement of non-existence, if meaningful, is false. Not good. Not good at all.

This is where the theory of descriptions comes in. Russell says: what takes the place of x in ⌜x does not exist⌝ is not a referring expression, but a definite description. And a sentence of the form ⌜The F does not exist⌝ is equivalent to ⌜It's not the case that there exists exactly one F⌝. Problem solved. But, you might say, *names* can also be substituted for the variable in ⌜x does not exist⌝. To this Russell responds: not all *apparent names* really do refer. Some apparent names aren't names *in the semantic sense* at all; instead, they're **disguised descriptions**. To take an example: Russell would say that 'Atlantis' isn't, strictly speaking, a name, though it looks like one. Rather, it's a short hand for 'The city which fell into the sea'. In which case, the theory of descriptions straightforwardly applies, offering a way of understanding sentence (96) so that it can come out meaningful *and* true, even within direct reference theories.

(96) Atlantis doesn't exist

I repeat the puzzle: if you think of 'Atlantis' as a meaningful name—i.e. as referring to ATLANTIS, whatever that might be—sentence (96) can't be true. The reason is, given that 'Atlantis' is meaningful, if it's a name, then it has a referent. (According to direct reference theories, anyway.) But if 'Atlantis' refers to something, that something must exist. And if that something exists, (96) is false. Fortunately, Russell would say, one can take 'Atlantis' to be a (disguised) definite description. Hence, (96) comes out as (97):

(97) The city which fell into the sea does not exist

And this, in turn, simply means that it's not the case that there exists exactly one city which fell into the sea. Which, of course, can unproblematically be meaningful *and* true. Hence, (96) can as well. That's another philosophical advantage of Russell's theory.

Summary

Let me summarize. Russell struggled long and hard to understand how, consistent with the direct reference theory of meaning, non-denoting descriptions (e.g. 'The person that Tracy lives with', 'The round square') could be meaningful. A solution he rejects is that these apparently non-denoting "complex names" actually refer to unreal individuals. He maintains, instead, that descriptions *don't* refer. Still, they're not nonsense. Rather, the various parts of the description each make a contribution to the sentence as a whole, in roughly the way quantificational expressions do. That's Russell's theory of descriptions. The result is a final change to the direct reference theory of meaning. This change, and its consequences, are summarized in the following table:

Expression Type	Semantic Type: Old Version	Semantic Type: Russellian Version
Names (E.g. 'Mary', 'Mathieu')	*Ind*	*Ind*
Predicates (E.g. 'smokes', 'is round')	*Ind→TV*	*Ind→Prop*
Sentences (E.g. 'snow is white')	*TV*	*Prop*
Quantifier Phrases (E.g. 'some cat', 'nothing')	*<Ind→TV>→TV*	N/A
"Complex Names" (E.g. 'the P.M. of Canada')	*Ind*	N/A
Articles & Bare Quantifiers (E.g. 'the', 'a', 'some')	N/A	*<<Ind→Prop>, <Ind→Prop>>→Prop*

Suggested Readings

The direct reference theory has a long history. But its modern incarnation begins with John Stuart Mill 1843 and Bertrand Russell 1905. See also Russell 1919, 1957 and elsewhere. For an elementary exposition of the direct reference theory, see Martin 1987. For a significantly less elementary one, see Davis 1976 and Devitt and Sterelny 1987. A rich and insightful discussion of where Russell differs from Frege can be found in Evans 1982. The direct reference theory has been developed and defended in recent times by David Kaplan (1978), Saul Kripke (1972), and Hilary Putnam (1973, 1975) among many others. On Russell's theory of descriptions, I would highly recommend Cartwright 1987. He, unlike me, works hard at getting the history right. See also Kaplan 1972 and Neale 1990. Stalnaker (forthcoming) discusses the contrast between semantics and metasemantics at some length, although he calls it the descriptive/foundational distinction.

Chapter Four:

Mediated Reference

1. Introduction

I pause to remind you of the game plan. The central theme of the book, you'll recall, is that language is a system of symbols which we know and use. At this point I'm still describing language from the system perspective. Simplifying (to a degree that would make many linguists shiver), it has emerged that, considered as a system, a language has three fundamental parts: a syntactic component, a phonological component and a semantic component. The first generates formulae. The second pairs these formulae with sounds. The last pairs them with meanings.

I'm currently focussing on this last fundamental part—the semantic component—highlighting especially some questions: what meanings are, what makes expressions meaningful, what gives an expression the particular meaning it has, and so on. One family of answers to this family of questions is the Thing Theory of Meaning—the view that meaning consists in relations between syntactic structures and sound patterns on the one hand, and "external objects" on the other. So far I've introduced the most straightforward version of the Thing Theory: the direct reference theory, according to which words are paired directly with worldly objects. In this chapter I'll consider two other options within the Thing

Theory. Both take reference to be **indirect** or **mediated**.

2. Frege

I begin with Gottlob Frege, a nineteenth-century mathematician, logician and philosopher, who—in the view of many—was the founder of philosophy in the analytic tradition.[23] By way of understanding Frege's theory of mediated reference, let's recall the **principle of compositionality**. It says that the meaning of an expression is completely determined by the meaning of the parts, plus the way those parts are ordered. So, if two expressions are non-synonymous, there can be only two reasons. Either their parts are not synonymous, or the parts are combined together differently.

For example, sentences (98a) and (98b) have different meanings. This is expected, because they are composed of different words, with different meanings.

(98)
(a) Mary kissed Phil
(b) Lucy hugged Jack

Sentences (99a) and (99b) also have different meanings, even though the parts of each are the same. In this case, the explanation is that the order is different.

(99)
(a) Mary kissed Joan
(b) Joan kissed Mary

In addition to the principle of compositionality, I also supposed in the previous chapter that the meaning of an expression is the thing it refers to. I will call this the **principle of extensionality**. Frege argued that the principle of extensionality and the principle of compositionality cannot *both* be true for natural languages. Here's a reconstruction of his argument: 'Samuel Clemens' and 'Mark Twain' refer to the same man. ('Mark Twain', in case you didn't know, was a pseudonym.) So, if the principle of *extensionality* is true, 'Samuel Clemens' and 'Mark Twain' have the same meaning. In which case, if the principle of *compositionality* is true, sentences (100a) and (100b) have the same meaning—because their parts are synonymous, and their parts are put together in the same way.

(100)
(a) It is common knowledge that Mark Twain was an author
(b) It is common knowledge that Samuel Clemens was an author

But, patently, (100a) and (100b) are not synonymous. So, either the principle of compositionality or the principle of extensionality is wrong.[24] Frege rejects the principle of extensionality; that is, he rejects direct reference theories. For, to give up compositionality is to forego all previous progress: semantics would have to start from scratch. (Besides, what else could contribute to sentence-meaning than part-meanings and their order? What else is there?)

If the meaning of a symbol isn't the object denoted, what can the meaning be? Frege says the meaning is the **sense** (German **Sinn**) of the "thing denoted" (German **Bedeutung**).[25] All objects have senses. Senses are the various ways people can think about the object, the ways in which the object is presented. In Frege's words, "the manner and context of presentation" of the object (1892a, 191). But objects aren't the only things which "have" senses. Words too are associated with senses—though in this case the association is conventional. This is what makes it possible for words to refer to external objects: a word w refers to an object o if w is conventionally associated with sense s, and s is a sense of o. That is, a word refers to (has as **referent** or **nominatum**) *whatever its sense determines*. Sense, then, mediates between a sign and what the sign refers to.

Frege gives a mathematical example of sense, which I reconstruct as follows. Suppose there are three streets, Main, Elm and Bank, which all meet at a single intersection. Now consider the following expressions:

(101)
(a) The intersection of Main and Elm
(b) The intersection of Main and Bank
(c) The intersection of Elm and Bank

Frege says that (101a-c) **designate** the same thing (i.e. they have the same nominatum, or referent); specifically, each designates the intersection of the three streets. However, they each **express** a different sense; that is, the ways in which they present their common referent are different. Frege would say the same about (102a-e). To use his terminology again, all five terms *designate* (i.e. refer to) the same planet, but each *expresses* something different (i.e. is conventionally associated with a different sense of said planet).

(102)
(a) Hesperus
(b) Phosphorus
(c) The evening star
(d) The morning star
(e) Venus

That is the basic idea. Here are some further details. First, senses are public and objective. As Frege (1892a, 191) writes, "The sense of a proper name is grasped by everyone who knows the language." Being public and not subjective, senses cannot be images or ideas inside individuals.[26] Also, to each sense there corresponds at most one referent. So you can't, according to Frege, have a single sense shared by distinct objects. On the other hand, "the grasping of a sense does not with certainty warrant a corresponding nominatum [i.e. referent]" (Frege 1892a, 191). This allows there to be meaningful expressions which do not denote.[27] (Examples: 'the heavenly body which has the greatest distance from the earth' and 'Atlantis' both have a sense, but probably lack a referent; 'the largest natural number' has a sense, but unquestionably lacks a referent.) Also worth stressing: numerous "signs" (e.g. words, sentences, etc.) can correspond to the same "way of thinking about an object"—the same sense. For example, the various other-language translations of the English name 'Plato' (e.g. 'Platon' and 'Platón') all correspond to a single sense of the philosopher in question. Ditto for synonyms *within* a language: though syntactically distinct, they nevertheless share the same sense. The picture which emerges, illustrated by the case of PLATO, looks like this:

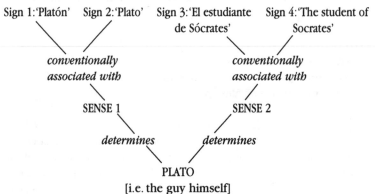

Sign 1: 'Platón'   Sign 2: 'Plato'   Sign 3: 'El estudiante   Sign 4: 'The student of
                                                de Sócrates'   Socrates'

conventionally   *conventionally*
associated with   *associated with*

SENSE 1   SENSE 2

determines   *determines*

PLATO
[i.e. the guy himself]

In short: there are lots of ways of "looking at" a single object. Each

is a sense of that object. And for each way of looking at an object—
for each distinct sense—there can be multiple symbols conventionally associated with it. This is how senses mediate between
objects and words.

Frege's insight is extendable: one can apply the doctrine
of sense and reference not only to proper names, but also to sentences, predicates, and all the rest. Frege's stated view is that
declarative sentences denote truth values. This is familiar from
the discussion of the direct reference theory. But what to take as
the *senses* of sentences? Propositions—though not quite
Russell's version.[28] For Russell (circa 1905), a name's denotation
is *an actual part* of the sentence's denotation. So, for example,
the man Noam Chomsky is part of the proposition expressed by
sentence (103).[29]

(103) Noam Chomsky is over 50

Fregean propositions, unlike Russellian propositions, don't contain
the objects themselves; they instead contain *senses* of objects. So,
for Frege, the man Chomsky isn't part of the proposition expressed
by 'Noam Chomsky is over 50'. Instead, "a manner of presentation"
of Chomsky is part of this proposition.

Frege would also endorse the idea that predicates *refer to*
functions from individuals to truth values. But what kind of thing
will serve as the *sense* of a predicate? Short (unhelpful) answer: the
manner in which such functions are presented. Long answer: the
sense of a *name* is a way of thinking about an individual, sometimes called an **individual concept**. Thus, if MARK is an individual, then MARK-AS-FAMOUS-AUTHOR is an individual concept. The
sense of a name combines with the sense of a predicate to give the
sense of a sentence. The sense of a sentence is a proposition. Given
this, you can easily figure out the semantic type of predicates, at
the level of sense: a predicate must express a kind of function—
one which takes individual concepts as input, and gives propositions as output.

The upshot of all this is that, on Frege's view, each meaningful linguistic expression corresponds to *two* bits of stuff,
namely, a sense (Sinn) and the referent (Bedeutung) which that
sense determines. Here's another table (read *Ind.Con* as 'individual
concept').[30]

Expression Type	Names	Predicates	Sentences
Reference Type	*Ind*	*Ind→TV*	*TV*
Sense Type	*Ind.Con*	*Ind.Con→Prop*	*Prop*

Where, I repeat, the sense always mediates between the expression and its referent.

Compositionality Again

So far so good. Frege explained the non-synonymy of (100a) and (100b) by introducing senses.

(100)
(a) It is common knowledge that Mark Twain was an author.
(b) It is common knowledge that Samuel Clemens was an author.

But so far isn't good enough. Recall the principle of compositionality: the meaning of an expression is determined by the meaning of its parts, and the way these parts are ordered. Given "two levels of meaning", so to speak—the level of sense and the level of reference—the principle now applies at each level. Of particular interest here: the principle of compositionality *for references* (as distinct from senses) says that the referent of an expression is determined by the referents of its parts, and the way these parts are ordered. And now there's trouble. For notice: by the principle of compositionality for references, if two sentences have different referents, that can only be because the referents of their parts are different, or the parts are ordered differently. Now, 'Mark Twain' and 'Samuel Clemens' may not be synonymous, but they *are* co-referential: they refer to the very same individual. Hence, one would expect the referents of (100a) and (100b) to be the same, because their parts have the same referents, and the parts are ordered in the same way. But, not only aren't these sentences synonyms; they don't seem to have the same referents. Sentence (100a) refers to the TRUE, whereas sentence (100b) refers to the FALSE.[31] (That is, it's widely known that Mark Twain was an author. But how many people know that Samuel Clemens was an author?)

Here is another example:

(104)
(a) 'Mark Twain' has nine letters
(b) 'Samuel Clemens' has nine letters

Again, the various parts of these two sentences have the same referents, and the parts share the same order. (The parts are the co-referential names on the one hand and "___' has nine letters' on the other.) But the whole sentences have different referents. Sentence (104a) is true, while sentence (104b) is false.

One could conclude that the principle of compositionality for references is wrong. But then, as before, the whole carefully constructed framework would fall apart, which would mean starting from scratch. Can this be avoided? Frege believed it could. What one has to say is: the following table is correct for the usual case. However, there are exceptions called **opaque contexts**.

Expression Type	Names	Predicates	Sentences
Reference Type	Ind	Ind→TV	TV

In effect, what Frege says is that *sometimes* the referent of a name isn't an individual. That, presumably, is what is going on with 'Mark Twain' and 'Samuel Clemens' in (100a) and (100b). Similarly, *sometimes* the referent of a sentence isn't a truth value. For instance, take (105) and (106). The first exemplifies **direct discourse**—that is, direct quotation. Sentence (106), on the other hand, exemplifies **indirect discourse**:[32]

(105) Alex said, 'John Wayne was a Nazi'
(106) Alex said that John Wayne was a Nazi

Start with direct discourse. The first task is to establish that 'John Wayne was a Nazi' in (105) does not denote a truth-value. This is easy enough because if it *did* denote a truth-value, then, by the principle of compositionality for references, one should be able to substitute any other sentence with the same truth-value for 'John Wayne was a Nazi', and preserve the reference (read: truth-value) of the whole. But it's pretty clear that such a substitution need not be truth-preserving.

Allow me to flesh out the example. Suppose that Alex really did say the sentence 'John Wayne was a Nazi'. Now, though Mr. Wayne was a hard-edged conservative, he was no Nazi. So the sentence 'John Wayne was a Nazi' is false. Next step: John F. Kennedy wasn't a Nazi either. And, I'll suppose, Alex never said he was. In these circumstances, (105) is true, but (107a), (107b) and (108) are false.

(105) Alex said, 'John Wayne was a Nazi'

(107)
(a) John Wayne was a Nazi
(b) J.F.K. was a Nazi

(108) Alex said, 'J.F.K. was a Nazi'

Applying the principle of compositionality for references, you can see that 'John Wayne was a Nazi' does *not* denote a truth-value in (105), because (107a) and (107b) have the same truth-value, and yet one cannot substitute 'J.F.K. was a Nazi' for 'John Wayne was a Nazi' in (105), while preserving truth. So, direct discourse is one context in which sentences don't refer to truth values.

Well then, what *do* sentences refer to in direct discourse? Frege's positive view is that, in direct discourse, a sentence refers to itself. He doesn't really argue for this in Frege 1892a, but it's a reasonable claim. Notice, for instance, that (105) can be paraphrased as (109).

(109) Alex said [the sentence 'John Wayne was a Nazi']

And notice too that what appears in the brackets in (109)—'the sentence 'John Wayne was a Nazi''—does indeed refer to the sentence 'John Wayne was a Nazi'. So it's natural to suppose that, *in this context,* 'John Wayne was a Nazi' is co-referential with 'the sentence 'John Wayne was a Nazi''.

Again, it's fairly easy to establish that in indirect discourse—roughly, cases not of quotation, but of recounting and paraphrase—sentences do not refer to truth values, either. Substitution of the false sentence 'J.F.K. was a Nazi' for the false sentence 'John Wayne was a Nazi' in (106) is *not* truth preserving.

(106) Alex said that [John Wayne was a Nazi] (=TRUE)
(110) Alex said that [J.F.K. was a Nazi] (=FALSE)

So, sentences in indirect discourse do not denote truth values. It's less easy to establish that, as Frege maintained, sentences in indirect discourse refer to their *usual or customary sense,* i.e. the proposition they ordinarily express. His argument for this conclusion is hidden away in a passage in Frege 1892a, 195. He there points out that truth-value *is* preserved in indirect discourse under substitution of sentences *with the same sense*—sentences that express the same proposition. This would be a surprising result, were it not the case that sentences in indirect discourse refer to the propositions they normally express.

So here's the picture: the referent of a whole expression is determined by (a) the order of the words in it, and (b) the referents of those words. In the standard case, the reference of a sentence is a truth-value: that's what a sentence usually contributes to the expressions in which it is contained. Similarly, in the standard case, a name refers to an individual. However, there are some exceptions. These are cases of **indirect reference**. The "indirect reference" of a sentence is either itself, or the proposition it normally expresses. It is one of these which, in the exceptional cases, a sentence contributes to the whole expression. And the "indirect referent" of a name is either itself or the individual concept which it normally expresses. Again, in the exceptional cases it is one of these which a name contributes as its referent. What exactly are the "exceptional cases"? Direct and indirect discourse are two. But there are others. Other *opaque contexts*.

More Opaque Contexts

A **context**, as I'll use the term, is simply a linguistic string with a gap in it. For example:

(111)
(a) The son of ____
(b) ____ is bald
(c) Snow is white and ____

A context C is an **opaque context** if and only if there are two expressions E_1 and E_2 which share their ("standard" or "usual") referent, such that the referent of the complex E_1-embedded-in-C is distinct from the referent of E_2-embedded-in-C. Symbolically, reading $\exists <E_1, E_2>$ as 'there exists an ordered pair $<E_1, E_2>$' and the symbol $\frown$ as 'is concatenated with':

(112) *Definition of 'Opaque Context'*[33]
A context C is opaque $=\text{Def}^n$
$(\exists <E_1, E_2>)\{[\text{Referent}\ (E_1) = \text{Referent}\ (E_2)]\ \&\ [\text{Referent}\ (C \frown E_1) \neq \text{Referent}\ (C \frown E_2)]\}$

It is in opaque contexts that expressions take their indirect referent.

There are many kinds of opaque context, including:

(113) *Quotational Contexts (Direct and Indirect Discourse)*
(a) Alex said, '___'
(b) Linda said that ___

(114) *Propositional Attitude Contexts*
(a) It is common knowledge that ___ is an author
(b) Joshua believes that ___
(c) Gita is awfully glad that ___
(d) Oedipus wanted to marry ___
(e) It is obvious that ___

(115) *Logical and Mathematical Contexts*
(a) It is a truth of arithmetic that two plus two equals ___
(b) It follows from such-and-such that ___
(c) It is logically true that ___

(116) *Explanatory/Causal Contexts*
(a) Anita lives in Ottawa because ___
(b) The damage was caused by ___

(117) *Performative Contexts*
(a) I command that ___
(b) Mary's father wouldn't let her buy ___
(c) Huang promised to ___

(118) *Semantic Contexts*
(a) '___' means that water is cold
(b) '___' is synonymous with 'snow'

(119) *Modal Contexts*
(a) It is possible that ___
(b) Necessarily, ___
(c) Given the laws of nature, it's not possible that ___

To show that these contexts are opaque, one need only find two expressions with the same referent—two sentences with the same truth value, or two names denoting the same individual—such that plugging one expression into the context gives one referent for the whole, while plugging the other into the very same context gives a different referent for the whole. I've already done this for direct discourse contexts—recall how Alex *did* say 'John Wayne was a Nazi', but *didn't* say (the co-referential sentence) 'J.F.K. was a Nazi'; and how 'Mark Twain' had nine letters, though 'Samuel Clemens' didn't, despite the fact that they both denote the same author. Recall too that Alex *did* say that John Wayne was a Nazi, but *didn't* say that J.F.K. was a Nazi. In all these quotational cases, the referent of the whole went from TRUE to FALSE under substitution of co-referential parts. I've also established that one propositional attitude context (i.e. 'It's common knowledge that ___ was an author') is opaque, using the two co-referential names 'Mark Twain' and 'Samuel Clemens'. There's not much point proving that *all* of the above contexts are opaque. But, to illustrate the form of argument, I'll do two more.

Take (115a), the context 'It is a truth of arithmetic that two plus two equals ___'. Fun physics fact: it now appears that there are four basic physical forces—gravitational, electromagnetic, strong nuclear and weak nuclear. That is, 'four' and 'the number of basic physical forces' are co-referential.[34] Take these as values for E_1 and E_2. (See the definition in (112) if you're puzzled.) The result is Premise 1, below:

Premise 1: Referent ('four') = Referent ('the number of basic physical forces)

Now, though it's a truth of arithmetic that two plus two equals four, facts about the number and variety of basic physical forces are not arithmetic truths. Hence:

Premise 2: Referent ('It is a truth of arithmetic that two plus two equals four') = TRUE
Premise 3: Referent ('It is a truth of arithmetic that two plus two equals the number of basic physical forces') = FALSE

From Premises 2 and 3 it obviously follows that,
Conclusion 1: Referent ('It is a truth of arithmetic that two plus two equals four') ≠ Referent ('It is a truth of arithmetic that two plus two equals the number of basic physical forces')

In short, the referent of the complex changes (from TRUE to FALSE) under substitution of co-referential terms. Hence, by the definition in (112), 'It is a truth of arithmetic that two plus two equals ___' is an opaque context.

A final example. The context 'Anita lives in Ottawa because ___' is opaque. Here's the argument: 'Ottawa is the capital of Canada' is true; ditto for 'Ottawa has very cold winters'. So, they are co-referential. This serves, once again, as Premise 1.

Premise 1: Referent ('Ottawa is the capital of Canada') = Referent ('Ottawa has very cold winters')

Now, as it happens, Anita moved to Ottawa to work in the federal civil service. This *despite* the fact that she abhors cold winters. So:

Premise 2: Referent ('Anita lives in Ottawa because Ottawa is the capital of Canada') = TRUE
Premise 3: Referent ('Anita lives in Ottawa because Ottawa has very cold winters') = FALSE

From Premises 2 and 3 one can immediately infer that,
Conclusion 1: Referent ('Anita lives in Ottawa because Ottawa is the capital of Canada') ≠ Referent ('Anita lives in Ottawa because Ottawa has very cold winters')

Hence, by the definition of 'opaque context', 'Anita lives in Ottawa because ___' is opaque.

It should now be clear what an opaque context is, and which sorts of contexts are opaque. Recall now why this matters: opaque contexts, according to Frege, are the places where expressions don't exhibit their usual or standard reference. Rather, in these contexts, expressions contribute their indirect referents. To repeat: in the ordinary course of events, proper names express individual concepts and denote individuals, sentences express propositions and denote truth values, and predicates express functions from individual concepts to propositions and denote functions from individuals to truth values. The non-ordinary cases divide in two. In direct discourse—actual word-for-word quotation—an expression refers to itself rather than to its usual referent. In the other opaque contexts, a proper name designates its usual sense (i.e. an individual concept), and a sentence designates *its* usual sense (i.e. a proposition).[35] This is Frege's doctrine of sense and reference, and its associated doctrine of indirect reference.

Philosophical Applications: Frege's Puzzle

You now have two versions of the Thing Theory of

Meaning before you. One, due to John Stuart Mill (1806-1873) and Bertrand Russell, takes meaning to be a matter of direct reference to external objects. The other, due to Frege, equates meaning with sense—i.e. that which determines the reference. There is a third version of the Thing Theory that I'll present shortly: the Possible Worlds theory. Before going on, however, I want to explore one of the important logical applications of Fregean semantics: the solution to his "Puzzle".

Allow me to indulge in a little bit of historical setting. Frege begins "On Sense and Reference" with a kind of metaphysical question:

> The idea of Sameness challenges reflection. It raises questions
> which are not quite easily answered, Is Sameness a relation? A rela-
> tion between objects? Or between names or signs of objects?
> (Frege 1892a, 190)

Frege is concerned with exploring the nature of Sameness, or, as it's sometimes translated, Identity. He says (1892a, 190) that in an earlier logical work (Frege 1879) he'd assumed Sameness was a relation between *names* or *signs* of objects, rather than a relation between objects themselves. This because, if identity is viewed as a relationship between—for example—the *objects* designated by the names 'Clemens' and 'Twain', then (120a) and (120b) express the same relation between the same individuals.

(120)
(a) Twain = Twain
(b) Twain = Clemens

But, it seems, sentences of the form $\ulcorner a=b \urcorner$ do not express the same relation as those of form $\ulcorner a=a \urcorner$, even where the appropriate instance of $\ulcorner a=b \urcorner$ is true. Frege notes that sentences of this form have different "cognitive value", that anything of the form $\ulcorner a=a \urcorner$ is knowable *a priori*, whereas examples of $\ulcorner a=b \urcorner$ needn't be; that anything of the form $\ulcorner a=a \urcorner$ is analytic, whereas sentences of the form $\ulcorner a=b \urcorner$ might well "contain very valuable extensions of our knowledge" (1892a, 190). Thus Frege's early view that Sameness was a relation between names of objects.

In "On Sense and Reference" (Frege 1892a), however, he reconsiders his earlier position. The problem is that at least *sometimes* an identity sentence expresses "genuine knowledge"—i.e. knowledge about *things*, not about words-for-things; knowledge about the way the world is, rather than knowledge about how certain people arbitrarily choose to talk. So, Frege is stuck between two untenable positions: identity doesn't look like a relation between objects, because $\ulcorner a{=}b \urcorner$ is informative in a way that $\ulcorner a{=}a \urcorner$ isn't, but identity can't be a relation between expressions either, if identity statements are to be about the world, rather than merely being about words. This quandry has come to be known as Frege's Puzzle.[36]

Frege eventually concluded that he'd fallen into this difficulty by mistakenly assuming that names for the same individual differ from each other *only* in terms of their form or shape. In fact, he realized, co-referential names might also differ "in the way in which the designated objects are given" (1892a, 190). In short, sense saves the day. $\ulcorner a{=}b \urcorner$ can be informative because the two names involved, though co-referential, may have different senses. Furthermore, what is recovered is not simply information about words. Senses are real things that objects have. So it's a discovery, and it's a discovery about the world—not merely about words.

All right, then, just what is "sameness" on this view? Is it a relation? A relation between objects? Here is the answer, as far as I can tell. Sameness (or identity) is indeed a relation between objects. But taking sameness as a relation between objects doesn't raise problems about analyzability, informativeness, and such, because senses explain the observed differences. Frege (1892a, 201) writes:

> Let us return to our point of departure now. When we discerned generally a difference in cognitive significance between "a=a" and "a=b" then this is now explained by the fact that for the cognitive significance of a sentence the sense (the proposition expressed) is no less relevant than its nominatum (the truth value).

That is Frege's Puzzle, and his solution to it. It's an important virtue of mediated reference theories that they allow this solution.

Summary

Before going on to Possible Worlds, I should sum up what I've been doing so far. At this point, I'm still treating language as a quasi-mathematical system of symbols—ignoring for the moment that the system is both known and used by speakers. I introduced the Thing Theory of Meaning as one candidate for the semantic part of the system, and began a survey of its simplest incarnation: the direct reference theory. Within the direct reference theory, I provided an appropriate reference type for each kind of expression (names, predicates, sentences, quantifier phrases, connectives, and so on), and then proposed an emendation to the original referential theory: Russell's theory of descriptions, according to which descriptions do not refer to individuals.

I began the present chapter by introducing a different kind of Thing Theory: the mediated reference theory of Gottlob Frege. Frege's version of the Thing Theory distinguishes sense (the way the object is presented) from reference (the object itself). According to mediated reference theories, it is not with referents, but rather with senses, that words are directly connected. This constitutes an improvement because, Frege says, two expressions may share the same referent *without being synonyms*. I then provided a kind of "thing"—at the level of sense *and* at the level of reference—for various expression types. Finally, I noted that what kind of thing an expression refers to is a bit complicated, since it varies with the linguistic context: sometimes expressions exhibit their indirect reference, rather than their customary reference.

3. Possible Worlds

Beyond the facts about how things actually are, there are facts about how things might be, or might have been. You might not have learned to read English. I might have written a book on history, instead of philosophy. There are also facts about how things could not be, or could not have been.[37] I could not have been a cactus, instead of being human—any *cactus* would not be me! Nor could I, given my actual physical abilities, possibly jump to the moon. These are **modal facts**.

Gottfried Leibniz (1646-1716) gave philosophers a powerful tool for understanding modality: possible worlds. Importantly, a possible world isn't another planet, or another dimension. Rather, a possible world is "a way things might have been".[38] Using this terminology: to say that something *could be* the case is to say that there is at least one "way things might have been" (i.e. one possible world) where it *is* the case. So, 'you might not have learned to read English' comes out as: there is a "way things might have been" (i.e. a possible world) in which you exist, but didn't learn to read English. And, 'I might have written a book on history' comes out as: there is "a way things might have been" (i.e. a possible world) in which I wrote a book on history. Similarly, there are possible worlds in which fish speak, possible worlds where cheese doesn't exist, possible worlds where I am named 'Jim', and so on. That is, these things are possible.

By the same token: to say that something *cannot be the case*, in possible worlds parlance, is to say that there are *no* possible worlds where that something *is the case*. For instance, there are no possible worlds in which red leaves aren't red (that's a logical impossibility), and no possible worlds in which, while remaining physically the same as I am in this world, I jump to the moon (that's a physical impossibility). Similarly, there are no possible worlds in which two plus two fails to equal four. Nor are there possible worlds in which the number two is odd, nor worlds where space is unextended, nor worlds where the number two speaks. That is, these things are impossible. (You might say: "'four' could have meant three, in which case two plus two would not equal four". But this confuses linguistic possibilities with mathematical possibilities. In a language in which 'four' meant THREE, the *sound pattern* 'two plus two equals four' would indeed be false. But this *would not* be a case in which two plus two failed to equal four. It would instead be a case of people uttering familiar sounds, with different meanings. A mathematical fact, by any other name, is precisely as necessary.)

Finally, to say that something *must be the case* is to say that it *is* the case in *every* possible world. In every possible world, two is even. In every possible world, space is extended. In sum:

(121)
(a) Sentence *s* is possible = $(\exists w)$ *s* is true at *w*
(b) Sentence *s* is impossible = $\neg\ (\exists w)$ *s* is true at *w*
(c) Sentence *s* is necessary = $(\forall w)$ *s* is true at *w*

(Some notation: '$\neg$' should be read as 'not'. '$\exists w$' means 'There exists at least one world'. '$\forall w$' means 'For every world'. Thus (121a) is equivalent to 'There exists at least one world *w* such that *s* is true at *w*'; (121b) to 'It's not the case that there exists a world *w* such that *s* is true at *w*'; and (121c) to 'For every world *w*, *s* is true at *w*'. That is: *s* is possible, *s* is impossible and *s* is necessary, respectively.)

So, there are modal facts. And Leibniz provided a tool for understanding modal facts: possible worlds. So what? Well, linguists and philosophers of language care about possible worlds because they are tremendously useful in semantics. A set of worlds determines a way things could be. Notice that that's also what propositions do. The proposition THAT MIAMI GETS LOTS OF SNOW, for example, is consistent precisely with those possible worlds in which Miami gets lots of snow. Given this, why not take this proposition to simply *be* the set of worlds in which Miami gets lots of snow? Why not indeed. Consider it proposed.

I stress: the idea is that propositions be equated with *sets* of possible worlds. Not with *a* possible world. For instance, the proposition THAT MIAMI GETS LOTS OF SNOW cannot be equated with "the world" in which Miami gets lots of snow, since there are lots of such possible worlds: the world where it snows lots in Miami and rains constantly in Los Angeles and Ottawa; the world where it snows lots in Miami and Ottawa, but only a little in Los Angeles; the world where it snows in Miami and no where else; and so on. So, instead of equating the proposition THAT MIAMI GETS LOTS OF SNOW with *a* world, this proposition is captured by *a set of worlds*—a set whose members share one crucial feature: Miami gets lots of snow in those worlds.

This insight—that sets of worlds do the same job as propositions—allows one to "cash out" Frege's notion of sentential sense in a revealing way. The sense of a sentence, in this updated alternative, is a set of worlds. Or, to put it more technically but more in line with previous developments, the sense of a sentence is a function from worlds to truth values. For example, the function which (122a) expresses yields TRUE for all and only those possible worlds in which Jean Chrétien was Prime Minister of Canada in 1995. What (122b) expresses yields TRUE for exactly those worlds in which Miami gets lots of snow.

(122)
(a) Jean Chrétien was Prime Minister of Canada in 1995
(b) Miami gets lots of snow

(Alternative formulation: Sentence (122a) expresses *the set* of possible worlds where Chrétien occupies Canada's Prime Minister's Office in 1995. Likewise, sentence (122b) expresses the set of worlds whose common feature is that Miami gets a lot of snow.)

If the *sense* of a sentence is to be a function from worlds to truth values, what can a sentence *refer to*? The answer is obvious, once you see it: the referent of a sentence is the value of the function it expresses, *taking the actual world as argument*. What will this value be? A truth value: either TRUE or FALSE, depending upon whether what the sentence says is true in the actual world. To continue with the examples: the function expressed by (122a) yields TRUE for the actual world as argument. So sentence (122a) denotes the TRUE. (That's because Jean Chrétien *was* the Prime Minister of Canada is 1995.) Sentence (122b), on the other hand, denotes the FALSE because Miami *doesn't* get lots of snow in the actual world: the function denoted by (122b)—from worlds in which Miami gets snow to the TRUE—yields FALSE for the possible world you and I inhabit.

This possible worlds treatment extends naturally to **singular terms**. (I.e. names and definite descriptions. To simplify exposition, I'll assume, contra Russell, that descriptions are name-like). As always, singular terms denote individuals. Their "sense"—sometimes called their **intension** (with an 's')—becomes a function from worlds to *individuals*. For instance, 'the P.M. of Canada' expresses a function which outputs, for each possible world, the individual (if any) who happens to be Prime Minister of Canada in that world.[39] The referent (or **extension**) of 'the P.M. of Canada' is—you guessed it—the value of this function, taking the actual world as argument.

I summarize with yet another table, taking $W{\to}X$ as representing a function from a possible world to an entity of type X.

Expression Type	Singular Terms (E.g. 'Jan', 'The President')	Sentences (E.g. 'Jan smokes')
Intension Type	$W{\to}Ind$	$W{\to}TV$
Extension Type	Ind	TV

Predicates are only slightly more complicated. The referent/extension of a predicate is, as always, the function from things which satisfy the predicate to the TRUE. Thus, 'smokes' refers to the function from smokers to the TRUE. (Important aside. Every propositional function determines a set of individuals: the set of individuals which yield TRUE when input into the function. And every set of individuals determines a propositional function: the function which yields TRUE for all and only members of the set. Which means that propositional function talk and set talk are effectively interchangeable. Hence one can, when desirable, eschew function talk and say that the extension of a predicate is the set of individuals which satisfy it. For instance, 'smokes' may be taken to refer to the set of smokers. I'll adopt this set terminology wherever it's useful.) Given that the extension of a predicate is (in effect) a set of individuals, what kind of *intension* does a predicate have? That function which outputs, for each possible world w, the predicate's extension in w. So, predicates express a function from worlds to a set of individuals. Continuing with the example: 'smokes' expresses a function which takes a world w as argument, and yields as value the set of smokers in w.

Let me illustrate further. Consider worlds w_1, w_2 and w_3. By stipulation, each shall contain exactly three individuals: Alex, Betty and Carrie. Their smoking patterns differ from world to world, as indicated.

(123)
(a) In w_1 Alex, Betty, and Carrie all smoke.
(b) In w_2 Carrie is the only smoker.
(c) In w_3 Alex and Betty smoke, but Carrie doesn't.

Given this, the extension of 'smokes' in w_1 is the set {Alex, Betty, Carrie}, the extension of 'smokes' in w_2 is the one-membered set {Carrie}, and the extension of 'smokes' in w_3 is the set {Alex, Betty}. Now, to simplify enormously, assume that w_1, w_2 and w_3 are the *only* possible worlds there are. In that case, the *intension* (also known as 'sense') of 'smokes' is:

(124) f: $f(w_1)$= {Alex, Betty, Carrie}, $f(w_2)$={Carrie} and $f(w_3)$={Alex, Betty}

(Read: the function f such that the value of the function for w_1 is {Alex, Betty, Carrie}, the value for w_2 is {Carrie}, and the value for w_3 is {Alex, Betty}.) Equivalently, using *function* talk instead of set talk, 'smokes' denotes the function g in w_1, it denotes the function h in w_2 and it denotes the function r in w_3.

(125)
(a) g: g(Alex)=TRUE, g(Betty)=TRUE, and g(Carrie)=TRUE
(b) h: h(Alex)=FALSE, h(Betty)=FALSE, and h(Carrie)=TRUE
(c) r: r(Alex)=TRUE, r(Betty)=TRUE, and r(Carrie)=FALSE

In which case, the intension of 'smokes' is f.

(126) f': $f'(w_1)$=g, $f'(w_2)$=h, and $f'(w_3)$=r

Possible worlds semantics can be quite easily extended to handle sentential connectives (e.g. 'and', 'or', 'implies'), "incomplete names" (e.g. 'Language most commonly spoken in ___', '___

squared'), quantifier phrases (e.g. 'someone', 'nothing'), bare quantifiers ('every', 'no'), and so on. As before, the semantic type of sentential connectives—at the level of reference/extension—remains
some function from two truth values to a single truth value. Their
semantic type at the level of intension, however, is some function
from *two sets of possible worlds* (read: two propositions) to a single set of possible worlds. An "incomplete name" was said, in
Chapter Three, to denote a function from one individual to another
individual. That still holds. What an "incomplete name" *expresses*, in
the possible worlds framework, is a function from worlds to a function from one individual to another. That is, "incomplete names"
express something of type $W \to <Ind \to Ind>$. Quantifier phrases, like
'someone' and 'everything', were said to denote functions of type
$<Ind \to TV> \to TV$. This remains the semantic type of their extension,
in possible worlds semantics. Their intensions become functions
from possible worlds to extensions of this type. And so on. Here is
one last table:

Expression Type	Semantic Type: Intension	Semantic Type: Extension
Singular Terms	$W \to Ind$	Ind
Predicates	$W \to <Ind \to TV>$ (or $W \to \{Ind\}$)	$Ind \to TV$ (or $\{Ind\}$, a set of individuals)
Sentences	$W \to TV$ (or $\{W\}$, a set of worlds)	TV
Quantifier Phrases	$W \to <<Ind \to TV> \to TV>$	$<Ind \to TV> \to TV$
"Incomplete Names"	$W \to <Ind \to Ind>$	$Ind \to Ind$
Articles & Bare Quantifiers	$W \to <<<Ind \to TV>, <Ind \to TV>> \to TV>$	$<<Ind \to TV>, <Ind \to TV>> \to TV$

Two things I want to stress. First, it should be clear why
possible worlds semantics counts as a *mediated* reference theory.
According to the possible worlds account, an expression's referent—or extension—is the output of its intension, taking the actual
world as argument. Hence, what determines the referent of an
expression is the nature of the actual world on the one hand, and
the expression's intension on the other. So intensions mediate
between expression and referent. It should be equally clear why
this is a Thing Theory of Meaning. The "things" are a little peculiar
(e.g. sets of possible worlds, functions from worlds to individuals in
those worlds, the TRUE and the FALSE, and so on). But they're
"things" nonetheless. And they are external to the mind.

Finally, I want to outline how possible world semantics answers some of the questions required of a theory of meaning. It says what meanings are (possible worlds and such); it says what meaningfulness consists in (being paired with a set of possible worlds, or a function from worlds to individuals, or...) and what meaninglessness consists in (*not* being paired with a set of possible worlds, nor with a function from worlds to individuals, nor with...); and, finally, possible worlds semantics has a story about why linguistic strings mean what they do, rather than meaning something else (it's a matter of *which set of worlds* the expression corresponds to).

Applications: Modal and Propositional Attitude Contexts

I'll end by illustrating an advantage which the possible worlds approach inherits from the Fregean theory. In brief, the possible worlds framework does a reasonably good job of dealing with opacity. In particular, it can be straightforwardly applied to modal contexts and propositional attitude contexts. Nevertheless, as will become clear at the very end, there are important and worrisome complications.

A **modal context**, to put it very crudely, is a linguistic string which contains both modal vocabulary and a "gap". Here, once again, are examples:

(127)
(a) It's possible that ___
(b) It's impossible that ___
(c) Necessarily, ___

Modal contexts are opaque. (Remember, a context is opaque if and only if there are two co-referential expressions E_1 and E_2 such that the result of embedding E_1 in the context is referentially distinct from the result of embedding E_2 in the same context.) This can be illustrated, as usual, with an example. I said earlier that 'four' and 'the number of basic physical forces' are co-referential. Now, sentence (128) is true. It's just *impossible* for two plus two to equal anything but four.

(128) Necessarily, two plus two equals four

But the result of substituting 'the number of basic physical forces' for 'four' in this sentence is false. Although there are *in fact* two-plus-two basic physical forces, there could have been three basic physical forces, or five, or just one. That is, in the context 'Necessarily, two plus two equals ___', identity of referents does not guarantee truth-preservation. Hence, the context is opaque.

What would a Fregean say about modal contexts? That, at the level of reference, what the embedded words contribute is their customary sense; so that the meaning of the whole is sensitive to the customary *senses* of the parts—not just their customary referents. Put another way: necessity, possibility, and impossibility are properties of propositions, rather than of truth values. This is an essential insight. A possible worlds theorist would capture it this way: in modal contexts, sentences denote the set of worlds they ordinarily express. Modal contexts, in turn, denote functions from sets of worlds to truth values, as follows:

(129)
(a) 'It's possible that ___' denotes a function from non-empty worldsets to TRUE
(b) 'It's impossible that ___' denotes a function from empty worldsets to TRUE
(c) 'Necessarily, ___' denotes a function from the set of all possible worlds to TRUE

Modal contexts are opaque, the possible worlds theorist explains, because what they denote isn't a function from truth values to truth values. Rather, what they denote are functions from sets of worlds (i.e. propositions) to truth values.

Psychological Contexts

The naturalness of the possible worlds treatment of modal contexts greatly recommends it. And possible worlds can be used elsewhere, though not always with equal naturalness. Consider psychological contexts. It's manifest that they're opaque because of examples like (130a) and (130b), taken from Martin 1987, 177:

(130)
(a) Arnold believes that snow is white
(b) Arnold believes that Bolivia is in South America

The embedded sentences—'snow is white' and 'Bolivia is in South America'—are both true. However, the resulting sentences (130a) and (130b) may nevertheless differ in truth value: imagine poor Arnold thinks Bolivia is in Africa, but he knows full well that snow is white. In that case, (130a) would be true, though (130b) would be false. So 'believes that ___' is opaque.

But *why* is it opaque? Well, a belief sentence like 'Arnold believes that snow is white' seems to express a *relation*—for example, the relation in (131).[40]

(131) Believes(Arnold)(The proposition that snow is white)

Notice that the relation expressed is between persons on the one hand, and *propositions* on the other. It is *this* which makes 'believes that ___' opaque. Intuitively, an opaque context is one whose output at the level of reference depends on the *meaning* of the embedded sentence—the proposition it expresses—not just its referent (i.e. not just its truth value). And belief contexts are classic examples of this. Similarly for all psychological verbs: 'hopes', 'fears', 'desires', 'imagines', and so on. (Opaque constructions are important to philosophers precisely because they suggest that meanings—something above and beyond referents—are required. Referents alone won't do.)

Now, taking a cue from the discussion of modal contexts, one can once again employ the notion of a possible world. A proposition, I said, is equivalent to a set of worlds. Hence, a psychological verb may be taken to denote a relation between a person and a set of worlds. In which case, (131) says that the relation in (132) obtains:

(132) Believes(Arnold)($\{w:$ snow is white in $w\}$)

The context comes out opaque because belief *isn't* a relation to a truth value. It's a relation to a set of worlds. And two sentences having the same truth value in the actual world needn't be true in exactly the same set of possible worlds—so two sentences with the same truth value may well express different sets of worlds. Yet another application of possible worlds to semantics.

I end with an important complication. One which threatens to bring the whole edifice down. Remember: a sentence expresses the set of worlds where it is true. Now, '2+2=4' is true at every world. So it expresses the set of all possible worlds. But here's the rub: (133) is *also* true at every world.

(133) For any right-angle triangle, the square of its hypotenuse is

equal to the sum of the squares of its two remaining sides.

Hence (133) *also* expresses the set of all worlds. Indeed, every necessarily true sentence expresses this set of worlds. So they're all synonymous, according to the possible worlds story!

The same holds for impossible sentences. '2+2=5' expresses the null set of worlds. As does 'The area of a circle is equal to its radius cubed'. Indeed, every sentence which is necessarily false expresses the null set of worlds. So, again, they're all synonymous according to the possible worlds account. This seems crazy enough. But consider its implications for the possible worlds approach to propositional attitude contexts. According to this approach, what a sentence contributes as its referent in a propositional attitude context is the set of worlds which it expresses. Now, I just said that '2+2=4' and (133) express the same set of worlds; namely, the universal set. Hence they must contribute the same thing as their reference in propositional attitude contexts. This has lots of bizarre consequences. For example, consider (134a) and (134b):

(134)
(a) Everyone who believes that [two plus two equals four] believes that [four equals two plus two]
(b) Everyone who believes that [two plus two equals four] believes that [for any right-angle triangle, the square of its hypotenuse is equal to the sum of the squares of its two remaining sides]

According to the possible worlds story, the parts of these sentences are co-referential in psychological contexts, because the parts are synonymous. (Remember: 'Four equals two plus two' and 'For any right-angle triangle, the square of its hypotenuse is equal to the sum of the squares of its two remaining sides' are both true at every world.) The parts are clearly ordered in the same way. So, by the principle of compositionality for references, the wholes must be co-referential. At least according to the possible worlds account. Hence, if (134a) is true, then (134b) must be true also. Now, (134a) is undoubtedly true. The possible worlds theorist must therefore conclude that (134b) is true as well. But this conclusion is absurd. Not everyone who believes that two plus two equals four believes the Pythagorean Theorem!

In fact the argument generalizes. Making suitable changes, one can show that, on the possible worlds account, anyone who believes *any* necessary proposition believes *every* necessary proposition, no matter how complex. Maybe worse: consider those unlucky souls who believe some necessarily false proposition. By similar reasoning, they must believe each and every necessary falsehood, no matter how laughable! Again, this seems absurd. This has led many philosophers to abandon the possible worlds theory altogether. Others have tried to fix it. I leave the issue open.

Summary

Recall the beloved slogan: Language is a system of symbols which we know and use. The system, I've insisted, has at least three components: phonology, syntax and semantics. An adequate semantics for a language *L* must determine which of *L*'s syntactic structures are meaningful. And it must assign, to each expression *E* of *L*, the meaning of *E* in the language. In the last two chapters, I have been scouting three ways of doing this: three Thing Theories of Meaning.

Thing Theories of Meaning—be they directly referential or mediated—all share a central feature: each locates meaningfulness in the relations between structures/sounds on the one hand and "external objects" on the other. As you've seen, however, they disagree about the nature of said relations. Direct reference theories—introduced in the last chapter—take the relation between words and things to be immediate. Not so mediated reference theories.

In this chapter I have been exploring two mediated versions of the Thing Theory of Meaning: Frege's sense and reference theory, and possible worlds semantics. What both assign *directly* to words are intensions, also called "senses". It's the job of these intensions/senses, in their turn, to determine a word's referent. Frege and possible worlds theorists agree on this, but they would disagree about *how* reference determination occurs. Frege took senses to be creatures of the actual world: something like attributes of actual objects. Possible world theorists, on the other hand, allow intensions to deal in mere possibilia.

Suggested Readings

The classic argument for sense as well as reference appears in Frege 1892a. See also Frege 1892b and his "Letter to Jourdain", reprinted in Moore 1993. To my mind, the single best secondary source on Frege is Dummett 1973. Dummett 1978, 1981, 1994 are also very useful. See also Geach 1962 and Kenny 1995. For a rather different point of view on Frege, see Chomsky 1993b. Quine 1956, 1960, Ch.4 and Kaplan 1968 contain difficult but rewarding treatments of opacity. Davidson (1967, 1968 and elsewhere), building on Tarski 1944, argues forcefully that, *pace* Frege, sense isn't required. Saul Kripke (1972) contends that, in the case of names anyway, it isn't even desirable. On a truly pessimistic note, Kripke (1979) worries that, in addition to lacking an adequate *treatment* of opacity (in particular, of propositional attitudes), philosophers have yet to even understand the *problem* aright.

Carnap's (1949) *Meaning and Necessity* lays the foundations for possible world semantics. Church 1951, Lewis 1970 and Montague 1974 carry the program forward. All three, however, are very heavy going. See Dowty, Wall and Peters 1981, Partee 1975, and Weisler 1991 for introductions to possible world semantics in the Montague tradition. Bach 1989 and Chierchia and McConnell-Ginet 1990 are good introductory sources for intensional semantics, broadly construed. On the problem of the possible equivalence of all necessary propositions, consult Stalnaker 1984, who works hard to overcome it. For general issues about possible worlds, see Lewis 1973, Lycan 1979 and Stalnaker 1976. All three are reprinted in Garfield and Kiteley 1991. Quine (1953a, 1961) is noted for expressing scepticism not only about possible worlds, but about modal notions generally.

Chapter Five:

Truth Theoretic Semantics

1. Truth and Meaning

Donald Davidson (1967) explicitly rejects semantics in Frege's style, with its postulation of senses for all meaningful expressions. Up until now, I have been thinking of theories of meaning as systematically pairing words and sentences with entities of some sort—these being their meanings. Davidson's intuition, however, is that thinking about meaning in this way is a mistake. Indeed, Davidson is vaguely hostile towards any theory of meaning which introduces meanings as *things* which expressions have. (This intuition is shared, incidentally, by W.V.O. Quine and Ludwig Wittgenstein (1889-1951).) How, then, can he give a theory of meaning? Well, Davidson notes, what is wanted is not necessarily a theory which pairs words with some kind of item, which is to serve as its meaning. Instead,

> The theory will have done its work if it provides, for every sentence *s* in the language under study, a matching sentence... that, in some way yet to be made clear, 'gives the meaning' of *s* (Davidson 1967, 23).

Notice that a matching *sentence* is wanted, not a matching external object. In short, what a semantic theory *really* needs to provide, for every meaningful sentence *s*, is an instance of (135), where what replaces p is not an external object but *a sentence*—one which gives the meaning of the target sentence.

(135) ⌜Sentence s means that $\bar{p}$⌝

A semantic theory which entailed all and only the true instances of (135) would indeed "give the meaning" of each sentence in the language. So this is what ought to be required.

But Davidson doesn't stop there. Ideally, a semantic theory should entail conclusions whose truth or falsity is *obvious*. But, he worries, the truth or falsity of instances of (135) won't inevitably be obvious, because 'means that ___' is opaque. As he puts it, since 'means that ___' is non-extensional, it may introduce "problems as hard as, or perhaps identical with, the problems our theory is out to solve" (Davidson 1967, 22). So, instead of 'means that ___', Davidson suggests substituting something non-opaque. That way, it will be self-evident when the semantic theory's entailments are correct. Insight one: meaning has a lot to do with truth conditions. Insight two: 'is true if and only if ___' is *not* opaque. Application: try replacing 'means that' in (135) with 'is true if and only if'. Here's the result: an adequate semantic theory for a language L must entail a true instance of (136) for every sentence of L. And it must entail no false instances of (136).

(136) ⌜Sentence s is true in L if and only if $\bar{p}$⌝

Many linguists and philosophers would agree that this is a *necessary* condition on a theory of meaning. To paraphrase Lewis (1970), a semantic theory without truth conditions isn't really a semantic theory. What sets Davidson apart from the crowd is his view that a theory of truth for a language *is sufficient* as a semantic theory. Allow me to explain.

A theory of truth for L is, in effect, a definition of the phrase 'true in L'. Now, there is a way of giving a definition which may not be familiar to you. One might call it 'definition by cases'. One way to define 'is a Uruguayan citizen', for example, would involving saying, for each candidate person, the conditions under which she would be a citizen of Uruguay. Or, to take a made-up example, suppose Fritz and Matilde, notorious weirdos both, set up a club. Call it Club Z. They invite three friends to join them. But, being notorious weirdos, they impose bizarre rules for entry into the club. The founders—Fritz and Matilde—become members simply by wishing to. (Hey, it's their club.) However, to become a member, Juan must pay 1000 Mexican Pesos, Gabriela must run five blocks in bare feet, and David must sing the Swedish National Anthem. Given these circumstances, one can define 'is a member of Club Z' by providing five instances of (137), as in (138a-e)—one for each candidate member:

(137) $\ulcorner x$ is a member of Club Z if and only if $p\urcorner$

(138) *Definition by Cases of 'is a member of Club Z'*
(a) Fritz is a member of Club Z if and only if he wishes to be a member of Club Z.
(b) Matilde is a member of Club Z if and only if she wishes to be a member of Club Z.
(c) Juan is a member of Club Z if and only if he pays 1000 Mexican Pesos.
(d) Gabriela is a member of Club Z if and only if she runs five blocks in bare feet.
(e) David is a member of Club Z if and only if he sings the Swedish National Anthem.

Taken together, the five instances of (137) provide a definition by cases of 'is a member of Club Z'. A "theory" of Club Z membership, if you like.

Now, look again at (136):

(136) $\ulcorner$Sentence s is true in L if and only if $p\urcorner$

By analogy, you can see that, taken collectively, the instances of (136) amount to a definition of 'is true in L'. Or, to use even fancier terms, the sum of the instances provides *a theory of truth* for L. Next step: a theory of truth for L gives the truth conditions of every sentence in L. In which case, Davidson conjectures, it may well give the *meaning* of every sentence in L—assuming meaning amounts to truth conditions. Hence—big conclusion—a theory of truth for L is a semantic theory for L. In which case, to give a semantic theory, one needn't provide either an extension or an intension for every expression. In contrast with all the Thing Theories of Meaning presented so far, in Davidson's formulation there's no requirement that there be a *thing* to which words correspond. On the contrary, to give a semantic theory, for Davidson, it is both necessary *and sufficient* to provide a system—a bunch of axioms and rules of proof, if you will—that generates all and only the true instances of (136).

This is the essence of Davidson's **truth theoretic semantics**.

2. Non-Declaratives and Truth

In the foregoing, the emphasis has been on **declarative** (also known as **indicative**) language. Sentences like:

(139) *Indicatives/Declaratives*
(a) Ottawa is really cold in the winter
(b) Jim Morrison died long ago

But a language is much more than a collection of declarative sentences. There are also **imperatives** and **interrogatives**, among other **syntactic moods**. Some examples:

(140) *Imperatives*
(a) Get the hell out of here!
(b) Pick up some milk on your way home
(c) Don't be fooled by imitations

(141) *Interrogatives*
(a) Is Lars at home?
(b) Where does Rita live?
(c) Why does television have to be so boring?

Evidently, any adequate theory of language must have something to say about imperatives, interrogatives, and other non-declarative moods. In particular, any truth theoretic semantics must accommodate them. But, as you'll shortly see, this is no easy feat.

An adequate theory of non-declaratives must, according to Davidson (1979), meet at least three conditions. First, it must capture what is common between declaratives and sentences in other moods. For example, it must explicate the sense in which (142a-c) all share a single semantic root.[41]

(142)
(a) The door is open [Declarative]
(b) Is the door open? [Interrogative]
(c) Open the door! [Imperative]

On the other hand, and here's the second condition, a satisfactory treatment of non-declaratives must also say what is semantically *different* about the distinct moods. To take the same example:

although (142a-c) share something in common, they clearly are not synonyms. The evidence that the moods are different, as if evidence were necessary: it is precisely because of the systematic differences in meaning between sentences of the various moods that such sentences are typically used in different ways. Indicatives are typically used to make assertions, imperatives are used to issue commands, interrogatives are used to ask questions, and so on. A theory of non-declaratives must somehow accommodate these differences. Final condition: if Davidson's project is to succeed, any account of non-declaratives must be consistent with his conjecture that a semantic theory for a language *L* is simply a theory of truth for that language. Meaning cannot be something other than truth conditions.

As Davidson points out, it's not easy to give an account of non-declaratives which meets all three conditions. Here's why: the first two conditions—that the differences and similarities be highlighted—suggest that non-declaratives be decomposed into a **mood indicator** and a **propositional content sentence**. Here's the picture:

(143)   Complete Sentence

     Mood Indicator   Propositional Content Sentence

The Mood Indicator captures the differences between the moods. The Propositional Content Sentence captures the commonality. For example, 'Is the door open?' would be captured by the following tree:

(144)   Is the door open?

     Interrogative Indicator   That the door is open

So far so good. But a difficulty arises because of the third condition. The problem has to do with how the two part-meanings combine. If truth theoretic semantics is to work—indeed, if *any* kind of semantics is to work—the Propositional Content Sentence and the Mood Indicator must combine somehow to give the meaning of the Complete Sentence. But the usual means-of-combination don't look promising, because the Propositional Content Sentence is a truth bearer, and the familiar functions which take truth bearers as input *also yield truth bearers as output*. This is, for example, what (145a) and (145b) do:

(145)
(a) It's true that ___
(b) It's not the case that ___

But this can't be how the Mood-Indicator-meaning meshes with the Propositional Content Sentence—with the Mood Indicator providing a function of type $TV{\rightarrow}TV$, and the Propositional Content Sentence contributing the TV argument—because then the complete sentence would be a truth bearer. But that wouldn't be right. For, as should be obvious, non-declaratives *are not capable of being true or false*. Recall, for example, (141b):

(141b) Where does Rita live?

To see that it's neither true nor false, imagine someone approaches you and says (141b). It would be absurd to reply 'I disagree'! That's because, in producing this interrogative, the speaker hasn't said anything truth-evaluable. (You might be tempted to insist that non-declaratives can be true or false. But if you say this, you run the risk of not satisfying condition two: capturing the differences between the various moods.) Conclusion: if non-declaratives are neither true nor false, then their meaning cannot result from a function whose output is a truth value. So the manner of combination of the Propositional Content Sentence and the Mood Indicator cannot be captured in the usual way. Davidson (1979, 117) concludes:

> Mood must somehow contribute to meaning...since mood is clearly a conventional feature of sentences. Yet it cannot combine with or modify the meaning of the rest of the sentence in any known way.

That is the difficulty. Here's Davidson's solution. There's more than one way for contents to "combine". One, which I haven't discussed at all, is the way the various contents in a *discourse* hang together.

(146) *A Discourse*
(a) The waiter: 'Hi, my name is Phil. I'll be your server today'
(b) The customer: 'I would like coffee, please'
(c) The waiter: 'I'll bring it right away'

The contents that make up (146) fit together—somehow. But they do not combine as function and argument. Notice too: though each utterance in the discourse is truth-evaluable, one might reasonably say that the discourse *as a whole* is not. (To see this, ask yourself: is the whole true or false if—with the exception of the fact that the waiter's name is really Floyd, rather than Phil—everything else is true? Bizarre question.) Davidson takes his cue from this. Basically, Davidson maintains that the Mood Indicator and the Propositional

Content Sentence are uttered *independently*, though as part of a single one-person discourse. So that, in saying 'Is it raining?', the speaker is effectively producing the following discourse:

(147) That it's raining. I am inquiring.

In short, the way a mood indicator functions is comparable *not* to an operator applying to a sentence—as in (148)—but to a second related "saying", as in (149).

(148) *Operators*
(a) It is not the case that [Fred smokes a lot]
(b) There's no doubt that [Nadia loves spaghetti]
(c) It's possible that [the Blue Jays will win]

(149) *Second Sayings*
(a) That Fred smokes a lot. It's not true.
(b) That Nadia loves spaghetti. There's no doubt about it.
(c) That the Blue Jays will win. It's possible.

This proposal of Davidson's satisfies his three conditions. Semantically related sentences in the distinct moods have something in common: namely, the same Propositional Content Sentence. However, something distinguishes the moods as well: the content of the Mood Indicator. Those are the first two conditions. As for the third: interrogatives, imperatives and so on are accommodated within truth theoretic semantics—despite the fact that non-indicatives are not truth bearers. The reason? Each part of the Complete Sentence has truth conditions: the Propositional Content Sentence clearly does, but the Mood Indicator part does too. (A token of 'I am inquiring', for example, is true if and only if its speaker is, in fact, inquiring.) But, because the two parts combine together as *two distinct sayings*, rather than as operator-sentence, the Complete Sentence *lacks* a truth value. Just as the discourse (146)—read not as a conjunction of statements, but as a mere collection of distinct claims—doesn't have a truth value.

To sum up, then: Davidson suggests giving a theory of meaning *not* by pairing expressions with things, but by pairing them with *other expressions*—where, importantly, these "other expressions" provide truth conditions only. One obvious problem is that many meaningful sentences—in particular, non-declarative sentences—are not capable of being true or false. Which suggests, contra Davidson, that meaning *isn't* truth conditions. Davidson's way around this is to divide non-declaratives into two parts: a propositional content part and a mood-indicating part. Each *part* has truth conditions—hence, there's nothing more to meaning than truth conditions. But non-declaratives aren't capable of being true or false, because their parts do not combine truth-functionally.

Suggested Readings

Davidson's truth theoretic semantics has its roots in Tarski's (1944) work on truth definitions. See Field 1972 for a clear and insightful discussion of Tarski's project. For telling (though difficult) criticisms of Davidson's program, see Dummett 1976, Foster 1976, and the other papers in Evans and McDowell 1976. The editor's introduction to this collection is also very useful. Introductions to Davidson's thought include Evnine 1991, Hernández Iglesias 1990, and Ramberg 1989.

The philosophical literature on interrogatives is growing rapidly. As a starting point, try Aqvist 1975 and Bromberger 1966. McGinn 1977 defends a view not unlike Davidson's (1979). It is carefully and critically examined by Gabriel Segal (1991). Belnap and Steel 1976 and Hamblin 1973 defend the idea that questions are sets of propositions. Hintikka (1974, 1976) offers a game-theoretic perspective. Higginbotham 1993, in addition to getting things just about right in my view, contains a useful overview and extensive bibliography.

Part Two:

The Knowledge Perspective

Chapter Six:

The Idea Theory of Meaning

1. Introduction

Until now, I have been treating language as a kind of quasi-mathematical system. A language, so considered, pairs abstract objects (syntactic structure types and sound patterns) with their meanings. This isn't a crazy view, but it is pretty narrow in focus. Oh, and by the way: meanings, from this system perspective, may be things like intangible propositions, obscure manners of presentation, or functions from two truth values to a single truth value. Abstract system indeed! From these lofty heights, I'll now bring the discussion down to earth a bit. To be precise, I'll place it firmly in the head.

I begin by returning to the central questions in the theory of meaning: what is it for a word or sentence to be meaningful? And what makes an expression mean what it does, rather than meaning something else? Put another way—a way more congenial to the knowledge perspective—what do you learn when you learn the meaning of an expression? For example, what is it for the word 'spaghetti' to have the meaning SPAGHETTI for me? Why is 'spaghetti' meaningful? And why doesn't 'spaghetti' mean FISH or HAIRCUT? When you learned the meaning of 'spaghetti', what did you learn?

One hypothesis I've discussed at length is that words get their meanings by being paired with something "out there", "something in the world". Here's a different view: linguistic meaning comes from pairing expressions with something "in the mind". This is the **Idea Theory of Meaning**. In this section you will encounter three versions of it. According to what I'll call the mental image version, meanings derive from (something like) pictures in the head. According to the second version, due to Paul Grice, meanings derive from intentions—that is, from commonsensical **intentional** or propositional attitude states. (Terminological aside: 'Intentions' (with a 't') is a term of ordinary language; anyone who intends something has intentions (with a 't'). 'Intensions' (with an 's'), on the other hand, is a technical term of philosophers and linguists. It is words, phrases and sentences which express intensions. The word 'intentional' lies somewhere in between ordinary talk and technical vocabulary. 'Intentional states' refers to states like believing, hoping, desiring and so on.) According to the third and final version of the idea theory, meaning comes from a **language of thought**. As we will see, none of these three is entirely satisfactory.

2. Mental Images

David Hume (1711-1776), always eager to root out meaningless philosophical jargon, suggests a way to do so. He writes:

> When we entertain, therefore, any suspicion, that a philosophical term is employed without any meaning or idea (as is but too frequent), we need but enquire, from what impression is that supposed idea derived? And if it be impossible to assign any, this will serve to confirm our suspicion (Hume 1748, 13).

In this passage Hume hints at a view he explicitly held: that, as he puts it in *An Enquiry Concerning Human Understanding*, words are "expressive of ideas" (1748, 11), where what is meant by "an idea" is something like a complex of remembered sensations/percepts.[42] In what follows, I will call these complexes **mental images**, since I'm reserving 'idea' as a cover term. Taking mental images—and not just visual images—to be meaning-givers yields the first version of the Idea Theory of Meaning.[43] Here's an example, culled from Martin 1987, 22:

> I assume that right now you are not having a pork chop dinner, but you are perfectly able to understand (or meaningfully say) the word 'pork chop', because the word calls to mind the sort of sense

experiences that you have had when a pork chop was actually before you.

The suggestion is that there are mental images associated with actual pork chop encounters. It is *these* which, collectively, give meaning to the term 'pork chop'.

Objections

The mental image view is obviously inadequate, especially when contrasted with the various Thing Theories. First of all, not all words are connected with mental images. For example, consider the words 'the', 'seven', and 'from'. What mental images—what collection of sights, sounds, smells, etc.—are associated with these? Apparently none. Or better: none which could serve as "the meaning" of these words. So, according to the mental image version of the Idea Theory of Meaning, they must be meaningless. But, patently, they're far from meaningless. Also consider that not every difference in meaning corresponds to a difference in mental image. What difference in sense experience is there between ten thousand hairs and 9,999 hairs? Apparently none. Yet there's a clear difference in meaning between the corresponding phrases. So again, not all meanings can be captured by mental images.

Furthermore, even if association with mental images is meaning-giving, only some associations count. Certain associations between words and mental images are accidental. That is, they are not a matter of meaning. Take Martin's example: there are lots of "mental images" I associate with the word 'pork chop'. I associate it with a stomach ache I once got from an undercooked pork chop; I associate it with sights from my Aunt's kitchen (she always makes pork chops), and so on. But these remembered sensations—despite their association with the word—aren't part of the meaning of 'pork chop'. Nor is there any obvious way of separating associations like these, which aren't meaning-giving, from those images that purportedly do give the meaning. At least, not without presupposing the very thing being sought: an account of meaning. (Also consider that if, for some peculiar reason, I mentally picture a banana while saying 'Hand me an apple'. What I request is nevertheless *an apple*, not a banana. In which case, it would appear that my word 'apple' means APPLE regardless of what image I token while saying it.[44])

Next objection. Images are too particular to serve as meanings. Every sense impression is specific. For instance, an impression of my cat Weeble involves a particular visual sensation (small, black, cute), sound sensation (whiny), tactile sensation (soft luxurious hair), and so on. Similarly for any cat *image* which I may call to mind. You can't perceive *or even imagine* a cat which is neither white, black, grey, or yellow; neither fat nor thin; neither Siamese nor Tabby, etc. Every mental image is specific. But—and here's the objection—meanings are not typically specific in this way. Moreover, an image, unlike a meaning, cannot correspond to a whole class of things that differ widely from one another. (What image, for instance, corresponds to all and only vegetables? I don't even want to think about it.)

One more problem. Hume and company want mental images to serve as the source of meanings for natural language expressions. One reason philosophers *need* a "source of meanings" is that words and sentences aren't inherently meaningful: that 'spaghetti' means what it does is not a basic fact about the universe. That's why one wants to tell a story about what *makes* linguistic expressions meaningful. Presumably, the hope was that images, unlike words, would represent inherently. In which case, words can get their meanings from images—and there the story ends. But, ultimately, it's not clear how this could work. You might think the answer to this is obvious: images manage to be inherently meaningful because they resemble what they stand for. For instance, one might say, a portrait of Queen Victoria is about *her*, in so far as it looks like her. In just the same way, my cat-image means CAT because it is actually quite like a cat. But think about it: can an *idea* really be similar to a cat? As Cummins (1989, 31) says:

> When I look at a red ball, a red sphere doesn't appear in my brain. If the ball is a rubber ball, it seems the brain will have to be made of rubber, or at least elastic. And what about furry tabby cats?

Images aren't furry, or overweight, or yellow. Which means they aren't really similar to furry, overweight, yellow cats. Which suggests that mental images don't represent because of similarity.[45] But, if you need to say what makes *an image* meaningful, you haven't yet provided an adequate theory of where linguistic meaning ultimately comes from. You've simply postponed that issue. (This is one reason one might favour the Thing Theory of Meaning. There's no "detour" through the mind. This will come up again.)

In sum, the problems with the mental image version of the Idea theory are several: not all meaningful words are connected to images; some images are only accidentally correlated with words; images are too particular to serve as meanings; and there's no account of how *images* represent what they do, since "similarity" won't do the trick. However, maybe the problem isn't with the Idea Theory of Meaning. Maybe it's with the kind of things chosen as "ideas"—namely, mental images.

3. H. Paul Grice

In a seminal article called "Meaning", H. Paul Grice (1957) distinguishes two sorts of meaning, one of which will underwrite his Idea Theory of Meaning. It will be worthwhile to get these sorted out early. Grice contrasts examples (150a-b) and (151a-b):

(150) *Natural Meaning*
(a) Those spots mean measles
(b) The recent budget means that we shall have a hard year

(151) *Nonnatural Meaning*
(a) Those three rings on the bell mean that the bus is full
(b) That remark, 'Smith couldn't get on without his trouble and strife', meant that Smith found his wife indispensable

It is the second kind of meaning—**nonnatural meaning** or **meaning$_{NN}$**—which linguistic expressions have, and hence this kind of meaning which will be the central topic of this section. Grice offers more information about this kind of meaning, namely:

(152) *Four Tests for Nonnatural Meaning*
(a) $\ulcorner x$ means$_{NN}$ that $p\urcorner$ does *not* entail that p
(b) $\ulcorner x$ means$_{NN}$ that $p\urcorner$ suggests that somebody meant something by x
(c) $\ulcorner x$ means$_{NN}$ that $p\urcorner$ can be rephrased as $\ulcorner x$ means 'p'$\urcorner$
(d) $\ulcorner x$ means$_{NN}$ that $p\urcorner$ *cannot* be rephrased as $\ulcorner$The fact that x means that $p\urcorner$.

Consider again Grice's original examples, to see if these tests work. Take (151a): that the three rings "mean" the bus is full does *not* entail that the bus actually *is* full, since someone could have rung the bell out of turn; and the sentence *does* suggest that somebody meant something by ringing; and it *can* be paraphrased as 'Those three rings mean 'The bus is full'"; but (151a) *cannot* be rephrased as 'The fact that those three rings means that the bus is full'. So, in the case of sentence (151a), the "meaning" in question is nonnatural meaning: the kind language theorists are interested in.

In contrast, sentence (153) *does* entail that John has measles: if the spots really mean measles, then John has measles.

(153) Those spots mean that John has measles

But (153) *does not* suggest that somebody meant something by the spots in question. (Indeed, if someone meant something by the spots, then they don't really "mean measles" at all, in the requisite sense.) Moreover, (153) *cannot* be rephrased as 'Those spots mean 'John has measles"; though it can be rephrased as 'The fact that John has those spots means that John has measles'. So (153) is a case of natural meaning—the kind of "meaning" language theorists *aren't* really interested in.

In sum: Grice's tests provide a good sense of what the difference is between these two senses of "meaning". Here's a further tip for keeping them apart. If x shows that p, x indicates that p, or x gives one grounds for inferring that p, *but that's all*, then x merely means$_N$ that p. For meaning$_{NN}$, something more is required: x must signify, connote or stand for p. (A warning about terminology: "natural meaning"—meaning$_N$—isn't meaning which is natural *in the sense of being independent of human beings*. The example of the budget should make this clear.)

Grice goes on to distinguish different varieties of meaning$_{NN}$, all of which are relevant to the philosophical study of language and communication. First: both tokens and types exhibit nonnatural meaning. But this isn't all. Grice writes that *an agent A* can also mean$_{NN}$:

> ... I include under the head of nonnatural senses of "mean" any senses of "mean" found in sentences of the patterns "A means (meant) something by x" or "A means (meant) by x that..." (Grice 1957, 73)

Notice: the things which are meaningful$_{NN}$ in these cases are neither linguistic expression types nor linguistic expression tokens. In this case of meaning$_{NN}$, it's not words, but rather *people* who mean$_{NN}$. So there are,

(154) *Varieties of Meaning$_{NN}$*
(a) Type meaning (Also called '**expression meaning**')
(b) Token meaning (Also called '**utterance meaning**')
(c) Speaker's meaning

Notice also that these three types of meaning aren't necessarily equivalent. To understand an utterance, or to recover speaker's meaning, generally requires understanding the meaning of the expression used *and then some*. For example:

(155)
(a) Steve bought it on sale [What is the "it" being talked about? When exactly was "it" purchased? Which Steve is being talked about?]
(b) Dear Prof. Smith: Mr. *X* has an excellent command of the English language and hands his work in on time. [Suppose Mr. *X* is applying for graduate school. What, in that context, would the letter-writer mean by this?]

In (155), the meaning of the linguistic expression—the meaning of the *type*—does not exhaust the meaning of any particular *token*. Put otherwise: knowing English isn't enough to understand *the token*, because the context partially determines its meaning. A token of (155a) could have any of the followings meanings, depending upon the context:

(156)
(a) STEVEN J. BROWN BOUGHT THE SILVER COIN ON SALE ON AUGUST 31, 1993
(b) STEPHEN R. LITTLE BOUGHT THE GREEN TOYOTA ON SALE ON MARCH 3RD, 1976
(c) LITTLE STEVIE WONDER BOUGHT THE BLACK PIANO ON SALE ON FEBRUARY 3RD, 1990

The type, on the other hand, typically has only one meaning: something like THE CONTEXTUALLY SALIENT PERSON *P* NAMED 'STEVE' PURCHASED THE INDICATED OBJECT *O* ON SALE AT INDICATED TIME *T*.

Similarly, of course, the meaning of the expression does not determine the *speaker's* meaning. For example, a speaker can mean any of (156a-c) by 'Steve bought it on sale'; but, as you saw, none of these is the meaning of that expression type. Curiously, it also seems that speaker's meaning and utterance meaning come apart—though this is much more a matter of debate. (The issue will be taken up at length in later chapters.) It's tempting, for example, to say that *the utterance* of (155b) just means that Mr. *X* has an excellent command of the English language and hands his work in on time. It's clear, however, that this does not exhaust what *an utterer* of this sentence would mean, in the context of a letter of reference. In such a context, a speaker would most likely mean something very unflattering.

So, to repeat, there is expression meaning (i.e. the meaning of the type), utterance meaning (i.e. the meaning of the token), and the speaker's meaning (i.e. what the agent meant when she produced the token). Each of these is, according to Grice, a variety of nonnatural meaning. And he intends his Idea Theory of Meaning to apply to each.

Grice begins his discussion of nonnatural meaning by rejecting an answer to the "What is meaning?" question—an answer he attributes to Stevenson (1944, Ch.3):

(157) *Stevenson's Proposal (Simplified)*: For x to mean that p, x must have a tendency to produce in an audience the belief that p.

The insight which informs this proposal is the following: saying an expression which means p has a tendency of getting people to believe that p. For example, saying 'Whales are mammals' tends to get people to believe that whales are mammals. So, thinks Stevenson, maybe to mean that p *just is* to have the tendency to make people believe that p. But there's an obvious problem with this proposal. As Grice points out,

> It is no doubt the case that many people have a tendency to put on a tailcoat when they think they are about to go to a dance, and it is no doubt also the case that many people, on seeing someone put on a tailcoat, would conclude that the person in question was about to go to a dance. Does this satisfy us that putting on a tailcoat means$_{NN}$ that one is about to go to a dance (or indeed means$_{NN}$ anything at all)? Obviously not (Grice 1957, 73).

It may be that putting on a tailcoat means$_N$ that one is going to a dance. That's because, as Grice says, there is a correlation between the two sorts of event. But it doesn't mean$_{NN}$ that. This isn't the kind of meaning—nonnatural meaning—which philosophers of language are after. What's more, there could be a correlation between saying an expression E and inducing a belief B which *does* rest on meaning$_{NN}$, but which rests on it in the wrong way. Take (158).

(158) Jones is an athlete

As Grice rightly observes, saying (158) will have a tendency to induce the belief that Jones is tall. And this time, the tendency does rest, at least in part, on the meaning of the expression. That's because there's a correlation between saying 'Jones is an athlete' and inducing the belief that Jones is an athlete. But, since there's *also* a correlation between believing that someone is an athlete and believing that they are tall, there's a correlation between saying 'Jones is an athlete' and inducing the belief that Jones is tall. But then, according to Stevenson's proposal, what 'Jones is an athlete' means$_{NN}$, in part, is that Jones is tall. This, I gather, is a mistake. In a nutshell, Stevenson's proposal is inadequate because it cannot distinguish simple correlation (meaning$_N$) from denotation/sense/etc. (meaning$_{NN}$).

What Meanings Are For Grice

Grice has sketched what meaning$_{NN}$ is not: having meaning$_{NN}$ is not simply a matter of having a tendency to produce some attitude or other in an audience. Some things have tendencies to induce the belief that p, but they do not mean$_{NN}$ that p (e.g. putting on tails, 'Jones is an athlete'). What's more, something can mean$_{NN}$ that p without having a *tendency* to induce p-beliefs: it might mean$_{NN}$ that p just once, or under very rare or special circumstances. There's no tendency, but there's (nonnatural) meaning. Having explained what meaning$_{NN}$ is not, however, Grice now owes a positive account of what meaning$_{NN}$ is. As a first pass, he suggests the following:

(159) *The First Pass*: $\ulcorner x$ meant$_{NN}$ $p \urcorner$ would be true if x was intended by its utterer to induce in the audience the belief that p.

How does this differ from Stevenson's proposal? Well, meaning$_{NN}$ that p is not a matter of the beliefs which the expression *actually* tends to induce; rather, what x means$_{NN}$ is a matter of what belief the speaker of x *intends* to inculcate. Does this first pass handle the cases which Stevenson's proposal couldn't? Well, the tailcoat doesn't always mean$_{NN}$ that its wearer is going dancing, because its wearer won't inevitably intend to induce this belief. Similarly, an utterance of 'Jones is an athlete' won't mean$_{NN}$ that Jones is tall, unless the speaker intends to induce this particular belief. Which, ordinarily, she will not. So, this proposal represents a marked improvement. But Grice rejects it on the grounds that

I might leave B's handkerchief near the scene of a murder in order to induce the detective to believe that B was the murderer; but we would not want to say that the handkerchief (or my leaving it there) meant$_{NN}$ anything or that I had meant$_{NN}$ by leaving it that B was the murderer (Grice 1957, 74).

You might call this "the sneaky objection". The problem is this: I can intend to induce a belief without wanting anyone to know that I'm trying to induce it. This isn't a case of communication, it's a case of manipulation. To deal with this problem, Grice adds a second condition:

(160) *Grice's Proposal*: ⌜x meant$_{NN}$ that p̄⌝ would be true if
(a) the speaker S intended x to induce the belief that p in some audience A
(b) S intended the audience A to recognize this intention, and to take it as grounds for believing that p.

The essential idea is this: communication consists in the "message-sender" intending to cause the "message-receiver" to believe something; *and* the message-sender hopes to achieve this just by getting the receiver to recognize that he, the sender, is wanting to induce this belief. Here's the crux: for a speaker to mean$_{NN}$ something is really a matter of that speaker having certain very complex intentions. And for *an utterance* to be meaningful$_{NN}$ is for some speaker to have meant something by it. This is Grice's account of what meaning$_{NN}$ is—for speakers and for linguistic tokens.

I hope it's clear why this is a version of the Idea Theory of Meaning. Meaning, in the first instance, comes from pairing sounds, marks or whatever with commonplace *mental states*. In particular, with intentions. As you'll shortly see, however, there are a number of difficulties with Grice's proposal, most of which he was very well aware of.

Objections

Problem One. There is something missing from Grice's account. He expresses *the hope* that elucidating utterance meaning and a speaker's meaning "might reasonably be expected to help us with" expression meaning (Grice 1957, 74). He writes:

"x means$_{NN}$ (timeless) that so-and-so" might as a first shot be equated with some statement or disjunction of statements about what "people" (vague) intend (with qualifications about "recognition") to effect by x (Grice 1957, 76).

But Grice never completed this program himself. Nor is it clear how to go about it, especially since the number of meaningful linguistic expressions is infinite—hence, most expressions are such that no one ever intends to do anything with them. Also consider: to give an adequate theory of meaning for the whole language, Grice needs to say what the "intended effects" of nouns, verbs, connectives, quantifiers, and so on might be, and how the "intended effects" of complex expressions are determined by the "intended effects" of these parts. How this might go remains mysterious—to say the least.

Problem Two: Grice's line requires ordinary everyday folks to have very complicated intentions. Even young children, the severely retarded and so on—who, I take it, mean things by the words they utter—are supposedly intending to induce complex beliefs, by getting their audience to recognize their intentions to induce said beliefs, and so on. To make matters worse, people on the whole aren't conscious of having such intentions. Should one really believe that all speakers have such intentions? It's not clear. But if speakers *don't* have such meaning intentions, said intentions can't be the source of meaning$_{NN}$.

Problem Three. Recall what was said in the Introduction, about thinking in language. There were reasons for believing that some thought, if not all, presupposes a language. This was especially true of very complex thoughts like PARTICLE ACCELERATORS COST MILLIONS OF DOLLARS. Of crucial importance for present purposes: it may be that having some if not all *intentions* requires already possessing a language. And already possessing a language would require already possessing something whose expressions are meaningful$_{NN}$. But if intentions presuppose meaningful expressions, then you can't explain the meaningfulness of expressions by appeal to intentions. Not without circularity, anyway.

These are problems that Grice knew about, and he worked hard at solving them. But I won't go into that. Sorry.

Suggested Readings

The origins of the mental image theory can be found in Bishop George Berkeley's (1685-1753) *A Treatise Concerning the Principles of Human Knowledge* (1710) and David Hume's (1748) *An Enquiry Concerning Human Understanding*. Robert Cummins' (1989) *Meaning and Mental Representation* contains an insightful discussion of its development, as does Bennett 1971. See also Robert Martin's (1987) *The Meaning of Language*. To repeat, Martin's book is a fine introductory discussion of many aspects of philosophy of language, including the mental image theory.

For more on Grice's own views, see the papers in H.P. Grice's (1989) *Studies in the Way of Words*, especially Grice 1957, 1968, 1969. Another excellent source-cum-critique is Schiffer 1972. See also Black 1973, Sperber and Wilson 1986, 1987, and Ziff 1967.

Chapter Seven:

The Language of Thought

1. Mentalese and the Idea Theory of Meaning

According to the Idea Theory of Meaning, linguistic expressions are meaningful because they are paired with "something in the mind" that endows them with meaning. So far I've discussed two versions of this: the hypothesis that the "things in the mind" are images, and Grice's proposal. The final proposal is that public words and sentences are meaningful because they are paired with *internal* words and sentences: expressions of the **language of thought**, also known as **mentalese**.

Grice, you just saw, tried to get meaning from intentions. His project had two parts: conventional linguistic meaning was to be cashed out in terms of speakers' meaning, and speakers' meaning was to be cashed out in terms of speakers' intentions. Please notice something important: talk of intentions, in Grice's sense, is part of everyday talk of **intentional states**. States which, according to *common sense*, everybody has—states like beliefs, desires and so on. Notice too that Grice doesn't offer *a theory* about what intentions (and intentional states generally) are, or where they come from. (We might say that although he gives an Idea Theory of Meaning, Grice doesn't really offer a theory of ideas.)

Hume and company, unlike Grice, didn't try to ground meaning in ordinary intentional states or **propositional attitudes** like belief, desire, etc. And, again in contrast with Grice, they *did* have an explicit theory of ideas, flawed though it was. Jerry Fodor, a contemporary philosopher and cognitive scientist, takes a leaf from both Hume and Grice. Like Grice, he grounds conventional linguistic meaning in belief-desire states. Like Hume, he offers a *theory* of the mental items that he appeals to.

What is Fodor's theory? Well, notice first that pictures aren't the only kind of symbol. Words and sentences are symbols too. So the way is open to suppose that mental representations— ideas in the head—are *sentence-like* rather than picture-like.[46] According to Fodor *and* Hume, there are "symbols in the head". And these are what get paired with natural language expressions to give them meaning. But according to Fodor, the symbols aren't pictures. They are **formulae**: strings of words.

Is this change so substantial? Well, yes. Pictures—the story goes—represent by being similar to the things they picture, in some respect. And similarity is, of course, a matter of more or less. This is **analogue representation**. Words and sentences, on the other hand, seem perfectly unlike pictures in this regard. The word 'spaghetti', for instance, doesn't look, feel or sound like spaghetti. Not even more or less. Another difference: sentences are built up compositionally—and what they mean depends entirely, exclusively and rigidly upon what their parts mean, and how those parts are assembled. Not so pictures. Finally: as any computer scientist will tell you, formulae can serve as the inputs and outputs of **computations**. Pictures can't. (This may be the most important difference of all.) So, the differences are substantial.

What Is The Language of Thought (LOT) Hypothesis?

By way of spelling out this final version of the Idea Theory of Meaning, I'll briefly consider what the language of thought hypothesis says. Then I'll discuss, at some length, whether it is correct. Considered as a theory about intentional states/propositional attitudes, the claim is that propositional attitude tokens are relations to symbol tokens: formulae in the language of thought.[47] These symbols can appear in different "boxes"—to use Schiffer's (1981) metaphor. There is, as it were, a belief box, a desire box, and so on. The *kind* of intentional state (e.g. belief, desire, or fear) is determined by the "box" that the symbol is in. The *content* of the intentional state depends upon the content of the symbol tokened. So, for example, to *believe* that everyone got an A on the exam is to have a token of the mentalese sentence /everyone got an A on the exam/ in your "belief box". To *desire* that everyone got an A on the exam is to have this same sentence tokened in your "desire box". (Notational convention: /everyone got an A on the exam/ should be taken as referring to a *mentalese sentence* synonymous with the English sentence 'Everyone got an A on the exam'. In general, an expression of the form /S/ will denote a mentalese expression whose meaning is given by S.)[48]

It's worth stressing: what's crucially different about the language of thought story is not that it posits meaningful representations, or even that these get put in "boxes"; rather, the central difference lies in the claim that, in addition to being contentful, mental symbols have **constituent structure**. They are—to repeat—quasi-linguistic. As Fodor (1987a, 138) says:

> The question we're arguing about isn't, then, whether mental states have a semantics. Roughly, it's whether they have a syntax. Or, if you prefer, it's whether they have a combinatorial semantics.

If the language of thought hypothesis is correct, then there are primitive mental symbols which are the minimal parts from which complex mentalese symbols are built, recursively. Just like in natural languages. And the very same mental symbol can be part of lots of different complex mental formulae. Furthermore, the meaning of a complex mental symbol is exhaustively determined by its syntactic structure and the meaning of its parts. Again, just like in natural languages.

Arguments for Mentalese

If the proposal of pairing public language expressions with language of thought (LOT) expressions is to work, there had better be a language of thought. So it's time to look at some reasons for positing one. One cluster of arguments centres on the parallels between natural language and thought: sentences and intentional states have a lot in common. Thoughts have truth values and are about things in the world. My thought that Uruguay is a republic, for example, is true. And it's a thought about Uruguay. The same holds of the sentence 'Uruguay is a republic'. Also, thoughts are made up of parts, sometimes called **concepts**. My thought about Uruguay involves the concept REPUBLIC and the concept

URUGUAY. In the same way, sentences are made up of words; e.g. the foregoing sentence contains the words 'republic' and 'Uruguay'. Thoughts enter into logical relations: the thoughts that URUGUAY IS A REPUBLIC and NO REPUBLIC HAS A KING together entail that URUGUAY DOESN'T HAVE A KING. In exactly the same way, the sentences 'Uruguay is a republic' and 'No republic has a king' entail the sentence 'Uruguay doesn't have a king'. Given these parallels, it's natural to suppose that thought is language-like.

There are two further language-thought parallels of particular importance. First, thought is productive. Humans can have indefinitely many novel thoughts. And, but for mortality, everyone could go on having new and different thoughts forever. Same for sentences: there are an unlimited number of them. Second, thought is systematic: if you can entertain the thought that BOB IS TALL, and you can entertain the thought that STEVE IS FAT, then you can entertain the thought that BOB IS FAT. Natural language is like this too. Any language which contains a translation of (161a) and (161b) will also contain a translation of (162).

(161)
(a) Bob is tall
(b) Steve is fat

(162) Bob is fat

What explains the productivity and systematicity of natural language? Well, as you saw in Chapter Two, natural languages have a syntax which is compositional and recursive. That is, every natural language has minimal elements, and rules for combining and re-combining these elements, such that the meaning of larger expressions is systematically dependent upon the meaning of its parts, and how they're combined. (Using the jargon: natural languages have a **combinatorial semantics**.) So, here's an explanation of why thought is systematic and productive: it too has a syntax, with its own lexicon and combinatorial rules.[49] As Fodor (1987a, 150-151) says:

> Linguistics capacities are systematic, and that's because sentences have constituent structure. But cognitive capacities are systematic too, and that must be because thoughts have constituent structure. But if thoughts have constituent structure, then LOT is true.

A second cluster of arguments: some philosophers have

114

motivated the language of thought hypothesis by trying to show that human representational capacities are so rich and complex that they require a medium. Gilbert Harman puts the point this way:

> We know that people have beliefs and desires, that beliefs and desires influence action, that interaction with the environment can give rise to new beliefs, and that needs and drives can give rise to desires. Adequate psychological models must reflect this knowledge and add to it. So adequate psychological models must have states that correspond to beliefs, desires and thoughts such that these states function in the model as psychological states function in the person modeled, and such that they are representational in the way that psychological states are representational. *Where there is such representation, there is a system of representation;* and that system may be identified with the inner language in which a person thinks (Harman 1970, 39. My emphasis).

Fodor, in his (1975) book, runs a similar argument. He focusses attention on decision-making, perception and concept-learning as examples of complex cognizing. For instance: to make a choice between options, it seems, the agent represents the various outcomes she would prefer, and she represents the various possible options available to her; she then selects the option whose total consequences are closest to her desired outcomes. Now, a person can consider an enormous number of hypotheses about how things are or might be, about how she would like them to be, and about how things could turn out, given such-and-such. Representation everywhere. Fodor, like Harman, supposes that an agent could not have these kinds of exceedingly powerful representational capacities without a medium for representing: a language of thought.[50]

Finally, there's the argument from **cognitive processes**. Most contemporary philosophers take for granted that, to put it crudely, contents can't be causes. For instance, suppose someone is describing a car accident. She grabs a salt shaker, and lets it stand for the car, and she lets a thin, fragile toothpick stand for the person walking. Given this, she can show how the car hit the pedestrian— poor defenceless soul! This is representation of a simple sort. The lesson to be drawn is this: coming to have a content doesn't change the *causal powers* of the salt shaker. It has no "extra powers" which the unchosen salt shakers lack. Ditto for the toothpick. That's because, as I said, contents aren't causes.

Now, if there's no **intentional causation**, how can thinking—decision making, perception, concept learning, belief fixation, etc.—work? There must be *something* which causes humans to move from one contentful state to another. For instance, there must be something which takes a detective from the thoughts that THERE'S BLOOD ON THE BLINDS, and that THE WINDOW IS OPEN, through a bunch of intermediate stages, to the thought that THE KILLER ESCAPED THROUGH THE WINDOW. But what underlies the inference cannot be content itself, if there's no content-based causation. The language of thought hypothesis may provide an explanation. Cognition (i.e. thinking) involves representations. And representations have a "dual aspect": they have both form/syntax and meaning/semantics. Thinking can't be content-based causation. But it might be form-based causation! On this view, change of belief is a matter of performing *syntactic derivations*: systematic and disciplined *manipulation of formulae*, transformations according to algorithms which pay attention *only to the symbol's form*, not its meaning. But—here's the crucial bit—the formulae stand for things. So, manipulating symbols ends up being a form of thinking. (Compare the syntactic rules from Chapter Two: you can combine the sentence 'Phil kissed Tim' with 'Tim kissed Phil' by placing 'and' in between. A syntactic manoeuvre. But, of course, this affects meaning as well.)

By treating cognition as **computational**—operations over symbols, paying attention *only* to form—one needn't assume that mental operations invoke content-based causation. Indeed, a computational process *just is* one in which representations have their causal consequences in virtue of form, not content (see Fodor 1980). No other theory of thinking seems to be in the offing. And if you want this one, you have to buy the language of thought, since, as Fodor puts it, "the cost of not having a language of thought is not having a theory of thinking" (Fodor 1987a, 147).

Here's a closely related point. Fodor's belief in LOT was, at the time of *The Language of Thought*, supported by a good deal of empirical work on cognition: cognitive psychologists, linguists (especially psycholinguists), and perceptual psychologists (e.g. Marr 1982), talked constantly about mental representations and computations in their theorizing. In the end, as Fodor has said, "the best reason" for believing in the language of thought is that it

> underlies practically all current psychological research on mentation, and our best science is ipso facto our best estimate of what there is and what it's made of (1987a, 17).

Barring reasons not to take these sciences seriously, philosophers ought to believe in what they claim is there. And what they claim is that psychological processes are transformations of mental representations. But you can't transform representations if there aren't any. In short: no computations without a system of symbols. So, Fodor thinks, philosophers should conclude—with the scientists—that there is a language of thought.

Time to sum up. There's a third version of the Idea Theory of Meaning, which goes like this: human cognition takes place in a medium, called **mentalese** or **the language of thought**. When you learn the meaning of an expression in a public language, what you learn is how to translate it into this language of thought. A public symbol is meaningful if it corresponds to some expression in mentalese; it is meaningless otherwise. And what the public symbol means is completely determined by which expression of mentalese corresponds to it.

Final Remarks

Let me end my discussion of the Idea Theory by contrasting it with the Thing Theory. First contrast: according to the Thing Theory, a symbol is meaningless if no *external object* corresponds to it. For such theories, the minimal requirement for meaningful symbols are: some things (not symbols); some symbols; and some pairing of these. But for "mentalists", something extra is required: namely, mental states and pairing of mental states with public symbols. This contrast between the Idea Theory and the Thing Theory can be highlighted with the following argument:

Premise 1: Linguistic expressions are meaningful.
Premise 2: Linguistic expressions get their meaning from mental states.
Premise 3: If linguistic expressions are meaningful, and they get their meaning from mental states, then mental states exist.
Conclusion: Mental states exist.

This argument underlines an important difference between the Idea Theory and the Thing Theory: only the former entails that mental states exist. Nor is this difference insubstantial. You can see its bite when you consider that some philosophers actually think the conclusion, that mental states exist, is *false*.

In short: the viability of the Idea Theories depends on

results in the philosophy of mind and psychology, in a way which the Thing Theory does not. Suppose, for instance, that psychologists become convinced that there are neither mental sentences, nor mental images. In that case, both the language of thought version of the Idea Theory and the mental image version *must be false*. For, according to them, if a collection of sounds or marks fails to correspond to an image/mental-formula, it is meaningless. But, if there are neither mental images nor mental formulae, then no word corresponds to such things. So no word would be meaningful. But, patently, words *are* meaningful. Or suppose, as **eliminative materialists** insist, that everyone becomes convinced that *commonsense psychology* is a radically false theory. So false that philosophers end up concluding that there are no such things as intentions, beliefs and such. In that case, Grice's theory would of necessity be false. For, again, it entails that there can be linguistic meaning only if there are intentions: if there are no intentions, there are no meanings. This is a striking contrast with Thing Theories.

Second contrast: "real semantics" versus translation. *Translation* of a sentence *S* involves finding a symbol in the "target language" which is synonymous with *S*. So, for instance, *translating* the Portuguese 'ele fala' into Spanish is a matter of finding a Spanish sentence synonymous with it. However, knowing that 'ele fala' and 'él habla' are translations of one another is not akin to knowing what 'ele fala' means: giving the meaning involves more than providing a translation, or paraphrase. Why? Because a translation won't help *unless it's a translation into a tongue which you understand*. Which brings out the contrast: unlike the Thing Theory, the Idea Theory of Meaning must take place in two steps. The first involves the "translation" of natural language symbols into ideas of some kind. The second step involves *giving the meaning of these ideas*. Failure to make the second step leaves you with mere translation, not real semantics. Thing Theories, on the other hand, do semantics in a single step. If the Idea Theory is to allow eventual connections between linguistic items and things, then a Thing Theory of Meaning *for ideas* is required. The need for a theory of meaning for ideas is especially pressing in the case of mentalese since, not being pictures, it's downright *obvious* that mentalese expressions don't represent inherently. So, Fodor and company must eventually explain why, for example, the mentalese word /cheese/ is meaningful, why it has the meaning it does, and so on. (Some initial attempts can be found in Fodor 1990, 1994. See also the papers in Stich and Warfield 1994.)

This point may be further illustrated with a diagram. Figure (163a) represents the Idea Theory. Figure (163b) represents the Thing Theory.

(163)
(a) *The Idea Theory*

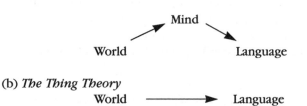

(b) *The Thing Theory*
World ⟶ Language

What defines the Idea Theory is that the arrow—representing the source of meaning, if you will—runs through the mind. In the Thing Theory, on the other hand, there is an arrow connecting language to the world, without a "detour" through the mind.

2. An Alternative to LOT: Connectionism

Fodor (1975, 27) has argued for the language of thought as follows:

Premise 1: The only psychological models of cognitive processes that seem even remotely plausible represent such processes as computations over representations.
Premise 2: Postulating computations over representations presupposes a medium of computation: a language of thought.
Premise 3: Remotely plausible theories are better than no theories at all.
Conclusion: We are thus provisionally committed to a language of thought.

As I said in the last section, at the time Fodor wrote, he was on safe ground in maintaining that the computational-representational theory of mind was the only serious theory of cognition. But the support for this is significantly less obvious nowadays. Indeed, there are now two alternative theories of cognitive processes, both of which have recently gained in popularity. Fairness demands that I introduce these two alternatives. And that's what I'll do in the remainder of this chapter. Be warned, however, that some readers will find it better to skip this discussion, since it breaks the flow of argument in a serious way. (It's not surprising that these alternatives stick out in a presentation of mainstream philosophy of language, since they're opposed to the tradition in important ways.)

The first alternative to the language of thought grows out of work in **connectionist artificial intelligence**. The second arises from Daniel Dennett's **Intentional Stance**. Each suggests that computations over representations may not be required for thinking. Which would mean that there's no need for a language of thought. In which case, philosophers should not appeal to the language of thought in the construction of theories of meaning for public languages.

I begin with an apparent digression, looking at some of the problems which **connectionists** have identified with Good Old Fashioned Artificial Intelligence (**GOFAI**), as John Haugeland calls it. GOFAI is the approach to artificial intelligence that grows out of the tradition I've been selling up until now: the idea that cognition—natural as well as artificial intelligence—involves computations over representations. The goal of artificial intelligence, from within the GOFAI framework, is to write sufficiently complex programs (i.e. sets of rules) over the right kinds of representations so that—when executed on a computer—the result will *be* a mind.

Notice a related claim: *human brains* are such computers. The job of human brains is to manipulate representations in terms of precise rules. Human thought consists in the manipulation of the appropriate kind of symbols in accordance with the appropriate kind of rules. Connectionists have recently argued that, whether or not there could be a form of intelligence that consisted in disciplined symbol manipulation, human intelligence isn't of this kind. Here are some arguments.

First of all, humans and GOFAI computers exhibit important differences in abilities. As Tienson (1988, 382) rightly says,

> ...there seem to be certain kinds of things that we are good at that are very difficult for computers, such as pattern recognition, understanding speech, recalling and recognizing relevant information, and making plans. It has also proven very difficult to program computers to learn in any domain. On the other hand, computers are much better than humans at other tasks, paradigmatically, number crunching, but in general, anything that involves many precisely specifiable computations or manipulating large amounts of data according to precise rules.

What's more, these "precise rules" seem incapable of replicating a natural feature of human cognition: the ability to respond to deformed inputs or thoroughly unfamiliar inputs. Taking speech comprehension as an example: ordinary people are all able to interpret non-native speakers of English—even though they don't follow exactly the rules that native English speakers have (supposedly) internalized. This seems to show that, whatever interpreters are doing, it's not simply a matter of following precise rules. The overall conclusion? Whatever human brains do, it's different than what conventional computers do—because the resulting skills and abilities are vastly different. That is, ours is a different kind of intelligence. Which means that language of thought models of cognition—based as they are on the classical computer metaphor—are inadequate.

Another difference lies in how computers and brains each achieve their phenomenal speed. Connectionists are fond of pointing out that human neurons are comparatively slow. For instance, a typical neuron firing takes about one millisecond. But human *brains*—even though they are composed of neurons—achieve things very quickly. To understand an utterance, for example, requires about one hundred milliseconds. One hundred milliseconds to understand; one neuron firing per millisecond. The arithmetic is simple: there can be only about one hundred serial neuron firings involved in understanding an utterance. Suppose further—as may well be the case—that the execution of one step in a program requires at least one serial neuron firing. One step for one neuron firing. And 100 neuron firings to perform all the steps. Once again, the arithmetic is pretty simple: it looks like at most 100 program steps can be executed in the time available to understand an utterance. So, on these assumptions, one would expect that processing an utterance would be done in about 100 serial steps. Maybe less. But, if you're familiar with the computer programs which are proposed for human parsing, you'll know that they require *thousands* of serial steps for a single utterance. Hence, these programs do not accurately capture what human brains do. Worse, programs which are short enough to be carried off in about one hundred steps (but complex enough to actually do the job) just aren't on the horizon. This leads connectionists to conclude that the way actual brains perform these cognitive tasks is vastly different from the way the computational model of the mind suggests.

In a nutshell: contemporary computer circuitry is about one million times faster than a typical neuron. Assuming neuron speed is a reliable guide to brain speed, this means that certain programs which are executable in "real time" by computers would take *years* for the brain to execute. But it doesn't take human beings years to do the tasks in question. Hence, it's argued, human brains can't be executing these programs. The thing is, no shorter programs seem to be in the offing.

There are other apparent differences between brain functioning and the functioning of classical computers. Brain processes suffer **graceful degradation**: the damaged brain functions less well, without "crashing" altogether; whereas classical computers simply fail when slightly damaged. Also, the brain seems to very effectively handle **the frame problem**: the problem of knowing what information is relevant in a given situation. But GOFAI research suggests that computational solutions to this problem are unlikely. (See Fodor 1987b and Haugeland 1979, 1985 for discussion.) What's the overall lesson? That the brain is very different from a conventional computer. Which likely means that brains and conventional computers do things in vastly different ways. So, one should not expect programs that work on the computer to greatly illuminate the functioning of the brain. In particular, one should not believe that human thought consists in the manipulation of the appropriate kind of symbols in accordance with the appropriate kind of rules, even if some future "computer thought" is like this. (Compare: don't expect rocket science to tell you much about the flight of birds, since the former is artificial while the latter isn't.)

The Connectionist Alternative to GOFAI

These are problems for traditional artificial intelligence, and for the associated computational theory of mind. In the last fifteen years or so, an alternative approach has emerged: **connectionism**. It attempts to supplant GOFAI by offering a computer model of the mind which more accurately reflects the way the brain works. An alternative which does without a language of thought. Simplifying enormously, the basic elements of a connectionist system are:

(164) *The Elements of a Connectionist Network*
(a) A bunch of nodes (or "units")
(b) Connections between these nodes
(c) Signalling patterns for the connections
      (i) Direction of signal (e.g. if A and B are connected, A may signal B, or B may signal A, or both)

(ii) Strength of signal (May be 0, 1, or some value
in between)
(iii) Nature of signal (Either inhibiting or exciting)
(d) Activation states for the nodes (These are completely determined by the number, source, strength and nature of incoming sig-
nals from connected nodes.)

These basic elements turn out to be pretty darn powerful. Shortly
I'll present an example. First a few notes. To begin with, notice how
connectionist systems resemble brain structure. In the brain, the
"units" are the neurons. Neurons are connected to one another in a
multitude of ways. And the activation of one can—through electri-
cal impulses—affect the activation of others. What's more, the paths
between neurons can be well-worn (i.e. strongly connected) or
barely present (weakly connected). And the direction of effect can
be variable. The similarity between connectionist systems and neural nets is not an accident, of course. The whole point is to create an
artificial system which more closely resembles the functioning of
the brain.

Patricia Churchland discusses a real example of a connectionist system that is highly effective: the NETalk system. This is a
system "which learns to convert English text to speech sounds"
(Churchland & Sejnowski 1989, 236). That is, roughly speaking, it's
a system that learns how to read aloud—though without understanding what it is reading. Here is what the system looks like:

(165) *NETalk*
(a) 309 processing units
(b) Three layers: input, one hidden layer, and output
(c) 18,629 connection strengths (weights) to be specified

The input layer receives the letters in the word as input. The output
layer yields the sound pattern. The intervening layer (i.e. the hidden
layer) performs the transformation of letters to sounds.

At the outset, when you give this network its first written
text, successful pronunciation is a matter of luck only. But the
researcher identifies the source of errors, and "changes connection
weights" to increase success. Indeed, one can even write an algo-
rithm—called "the teacher"—which readjusts the weights on its
own. The training period of the network goes on for thousands of
trials, until the network settles into "the right" pattern—in which
the text that serves as input and the sounds which serve as output

are appropriately related. At this point, one can say that the system has learned to "read aloud". It has solved the problem posed to it.

Notice some of the interesting properties of connectionist systems. First, there are multiple signalling patterns which will achieve the same input-output result. If the initial weights are set differently, the system can end up with different connection strengths between nodes—but the same input-output behaviour. Even *within* a single network, there are lots of different weight distributions that will, for example, correctly pronounce written text. So if you ask, of the variously trained networks, how certain information is stored, the answer will be different for each one.

Second, there aren't really *formulae* being manipulated. As Churchland and Sejnowski (1989, 237) say, the learning process—and the resulting "skill"—do not involve "manipulating symbols and accessing rules". (Still less is the organization which emerges *programmed* or coded into the network.) That is why talk of formulae seems out of place when talking about such systems. What's more, whether or not there is symbol manipulation, there isn't symbol *storage*. The content of the system—what its states represent—is distributed across the network. It's not located in any one "place". For example: you can't isolate a node in NETalk which represents the correct pronunciation of 'r-e-d'. The information is in there, but the system globally represents it: the "knowledge" of how to pronounce 'r-e-d' consists in the weights of the connections between nodes being at a certain level, even when said nodes are not activated. This contrasts sharply with conventional architectures, in which, "when information is being used, a certain structure—a syntactic object—is in the [Central Processing Unit]. When it is not being used, the same data structure is stored in memory" (Tienson 1988, 392).

Third, representations in connectionist systems have no syntactic structure. They don't have *parts* which are themselves representations. Here's a comparison. The sentence 'Elvis kissed Phil' is composed of three meaningful words. The meaning of the whole sentence is completely determined by the meaning of these parts, and the way the parts are ordered. As I've said repeatedly: meaning changes systematically if you replace any part with another part, or if you re-arrange the parts. Notice too: every *token* of this sentence would also have token parts. And each of those token parts would be meaningful. States of a connectionist machine, on the other hand, are *simple representations*. They represent stuff in the way that names do. Names—e.g. 'Aristotle'—may have parts (e.g. letters), but the meaning of the whole isn't determined by these parts. (More on this later.)

The punch line: if *this* is how the brain works, then the language of thought hypothesis (with its commitment to brittle, explicit and determinate processing/storage of individually meaningful structured formulae) is mistaken, and mentalese probably doesn't exist. In which case, it can't be the immediate source of linguistic meaning.

The Language of Thought Strikes Back

Time for some replies, on behalf of the language of thought. Fodor and Pylyshyn (1988) have argued that connectionist systems aren't really an *alternative* to GOFAI (and hence to the language of thought hypothesis). What connectionist networks offer, at best, is a way of *implementing* programs. In the first place—as even Patricia Churchland and crew would concede—connectionist systems are not representation-free. After all, theorists must supply interpretations either to the input and output units, or to patterns of activation over these. So connectionism does *not* eschew representations, i.e. symbols. Okay, so they have representations. But do they also have rules? Well, seen at the level of units, they don't appear to. But then again, at that level of grain, neither do conventional computers! If you look at the *circuits* of conventional computers, you won't see any rules. The rules transform the *system* from one representational state to another, and such transformations are indeed present in connectionist systems. Here's a related point. Ironic as it may seem, the only currently running connectionist systems (that I know about, anyway) are executed on traditional computers! As Bechtel (1988) says:

> In a simulation of a connectionist system in a traditional computer, the computer calculates the equations governing the changes of activations of units in a connection system, and thereby determines what will be the activation strengths of all the units in a connectionist system.

He continues:

> If the traditional computer can simulate the connectionist system, how can we maintain that the two are fundamentally different? (Bechtel 1988, 258)

125

A very good question indeed! I can't go into this topic. But I want to leave you wondering whether connectionist systems really offer an *alternative* to the language of thought, at the cognitive level.

One last objection to connectionism as a real alternative to the language of thought model. Fodor and Pylyshyn (1988) have argued that *if* connectionist systems really are radically different, then they must be inadequate as theories of human cognition. The argument should be familiar from the last chapter. Here's how it goes. First premise: human thought is productive (i.e. anyone can "build up" ever more complex thoughts); human thought is systematic (e.g. anyone who can think that John loves Mary is also able think that Mary loves John); and human thoughts are composed of parts (e.g. the thought that Aristotle was tall and the thought that Aristotle was a philosopher share an important property: they're both *about* Aristotle). Second premise: at the moment, the only account of the productivity, systematicity and compositionality of thoughts requires taking thoughts to be structured representations, related to one another by computational rules. So, human thoughts involve computations over representations. In which case, if connectionist systems *don't* have computations over representations, they offer poor models of human cognition.

Given all of the above, how secure is Fodor's premise that the only psychological models of cognitive processes that seem even remotely plausible represent such processes as computational? That depends, in part, upon how successful connectionism is in producing human-like intelligence in a wholly different way. Tienson (1988) remained sceptical but vaguely optimistic:

> To my mind, no connectionist system produced so far should be interpreted as a serious attempt to model or simulate any aspect of human cognition. Connectionist systems I have seen are too simple, too artificially constrained, and have been given too much help by the artificial specification of the task domain. Furthermore, there is no prospect that these systems will "scale up" to model some aspect of real cognition. However, these systems show that connectionist systems can do at least some of the right kinds of things (1988, 394).

I think this is still the right attitude. All in all, then, the language of thought version of the Idea Theory of Meaning remains a contender.

Before going on, it's time to take stock. The slogan is: language is a system of symbols which we know and use. I'm now considering language as something *known*—an aspect of the mind. In particular, I'm exploring the idea that linguistic meaning resides, in the first instance, in relationships with mind-stuff; natural language meaning arises from mental items being paired with public sound patterns. (How, in turn, the mental items get *their* meaning is left open.) I have canvassed, as meanings, several candidate "mental items": Humean images, Gricean common sense intentions, and Fodorian internal formulae. I'm still working through the latter. (Patience.)

3. Another Alternative to LOT: Dennett's Intentional Stance

If meaning is to come from the language of thought, there had better *be* a language of thought. Above, I gave arguments that, as a matter of fact, the language of thought *does* exist. The most powerful one went like this: the language of thought is the only game in town. So there's no alternative but to play it. Now, however, that argument is coming under serious scrutiny. For, it turns out, there may be other games worth playing. In particular, Dennett (1981) offers an account of ordinary intentional states—including especially belief—which eschews internal representations. Insofar as his account is successful, agents can have *representations* without *a system of representations*. In effect, then, Dennett offers an alternative to Fodor's language of thought approach. In this final section, I introduce Dennett's alternative.[51]

Dennett begins "Three Kinds of Intentional Psychology" with a rough and ready intuitive characterization of "folk psychology", and of its central notion, belief. Then he progressively makes refinements. Here's the first pass:

> What are beliefs? Very roughly, folk psychology has it that beliefs are information-bearing states of people that arise from perceptions and that, together with appropriately related desires, lead to intelligent action (Dennett 1981, 91).

Notice the central elements: beliefs are information-bearing. They are, therefore, contentful. Next, what one believes depends, in part, upon what one perceives. Hence upon the environment, and how one processes it. Notice too: beliefs aren't inert informational states. Rather, they lead to rational actions; beliefs serve as reasons for actual deeds.

But this first pass remains pretty vague about the exact nature of belief. Because this vague characterization is unsatisfactory, Dennett offers a second pass. He says that folk psychology is: (a) Rationalistic, (b) Idealized, (c) Instrumentalistic and (d) Abstract. I'll go through these in turn.

First point:

> ...explanations of actions citing beliefs and desires normally not only describe the provenance of the actions, but at the same time defend them as reasonable under the circumstances. They are reason-giving explanations, which make an ineliminable allusion to the rationality of the agent (Dennett 1981, 92).

To take an example: if I attempt to explain why Alice went to the store using belief-talk, my explanation will fail if Alice isn't rational. Put another way, the following argument is incomplete as it stands:

Premise 1: Alice wants cigarettes
Premise 2: Alice believes The Corner Store sells cigarettes
Premise 3: If *x* wants cigarettes, and believes that store *s* sells cigarettes, then (all else being equal) *x* will go to store *s*
Conclusion: All else being equal, Alice will go to The Corner Store

First of all, Premise 3 holds only for rational agents, not for any *x*. Secondly, there is an essential missing premise: that Alice *is* a rational agent. Without this extra premise, the argument doesn't go through. Hence, without this extra premise, the explanation of Alice's behaviour is incomplete.

This "extra requirement" of rationality is easily hidden from view because people simply do not attribute beliefs and desires to things which aren't (at least in large part) rational agents. So adding that Alice is rational may seem unnecessary. But notice how a reason-giving explanation fails if the resulting action requires highly sophisticated deliberation, and the agent is very severely retarded. Here the presupposition of rationality becomes explicit. So, says Dennett, folk psychology is rationalistic.

Belief attribution is idealized, according to Dennett, in that a system has the beliefs which it *ought* to have—where this means the beliefs it "would have if it were *ideally* ensconced in its environmental niche" (Dennett 1981, 93). It's further idealized in that, though individuals really aren't entirely rational, belief attribution presupposes that they are. As Dennett puts the point:

> We aspire to rationality, and without the myth of our rationality the concepts of belief and desire would be uprooted. Folk psychology, then, is idealized in that it produces its predictions and explanations by calculating in a normative system; it predicts what we will believe, desire and do, by determining what we ought to believe, desire, and do (1981, 95).

Though idealized, folk psychology still works. It works because humans really are pretty well designed (by evolution), which means that what they ought to believe, and how they ought to reason, effectively predict their actual behaviour.

Which takes me to the third point. Belief attribution, according to Dennett, is also **instrumentalistic**: the beliefs which an agent "really has", on Dennett's view, are simply those whose attribution allow an observer to predict its behaviour. In the form of a slogan: what works for the folk theorist determines what's true of the folk theorized. I'll come back to this. First, the final element of Dennett's treatment of folk psychology.

Dennett says that,

> Folk psychology is abstract in that the beliefs and desires it attributes are not—or need not be—presumed to be intervening distinguishable states of an internal behavior-causing system (1981, 95-96).

This could do with some explaining. Dennett compares the notion of belief, in the domain of folk psychology, to notions like centre of gravity, or earth's equator. The latter, he says, are **abstracta**—defined as "calculation bound entities or logical constructs". I'm not sure what he means by this, but here's a guess. "Concreta" are physical objects: both everyday ones (chairs, tables, bicycles, etc.) and fancy ones (gravitational force, electrons, spin, etc.). Abstracta are "objects" (if you will) whose existence is "reducible to the existence of concreta". (Reichenbach 1938, 211-212. Cited by Dennett.) That is, an object will be called an abstracta if it is the (apparent?) referent of a term which can be translated without loss into physical object talk. What Dennett calls abstracta, then, are not objects (physical or otherwise) *over and above* concreta. (In fact, I suspect that for Dennett they're not really objects at all.)

This is probably better put in the **formal mode**—mentioning language, rather than using it. Here goes: sentences containing "abstracta-names" express, in an abbreviated form, propositions about concreta. But the "abstracta-names" don't themselves refer to concreta. Take (166) as a helpful comparison.

(166) The average woman will have 1.6 children

The expression 'the average woman' is an abstracta-name. Though a "name", it *does not* refer to a physical object. Indeed, I suspect it doesn't refer to anything at all. This sentence is an abbreviated form of discourse, not really "about" some object called 'the average woman'. (Shades of Russell? You bet.) Rather, what (166) says is something like:

(167) The number of children divided by the number of women equals 1.6

Dennett, as I read him, thinks that the terms of belief-desire psychology (e.g. 'belief', 'desire', 'inference') are similarly "abstracta-names": they don't actually refer at all.

In summary, then: Dennett takes folk psychology to be a rationalistic and idealizing device for predicting behaviour by introducing abstracta. Having described his own position, Dennett notes the view of the orthodox opposition:

> Beliefs and desires, just like pains, thoughts, sensations and other episodes, are taken by folk psychology to be real, intervening, internal states or events, in causal interaction, subsumed under covering laws of causal stripe. Folk psychology is not an idealized, rationalistic calculus but a naturalistic, empirical, descriptive theory, imputing causal regularities discovered by extensive induction over experience. To suppose two people share a belief is to suppose them to be ultimately in some structurally similar internal condition, e.g. for them to have the same words of Mentalese written in the functionally relevant places in their brains (1981, 96).

Thus stated, it appears that Dennett and his opponents (Dennett clearly has Fodor in mind) are completely at loggerheads. In fact, Dennett suggests, the disagreement need not be so stark. To achieve a rapprochement with his opponents on the nature of folk psychology and its central notion of belief, Dennett distinguishes and separates two tasks. One task is **rational reconstruction**. Dennett calls this a "proto-scientific" quest, and describes it as an attempt to prepare folk theory for subsequent incorporation into, or reduction to, the rest of science, [an attempt which] should be critical and should eliminate all that is false or ill founded, however well entrenched in popular doctrine (91).

Another task is **anthropology of the phenomenon**. Here, the inquirer cares not the least about whether folk psychology is *correct*; she will include in her description whatever ordinary folk include in *their* theory, "however misguided, incoherent, gratuitous some of it may be" (Dennett 1981, 91). For the anthropologist of folk psychology, even if folk psychology is a myth, it is a myth people live by. For the proto-scientist, on the other hand, the mythical part of folk psychology is of no interest; what he cares about is what's right about folk psychology.

Keeping this distinction in mind, Dennett makes two refinements to his view, thus achieving the aforementioned rapprochement. The first refinement is on the anthropology front. Dennett says he is "prepared to grant a measure of the claims made by the opposition". For instance, real folk do sometimes attribute less-than-ideal beliefs and desires, and less than perfect rationality. The second refinement is on the reconstruction front. Dennett is interested in both tasks: reconstruction and anthropology. But he's *most* interested in what's best about folk psychology, and what's best about belief. And he thinks that his characterization, in the second pass, captures what is best—and ditches the rest. So, even if he's slightly wrong in his anthropology, he insists he's right about what folk psychology *as precursor to science* is like. Hence he's right about what belief *really is*, as opposed to what our folk theory thinks it is. (And, he would add, given what belief *really is*, there's no need for a language of thought—even though the anthropology of belief suggests the contrary.) The apparently stark disagreement with the opposition (e.g. Fodor) diminishes, then, because while fans of LOT are wedded to anthropology, Dennett is (mostly) doing proto-science.

Here, then, is Dennett's final view about the nature of folk psychology: anthropologically speaking, folk psychology is flawed in that ordinary folk sometimes attribute less-than-ideal beliefs and imperfect rationality. Proto-scientifically speaking, however, folk psychology at its best is entirely rationalistic, idealizing, and instrumentalist. And it introduces only abstracta, not concreta. On all four counts there are no grounds for introducing a language of thought. Hence philosophers ought not appeal to a language of thought in giving a theory of meaning for public languages.[52]

Suggested Readings

Interested in the language of thought? You've got a lot of reading to do. The book that initiated the flood is Jerry Fodor's (1975) *The Language of Thought*. He's authored many books and articles on the topic since then. See especially Fodor 1978, 1985, 1987a, as well as Fodor and Pylyshyn 1988. Another classic is Field 1978. It's difficult, but worth the effort. I'd also recommend Lycan 1981 and Pylyshyn 1980. For alternative views, see Dennett's (1977) "A Cure for the Common Code", Churchland and Churchland 1983 and Stalnaker 1984. As a general introduction to these topics, I highly recommend Kim Sterelny's (1990) *The Representational Theory of Mind*.

Introductions to connectionism include Paul Churchland's (1988) revised edition of *Matter and Consciousness*, Andy Clark's (1989) *Microcognition* and Rumelhart 1989. My exposition follows Bechtel 1988 and Tienson 1988. An excellent primary source is Rumelhart and McClelland 1986. For a critical view, see the papers in Pinker and Mehler 1988. Fodor and Pylyshyn's (1988) "Connection and Cognitive Architecture: A Critical Analysis" appears there.

For more on Dennett, go to the source. See especially his (1978) *Brainstorms* and *The Intentional Stance*, from 1987. Both are collections of seminal papers.

Chapter Eight:

Knowledge Issues

I've said it before; I'll say it again: language is a system of symbols which we know and use. In this chapter I continue to focus on the knowledge perspective. In particular, I discuss two pressing issues about linguistic knowledge. The first is largely empirical, but it has important philosophical implications: is knowledge of language mostly learned, or is it mostly innate? The second is about the very idea of linguistic knowledge: does it really make sense to say that language users *know* the rules of their language?

1. Innateness

Many linguists, Noam Chomsky being foremost among them, now believe that much of linguistic knowledge is innate. Call this "the innateness hypothesis". Before introducing the arguments in favour of this hypothesis, allow me to explain it. It is *not* simply the uncontroversial claim that humans are born with the capacity to acquire language. That much is common ground for all sides. Everybody agrees that dogs don't acquire language, and humans do. What's more, everybody agrees that the reason has something to do with innate differences between the species. Those who affirm and those who deny "the innateness hypothesis" differ about the exact nature of the innate differences between humans and other species; they *do not* disagree about whether there are any.[53] Of course there are.

Nor is the dispute really about whether the key difference between humans and other species is a mental one. An empiricist hostile to the innateness hypothesis might nevertheless agree that the human *mind* is innately different from all others, and further concede that this mental difference is what permits humans to acquire language. But this very empiricist could, in the same breath, deny that much of linguistic knowledge is innate. For, she might say, what is innately different about human minds is simply that humans are *smarter*. In fact, traditional empiricists—including Locke and Hume—admitted (indeed, *insisted*) that there were innate learning mechanisms. The mind, even at first breath, was (according to the empiricists) endowed with the capacity to perform mental operations. So, the issue between **nativists** (e.g. Chomsky) on the one hand, and anti-nativists on the other isn't over whether there's something innately different about humans, nor is it about whether there's some aspect of the human mind which is innate.

Okay then, where does the disagreement lie? Over whether there is *knowledge* at birth: whether the mind has any contents, if you will, when it comes into being. Applied to the case at hand, it's whether there is *knowledge of language* at birth. And what really sets Chomsky apart is his view that, not only is there *some* knowledge of language at birth, there's *lots of it*. That is, *much* of linguistic knowledge is innate. Put negatively: the "innateness hypothesis" is false if there is little or no linguistic knowledge at birth. Now that that's cleared up, here are the arguments for and against.

First argument for the innateness hypothesis: if cognitive theories of learning are anywhere near the mark, learning requires a representational medium of significant power. A language, if you will. So, to learn a language, you need a language. In which case, not all language can be learned (see Fodor 1975, 1981a).

Second argument: many features of human languages are widespread, and perhaps universal. These include "negative features": attributes which *no* language actually exhibits. So, to give a reasonably simple example, no human language allows wh-elements to be fronted out of conjunctive Noun Phrases. A case in point: sentence (168a) is well-formed. And sentence (168b), got by fronting the wh-element in (168a), is fine as well. (The letter 't' indicates the place where the element was moved from.)

(168)
(a) Alice saw what?

(b) What$_1$ did Alice see t$_1$?

In contrast, the result of moving the wh-element in (169a) to the front is ill-formed, as (169b) illustrates.

(169)
(a) Alice saw a dog and what?
(b) *What$_1$ did Alice see a dog and t$_1$?

That's because 'a dog and what' is a conjunctive Noun Phrase. So, you can't extract the wh-element (here: 'what'). This sort of rule seems to apply to every known language. Such commonalities, and hundreds more like it, can be explained by positing significant innate linguistic knowledge. It cannot, goes the argument, be explained otherwise. So, one ought to assume that humans are born knowing a great deal about human languages.

Third nativist argument. There is a **poverty of the stimulus**. Languages are extremely complex and subtle. (Could *you* have stated the rule about not moving wh-elements out of conjunctive Noun Phrases?) So much so that, even after constant research by hundreds of great minds, linguistics still lacks an adequate description of *English*! Linguists know even less about other tongues. Yet small children learn their first language in little time, on the basis of fractured and fragmentary evidence, and with effectively no training. How can language acquisition occur, given the richness of cognitive state arrived at, the rapidity of the process, and the poverty of the evidence available? Again, the best explanation is that much of linguistic knowledge is innate: infants have a "head start". (One might respond: the best explanation of rapid language acquisition is that babies are *very smart*. But this cannot be right, since developmentally challenged children—including very severely retarded children, who can learn little else—are capable of normal language learning.)

Before going on, let me introduce a rather sweeping version of the poverty of the stimulus argument. (I here borrow from Martin 1987.) Consider the following number series:

(170) 1, 4, 9, 16, 25, 36...

What are the next two numbers? You are likely to think they are 49 and 64. But that isn't exactly correct. The next two numbers could be anything at all!

The reason you want to say that the next two numbers must be 49 and 64 is that you've seen the following pattern:

(171) $1^2, 2^2, 3^2, 4^2, 5^2, 6^2...$

In which case, the next values must be 7^2 and 8^2, i.e. 49 and 64. It's natural to think this. But it's importantly wrong. In fact, though your math teacher didn't tell you this, no series of numbers uniquely determines the next member. That's because every finite series is generated by a variety of rules. For instance, the series in (170) is generated by "Martin's Rule" below.

(172) *Martin's Rule*
(a) For $n=1...6$, the nth member of the series is n^2
(b) For $n=7$, the nth member is 322
(c) For $n\geq8$, the nth member is the $(n-1)^{th}$ member plus two.

Notice: this (bizarre) rule does indeed generate the series in question. But the seventh member of the series, using Martin's rule, will be 322. Not 49. And the eighth number will be 324 (i.e. 322+2), not 64. Here's another rule which generates the same initial six-membered sequence.

(173) *Stainton's Rule*
(a) For $n=1...6$, the nth member of the series is n^2
(b) For $n\geq7$, the nth member is five.

Again, this rule generates the series in (170):

(170) $1, 4, 9, 16, 25, 36$

But the seventh member of the series, according to this rule, is five. Ditto for the eighth, ninth, and so on.

Martin states the lesson of this example as follows: "a series of examples does not in itself contain the information of what constitutes going on in the same way" (36). Now, apply this lesson to language learning. When a child learns a language, what happens? She encounters a finite array of language use, and she projects, from this body of cases, a rule—a rule which applies to all past cases and also to all future cases. These linguistic rules are much more complex than the simple algorithms in Martin's Rule and Stainton's rule. But the idea is the same. The phrase structure rules from Chapter Two, for instance, apply not just to all expressions that you've heard until now. They are also supposed to apply to hitherto unencountered cases. So, here is the idea: somehow, on the basis of a finite sample, a child arrives at the right rule—the rule which applies to past *and* future uses. This suggests a version of the poverty of the stimulus argument for the innateness hypothesis: as a matter of fact, all children in a given linguistic environment settle on roughly the same rules. There are many rules which are consistent with the data, but which are rejected. The basis for their rejection cannot be something *observed*, precisely because, by hypothesis, the available data does not select between them. Therefore, there must be some innate mechanism which eliminates the 'wrong' rules from consideration.

Three nativist arguments. Three anti-nativist replies. First reply: the data regarding language structure remain incomplete. Which raises the distinct possibility that, *pace* Chomsky, languages are *not* uniform. Second reply: even if linguists claim to observe universally shared, or just typically widespread features, this needn't show that these traits are, in fact, had in common. It may instead indicate that when linguists "observe" other languages, they are biased by their own, and hence see the structure of their language everywhere they look. Third reply to the nativist: even if certain attributes are really universal, it isn't true that the best explanation of this would be innate knowledge of language. Instead, the best explanation goes like this: certain structures are universal because they are useful (for communication), others are universal because all human languages share a single common "ancestor", some of whose characteristics have been passed down to all present languages (Putnam 1967, 296). In summary, there probably aren't universals (replies one and two), but even if there were, that wouldn't show that much of linguistic knowledge is innate (reply three).

Three anti-nativist replies, numerous pro-nativist rebuttals. First, the foregoing three replies to the nativist address the argument from universality. They don't touch the two other arguments: that there is no learning without language, and that the best explanation of observed language acquisition by children—including severely retarded children—is that many facts about human language are innately given.

Second: if you think the data for universals is in principle inconclusive, you're right. But no data in *any* science is ever truly conclusive. On the other hand, if you imagine the data isn't very highly suggestive, think again. Looked at from an unjaundiced point of view, the evidence for a significant innate linguistic endowment is striking. (See Pinker 1994 for much more.)

As for worries about **linguistic imperialism** (i.e. imposing the structure of one's own language on the target language), they are either justified or unjustified. If justified, they're surely applicable to sciences generally. In which case, linguists ought to continue with standard scientific practice, which amounts to *watching out for prejudices*. What linguists *ought not* do is abandon linguistics, or conclude that all previous work is unreliable—any more than scientists generally should abandon their work. On the other hand, if worries about linguistic imperialism are unjustified, then they're—well—unjustified.

The final reply to the nativist—i.e. that even if there are universals, the best explanation is function on the one hand, and history on the other—deserves significantly more attention. Here goes. Beginning with the "history gamut": the idea is to explain linguistic commonalities by appeal to a common ancestor. To the question, "Why are languages alike in feature F?" the reply comes: "Because the mother-of-all-languages had property P, and linguistic evolution occurred in manner M. And that resulted in many (all) languages having F". But this really isn't a complete explanation: it leaves unanswered as many questions as it addresses. For example, why did the mother language have property P? And why did evolution occur in manner M, so that certain properties like F end up being shared today, while other properties of the mother language are not shared? That is, why has language change been circumscribed in the ways it has? And why *hasn't* it been circumscribed in others? These questions deserve an answer. The answer which comes immediately to mind is that part of what drives linguistic evolution over time, and part of what determined the nature of the mother language, is precisely the innate linguistic knowledge shared by all humans. That is, the explanation falls back on the innateness hypothesis. Although this time the explanandum is somewhat different.

But what about function? Couldn't that explain the commonalities? Here's my view. Functional explanations may be in the offing for certain universals. For example, as Putnam (1967, 296) notes, the fact that all natural languages contain proper names is not surprising, precisely because names are enormously useful. But the universals which linguists have pointed to are by no means uniformly useful—things could have been otherwise, without decreasing the functionality of language as a whole. Recall the two "fake rules" from Chapter Two:

(20) *Rules not observed*
(a) *Fake Rule 1*: Invert the first and second word in a declarative sentence to form a question.
(b) *Fake Rule 2*: Delete every third word, if its meaning can be recovered.

English doesn't exhibit these or similar rules. Nor does any known language. But in what plausible sense are these rules less functional than subject-aux inversion or Verb Phrase ellipses? For that matter, what is *functionally* wrong with moving a wh-element out of a conjunctive Noun Phrase? Nothing, so far as I can see.

In sum: I doubt that either shared ancestors or "evolutionary fitness" can adequately explain the observed universals. In which case, the best explanation remains the innateness hypothesis. So, barring further evidence, it looks as though human beings may have a rich innate endowment when it comes to language.[54]

2. Rules and Regularities

Part of the point of introducing knowledge of language is that it explains linguistic behaviour: people produce the sounds they do because they know certain linguistic rules, and they apply this knowledge. But the idea that people know the rules of their language has seemed odd to some. I want now to introduce two possible problems with the idea of linguistic knowledge, innate or otherwise.

First worry: not all regularities derive from rules. For instance, objects don't fall because they are following rules, just as wings don't grow on birds because the birds follow wing-growing rules. A question, then: are rules really responsible for linguistic regularities? Using a language is regular behaviour. But is it **rule-guided**? If not, then the attribution of linguistic knowledge is fallacious: it's like proposing that rocks know the rules of gravity, and that's why they fall!

Two examples, from Martin 1987, to illustrate the distinction between rule-guided and merely regular behaviour. It's a regularity that truck drivers tend to stop at red lights. It's also a regularity that truck drivers tend to rest their left arms on the ledge of their truck window. The first regularity is clearly rule-guided. Indeed, the rule being followed is actually written down somewhere, with other traffic laws. (Look it up, if you don't believe me!) But what about the second regularity? This exemplifies a mere regularity. (I.e. there's no official rule—not in the law books, anyway—stipulating where drivers should rest their arms.)

The question was this: are regularities in linguistic behavior rule-guided, or are they *mere* regularities? It's less easy to say in this case. Stopping at red lights is an official rule; that's one clue that it's no mere regularity. But, clearly, the rules of our natural languages—if there be such—are not official in this way. There haven't been any ceremonies establishing the rules, nor are they written down somewhere. (Or, if they are, this is a matter of *recording* the rules, not establishing them.) So, one piece of evidence for rule guidance is missing: the rules aren't official.

Still, linguistic regularities might result from guidance by informal rules. Informal rules don't *have* to be codified to be followed. For example, the rule 'wear wedding rings on the third finger of the left hand' is informal, but guides human behavior. And yet, how do you know that this is rule guidance? Answer: this rule is *conscious*. Everyone can easily state it. Not so the rules which supposedly guide linguistic behavior. They are typically unconscious. And so complex that only a trained linguist can come close to stating them.

I pause to sum up: the red light regularity is rule-guided because it is official (i.e. codified somewhere) and it is conscious. But this will not serve as the model for linguistic rules. The wedding ring regularity is rule-guided because it is conscious, even though it is unofficial. But again, this won't serve as the model because linguistic rules—if there be such—are not conscious. So, what can serve as a model for rule-guiding in language?

Another attempt: one of the marks of regularities which are rule-guided is that one can fail to apply the rule correctly. Compare the "rules" in (174):

(174) *Two "Rules"*
(a) Stop at red lights, truck drivers!
(b) Rest your left arm on the window ledge, truck drivers!

Nobody thinks that it's *wrong* for truck drivers not to rest their

140

arms on their windows; yet people certainly do think that it's wrong not to stop at red lights. This may provide a test for rule-guided behavior: if you can do it wrong, it's rule-guided; otherwise, it's a mere regularity.

What implications would this have for the question at hand—i.e. whether linguistic regularities result from rule guidance? Well, in some sense there is a right and a wrong way to speak English. Foreign speakers and children get it wrong. So, linguistic regularities look rule-guided—at least in this sense. But there's a catch. As Martin observes, "it is not clear that the fact that we detect what we count as right and wrong ways of doing things is a good sign of the existence of rules" (1987, 70). The reason is this: some non-rule-guided behavior garners disapproval. (An obvious example: walking around with your finger up your nose will be considered wrong. But avoidance of this behaviour is a mere regularity.) So the questions arises: is the wrongness of saying, 'I am wanting to buy this' the requisite *kind* of wrongness? It's not unethical to speak this way. And there aren't any punishments for speaking this way. (Failure to communicate is not a punishment.) Maybe, then, the wrongness of 'I am wanting to buy this' is the wrongness of simple non-conformity, like the wrongness of nose-fingering. In which case, linguistic regularities don't count as rule guidance.

There may be a way out. It's a way favoured by Chomsky. Linguistic regularities, you've just seen, lack many of the features of common sense rule-guided regularities. The linguistic rules aren't codified anywhere; they're not official; they're not conscious; nor are they exactly normative. This suggests that linguistic rule following isn't a paradigmatic case. To some, this suggests that talk of rule following in the case of language is wrong-headed and confused. To others, it suggests that linguists and philosophers should set aside the ordinary concept of 'rule' and adopt a technical one. Which technical one? Quine, a trenchant critic of rule guidance in the case of language, nevertheless points the way. He says (though not in so many words) that guiding is a matter of *cause and effect*: if linguistic rules *cause* the observed linguistic regularities, then the behavior is rule-guided. Otherwise, the behavior is merely regular. This, I think, is the crucial issue.

Well then: is language behavior rule-guided? That, it turns out, is (in part) an empirical issue. It depends on whether the rules discovered by linguists *produce* the observed behaviour—in the way, for example, that computer programs produce the behaviour of computers. Or whether, on the contrary, the rules simply describe the behaviour correctly. In the first case, linguistic behaviour is rule-guided, and the attribution of knowledge of language is appropriate. In the latter case, linguistic behaviour is merely regular, and the attribution of linguistic knowledge is deeply misguided.

3. Radical Translation

The conclusion of this section can be stated simply: without the standard background beliefs garnered from one's own language, a linguist cannot arrive at a uniquely correct grammar for the language under study. The implications for the knowledge perspective on language are, some say, enormous. Assuming there are rules guiding the speakers under study, the linguist ought to be able to discover them—and rule out all other alternatives. Or so one might argue. Since, as Quine (1960) contends, the linguist *can't* do this, it seems that there really aren't rules which guide verbal behaviour. In which case one arrives, once again, at the conclusion discussed in the last section: talk of *knowing* linguistic rules is entirely out of place.

The argument has two crucial steps. The first: **radical translation** (the term will be explained shortly) cannot succeed. The second: because radical translation fails, attribution of linguistic knowledge is misguided.[55] I begin with the first.

Most of the time, when, as linguists or language learners, people encounter an unfamiliar language, they know something about it. They might know the words for 'yes' and 'no', 'good morning' and so on. And they typically recognize certain words as being like words in their native tongue. (E.g. 'crème', 'transport', and 'télévision' would be familiar to English speakers learning French.) What's more, even where the language being learned shares no obvious common ancestor with the native language—think of learning Mohawk as a native English speaker—there are still many behavioural similarities one can take for granted: pointing with the index finger, nodding for 'yes', and smiling when things go well. But—a thought experiment owing to Quine, 1960—suppose you had to write a grammar for a wholly alien culture, such as some Brazilian tribe who have only now encountered the outside world. This is *radical* translation.

Quine's point is that radical translation cannot entirely succeed. You cannot, without making questionable assumptions about similarities between yourself and the subject culture, arrive at the one true grammar of the language in question. Quine illustrates this with an example. In pursuing radical translation, you might begin by finding what terms referred to medium-sized physical objects. You might notice, for example, that the natives say the one-word sentence 'Gavagai' when—as *you* would put it—there's a rabbit in the environment. Of course, having them say 'Gavagai' once in the presence of a rabbit doesn't establish much. In particular, it doesn't establish that 'Gavagai' means 'Lo, a rabbit!' As Martin says,

> The native might 'really' have been meaning any one of a number of things, including:
> (175)
> (a) Lo, a fuzzy animal
> (b) Lo, an animal
> (c) Lo, an alligator [the native is confused about animals]
> (d) I saw that thing yesterday
> (e) Hand me my bow and arrows
> (f) I sure am hungry
> (Martin 1987, 54. The numbering is mine.)

But repeated correlations of rabbit appearances with utterances of 'Gavagai' would eliminate some of these as hypotheses. For instance, if the natives say 'Gavagai' in the presence of previously unseen rabbits, then (175d) is out. If they say 'Gavagai' when they already have their bow and arrows, while you are bow and arrow free, then (175e) can be rejected. And, if they say 'Gavagai' and then refuse food, that militates against taking 'Gavagai' to mean (175f).

Another way of making progress is to ask the natives, 'Gavagai?'—hoping that rising intonation and uplifted brow indicate questioning in their culture. But, of course, you need some way of interpreting their response. Suppose you hold up a rabbit, and say 'Gavagai?'. The native says 'Evet'. Does she mean yes or no? Quine proposes a way to find out:

> But how is [the linguist] to recognize native assent and dissent when he sees or hears them? Gestures are not to be taken at face value; the Turks' are nearly the reverse of our own. What he must do is guess from observation and then see how well his guesses work. Thus suppose that in asking 'Gavagai?' and the like, in the conspicuous presence of rabbits and the like, he has elicited the responses 'Evet' and 'Yok' often enough to surmise that they may correspond to 'Yes' and 'No', but he has no notion which is which. Then he tries the experiment of echoing the native's own volunteered pronouncements. If

thereby he pretty regularly elicits 'Evet' rather than 'Yok', he is encouraged to take 'Evet' as 'Yes'. Also he tries responding with 'Evet' and 'Yok' to the native's remarks; the one that is the more serene in its effects is the better candidate for 'Yes' (Quine 1960, 29-30).

Suppose that, using this technique, you hypothesize that 'Evet' likely means yes. So far so good. But there are difficulties ahead—philosophical difficulties. The example seems to show that one cannot learn the meaning of one word in isolation from all others. For instance: your learning what 'Gavagai' means depends, at least in part, in figuring out what 'Evet' and 'Yok' mean. Put another way, your experience of the language, including your "experiments" of prompting assent and dissent, confirm (or refute) a *system* of hypotheses about the language. In the case of the rabbit example, the (partial) systems are:

(176)
(a) *System One*: 'Evet' means YES and 'Gavagai' means THERE'S A RABBIT NEARBY
(b) *System Two*: 'Evet' means NO and 'Gavagai' THERE ISN'T A RABBIT NEARBY

Notice: System One makes sense of the native's saying 'Evet' when she sees a rabbit, since saying 'Evet' in this system affirms an obvious truth. But System Two *also* makes sense of the native's saying 'Evet' in the presence of rabbits, since in this system 'Evet' is used to deny an obvious falsehood. The lesson: your hypothesis about what 'Evet' means depends (in part) on what you take 'Gavagai' to mean, and vice versa.

For Quine, there is no crucial "experiment" or experience that would force you to reject any single entry in your translation manual. Each entry depends evidentially on the system as a whole, in the sense that every possible experience could be made consistent with a given entry by making changes elsewhere. (Especially since changes are allowed with respect to what one takes the natives to believe: you can always conclude that, in a particular instance, your informant is trying to mislead, or that she disagrees with you about the facts, or that she's just being polite, etc.) In sum: the entry you provide for any single item in your lexicon is not independent of the other entries. You cannot test the correctness of any one entry in isolation.[56]

To Quine, this suggests that—in principle anyway—the linguist could provide various *incompatible* systems which make equally good sense of the speakers in question. Each would accord with the overall patterns of actual speech. But, despite making the same predictions, the grammars would differ internally. Quine writes:

> The thesis is then this: manuals for translating one language into another can be set up in divergent ways, all compatible with the totality of speech dispositions, yet incompatible with one another (Quine 1960, 27).

In which case, the linguist in the situation of radical translation cannot arrive at the "one true grammar" of the language in question.

There are two ways of understanding this result. First: there's a fact about what rules are being employed by the natives, including facts about what individual items mean in their language, but there's no way to find out. That is, there is **underdetermination** of the linguist's grammar by the evidence. In cases of underdetermination, the scientist cannot rationally decide between the competing theories. But only one theory is right. Reading Quine's radical translation result this way: the linguist cannot be certain about what rules are guiding the natives' speech. But there are such rules.

There is, however, another way of understanding Quine's conclusion about the failure of radical translation. Sometimes, when two competing hypotheses appear equally good, philosophers conclude that *neither* is "the correct answer". Indeed, they conclude that there *is* no correct answer. Here are some example questions where, it might be thought, no one answer is right.

(177)
(a) Is the earth is upside down or right side up?
(b) Is Mozart better than ice cream, or vice versa?
(c) Given a subject who no longer knows what murder is, nor what presidents are, can she nevertheless believe that President McKinley was assassinated?[57]
(d) Is France octagonal?

It's not as if, by learning more, one would be able to settle these questions. Answers to them are, to use the jargon, **indeterminate**. This is how Quine suggests taking his result: as showing that there is no fact about which rules are guiding the natives. Not only can't the linguist *tell* which of the competing theories is the right one—there is no right one. The reason for drawing this conclusion is that, according to Quine, no *possible* evidence could ever lead the linguist to opt for one set of rules above all others.[58] To paraphrase Quine: two theories could be just alike in all predictions about dispositions to verbal behaviour *under all possible circumstances*, and yet diverge radically (see Quine 1960, 26). Given this, one should not conclude that there are rules known by the speaker, though linguists in the situation of radical translation could never find them; instead, Quine urges, one should conclude that such rules don't really exist. In short, because radical translation will not decide between competing hypotheses about what the speaker knows, attribution of *exactly one* body of rules-known is misguided.

Suggested Readings

The literature on the "innateness hypothesis" is vast. As a beginning, see Chomsky 1962, 1975 and Putnam 1967. Those and related papers appear in Part Four of Block 1981. The idea that learning a language requires a language is defended in Fodor 1975. Pinker 1994 provides a semi-popular defense of the innateness hypothesis. For much more see Devitt and Sterelny 1987, Hook 1969, Martin 1987, Piatelli-Palmarini 1980, Searle 1971, and Stich 1975.

Martin 1987 contains a useful introduction to problems about rule following and indeterminacy. For primary sources, see Quine 1951, 1953b, 1960, 1969. Gibson (1982, 1986) is an excellent expositor of Quine's views. Chomsky (1969, 1980, 1986) responds to many of the standard criticisms. Indeterminacy is taken up again in Chapter Nine of this book.

Part Three:

The Use Perspective

Chapter Nine:

The Use Theory of Meaning

According to the Thing Theory of Meaning, a linguistic symbol gets its meaning from the external object that corresponds to it. According to the Idea Theory of Meaning, linguistic symbols correspond to internal mental items. (And these, in turn, may correspond to something external.) These are two views about what meaningfulness amounts to. I turn now to a third alternative: the Use Theory of Meaning.

1. Meaning and Use

First point: words come in lots of varieties. There are abstract nouns ('symphony', 'honesty'); concrete nouns ('dog', 'fig'); proper names ('Ottawa', 'Joshua'); mass nouns ('water', 'gold'); and others. There are verbs of action ('run', 'jump'); verbs of mentation ('think', 'calculate'); statal verbs ('to tower', 'to like'); and others. There are prepositions ('at', 'from'); question particles ('who', 'where'); quantifiers ('many', 'each') and conjunctions ('whereas', 'furthermore'). And on and on. There are also many kinds of sentences. Despite this obvious multiplicity, there is a tendency—noted by Wittgenstein (1953), among others—to assimilate all linguistic expressions to a single kind. In particular, Wittgenstein thinks philosophers have routinely made the mistake of supposing that all expressions—words and sentences—are name-like.[59]

Giving in to this tendency, philosophers look for an object or thing for every expression—the item which the expression stands for. This is to be its meaning. (Indeed, the Thing Theory of meaning as presented in Chapters Three and Four would have struck Wittgenstein as a perfect example of what *not* to do.) To combat the simplifying tendency, Wittgenstein continually stresses the very different uses for the many varieties of linguistic symbols. I quote him at length:

> But how many kinds of sentence are there? Say assertion, question, and command?—There are countless kinds: countless different kinds of use of what we call "symbols", "words", "sentences". And this multiplicity is not something fixed, given once for all; but new types of language, new language-games, as we may say, come into existence, and others become obsolete and get forgotten... Review the multiplicity of language-games in the following examples, and in others:
>
> Giving orders, and obeying them—
> Describing the appearance of an object, or giving its measurements—
> Constructing an object from a description (a drawing)—
> Reporting an event—
> Speculating about an event—
> Forming and testing a hypothesis—
> Presenting the results of an experiment in tables and diagrams—
> Making up a story; and reading it—
> Play-acting—
> Singing catches—
> Guessing riddles—
> Making a joke; telling it—
> Solving a problem in practical arithmetic—
> Translating from one language into another—
> Asking, thanking, cursing, greeting, praying. (1953, 11-12)

There are, notes Wittgenstein, as many different linguistic activities as there are games. And notice: there's no essential feature shared by all games—some are played for fun, some for profit; some set teams against one another, others have individuals as participants, and some (e.g. solitaire) are played alone; some games have a termination built in (e.g. chess, bridge and baseball), others last a fixed time (e.g. football), and still others go on until the participants decide to stop (e.g. poker and roulette). Wittgenstein makes the same point about language: there is no single essence. In particular, having a denotation, or corresponding to a mental something, is *not* what all meaningful linguistic expressions share.

That's the first point, then: that language is used in a multiplicity of ways. Here's the second point. The fundamental criterion for whether a speaker S understands an expression E has to do with how S employs E. If you use E in the right sorts of ways, and in the right circumstances, then you can correctly be said to understand E. This suggests that, as Strawson (1954, 74) notes in a slightly different context, "to grasp a meaning is to be able to practise a technique..." So, when you grasp the meaning, what you grasp is *a procedure*—a way of acting. In which case, the meaning might as well *be* a way of acting. Hence, meaning *is* use. That, in a nutshell, is the use theory of meaning: the meaning of a symbol is determined by how it is used; and, since there are lots of different uses, there are many different meanings. I will now spell out the Use Theory, by applying it to a number of different cases; in particular: indexicals, referring expressions, and **performatives**.

2. Indexicals

A theory of meaning typically has a case for which it works particularly well. The Thing Theory works particularly well for names, while the Idea Theory captures sensation words. One place where the Use Theory really shines is **indexicals**. As Martin (1987, 191) says, an indexical is a 'pointing term'. Here are some examples:

(178) *Demonstratives*
(a) this
(b) that

(179) *Locatives (Spatial and Temporal)*
(a) here
(b) there
(c) now
(d) then

(180) *Pronominals*
(a) I
(b) she
(c) you
(d) they
(e) it

There are lots of others. However, this list should give you an idea of what indexicals are for: they are used to pick out an individual, place, time, or whatever *in the context*.

Whether or not names and definite descriptions refer, one can't help but agree that *indexicals* don't. Or, more precisely, though *tokens* of indexicals may refer, indexical *types* do not. Take sentence (181):

(181) She is hungry

The word type 'she' clearly doesn't refer to anything. Indeed, it's of the essence of this word that its referent changes from one context to the next. (Contrast a *token* of 'she'. For example, suppose I say sentence (181), pointing at my cat Weeble. This token of 'she' *does* refer: it refers to Weeble.)

Despite the fact that indexical types don't refer, they do have some **descriptive content**. For instance, using 'that' rather than 'this' presupposes that the object referred to is distant; using 'he' suggests that the object referred to is male and animate; using 'now' suggests (pretty strongly!) that the time referred to is present. So, indexicals are pointing devices and they pick out their object by using features of it. Which suggests that the meaning of an indexical can be split in two: the descriptive content part and "the pointing part". Here's the picture.

(182)   Indexical Expression

Descriptive Content Part   "Pointing Part"

The "pointing part" is constant across indexicals. Indeed, having a "pointing part" is what makes something an indexical. The descriptive content part, on the other hand, varies from one indexical to the next.

So far so good. But suppose you wanted to give the meaning of a particular indexical. 'This', for instance. How would you go about it? Clearly, you'd have to specify the content for both parts, to capture the meaning of the whole. The descriptive content part might be handled in the usual way. If you're a *thing theorist*, you would assign some external object as the descriptive content of 'this'. (In the possible worlds framework, for example, the descriptive content of 'this' might be a function from *nearby objects* to TRUE, at the level of extension.) If you're an *idea theorist*, the descriptive content of 'this' would need to be some mental item: an image, an expression in mentalese, or what have you. Again, it's easy enough to imagine how this would go. However, what bizarre "stuff", external or otherwise, could *the pointing part* correspond to? Here, both the Thing Theory *and* the Idea Theory look unpromising. The Use Theory, on the other hand, works exceedingly well: what a use theorist would say, to capture the meaning of "the pointing part", is that indexicals *are used to talk about objects in the environment*. That completely specifies the meaning of the pointing part. In short: giving the use, in this instance, is giving the meaning.

3. Strawson on Referring

As a second illustration of the Use Theory's power, consider Strawson's (1950) criticism of Russell (1905, 1919). Strawson begins his article as follows:

> We very commonly use expressions of certain kinds to mention or refer to some individual person or single object... (1950, 219)

Notice: *we* use expressions; *we* refer, using these expressions. Which expressions are so used? Demonstratives (e.g. 'this', 'that') and indexicals generally, proper names ('James', 'Paula', 'Venice'), pronouns ('she', 'they', 'it') and—contra Russell—definite descriptions, like those below:

(183)
(a) The table
(b) The King of France
(c) The invention of the telephone
(d) The southernmost city in England

Strawson insists that these descriptions can be used *by speakers* to refer to objects, individuals, places, events, and so on. It's not words which refer: it's *people*—in their use of language. (Only someone blind to the various uses of language would think otherwise.) Why is this an attack on Russell? Well, according to Russell 1919, sentences containing descriptions are actually disguised existentials. Sentence (184), for example, is supposedly equivalent to the conjunction of (185a-b):

(184) The present king of France is sexy

(185)
(a) There exists exactly one present king of France
(b) Every present king of France is sexy

Strawson thinks Russell is flatly wrong about this: (185) does *not* capture the meaning of (184). He writes:

> To give the meaning of an expression...is to give general directions
> for its use to refer to or mention particular objects or persons; to give
> the meaning of a sentence is to give general directions for its use in
> making true or false assertions (223).

> But the meaning of an expression is not the set of things or the single
> thing it may correctly be used to refer to: the meaning is the set of
> rules, habits, conventions, for its use in referring (Strawson 1950, 224).

In short: to give the meaning of an expression is to explain and illustrate the conventions governing *the use* of that expression. And this holds for all expressions: sentences, proper names, definite descriptions, pronouns, and so on. To repeat the slogan: words don't refer, people do; similarly, it's not sentences but speakers that express propositions. So, Strawson maintains, although (185) might capture what *a speaker* means in saying (184)—in producing a token of it—Russell was wrong to suppose that this is what *the sentence* means.

One advantage claimed for the Use Theory of Meaning is that it overcomes Russell's ontological difficulties, without imposing implausible semantic hypotheses. Russell (1919) reasoned roughly as follows:

(186) *Russell's "Not-Meaningful" Argument*
Premise 1: If 'the present king of France' is a meaningful group of symbols, then the present king of France has some kind of being.
Premise 2: It's not the case that the present king of France has some kind of being.
Conclusion: 'The present king of France' is not a meaningful group of symbols.

In short, if 'the present king of France' is meaningful—in Russell's peculiar sense of that word—there must be some thing which it refers to. So, to avoid ontological commitment to contemporary French kings, Russell drew the conclusion that descriptions *are not meaningful in isolation*: that is, there is no entity which descriptions stand for. The sentence ⌜The F is G⌝ gets cashed out as ⌜There is exactly one F and every F is G⌝. And, it appears, this latter sentence contains no part which can serve as "the meaning" of ⌜The F⌝ on its own.[60]

Russell's solution—i.e. denying that descriptions are meaningful in isolation—has seemed counter-intuitive to many. Strawson offers a different way out. On his view, being meaningful *does not* amount to having reference. Hence, Premise 1 in Russell's "Not-Meaningful" argument is false: the meaningfulness of 'the present king of France' does not entail the existence of any referent—let alone the existence of a present king of France. To call this expression meaningful is just to say that there are general conventions governing its use in speech. So, Russell's argument is valid, but it is not sound. Strawson concludes:

> The sentence, "The king of France is wise," is certainly significant; but...the fact that the sentence and the expression ["the king of France"], respectively, are significant just is the fact that the sentence could be used, in certain circumstances, to say something true or false, that the expression could be used, in certain circumstances, to mention a particular person; and to know their meaning is to know what sort of circumstances these are. So when we utter the sentence without in fact mentioning anybody by the use of the phrase, "The king of France," the sentence does not cease to be significant: We simply fail to say anything true or false because we simply fail to mention anybody by this particular use of that perfectly significant phrase (Strawson 1950, 225-226).

Meaning isn't reference. It's use. So lack of reference does not entail meaninglessness. In short: the Use Theory of Meaning saves our metaphysical bacon while preserving the intuition that 'the present king of France' is meaningful.

4. Speech Act Theory

According to J.L. Austin, philosophers used to assume that "the sole business, the sole interesting business, of any utterance—that is, of anything we say—is to be true or at least false" (1961, 105). Austin thought this a mistake, and a dangerous one. Ignoring non-assertive uses, Austin maintained, encourages philosophers to look for a *fact* being described whenever an utterance is made. Some examples:

(187) *Apparently Descriptive Language*
(a) I take this man to be my lawfully wedded husband
(b) I apologize
(c) I name this ship the Queen Elizabeth
(d) I bet you five bucks it will rain tomorrow
(e) I promise to be there tomorrow

Trapped by the **descriptive fallacy**—the idea that all language use involves making statements which are true or false—philosophers may look for something which makes (187a-e) true or false. Not finding any outwardly observable fact, some might suppose that sentences (187a-e) describe an "inner act": the utterance is true if the inner act really occurred; it is false otherwise. (Just as 'I jumped' is a sentence which describes an *outer* act; it's true if the act occurred, false otherwise.) This supposed analogy, Austin says, does not hold. For example, he emphatically denies that (187e) describes something about the speaker's internal machinations: for instance, that the speaker has mentally resolved to go.[61] It's a confusion to suppose that (187e) is true if and only if the speaker *really intends* to show up—a confusion encouraged by ignoring non-assertive uses.

What Austin maintains, on the contrary, is that in the case of promising (and elsewhere) instead of *saying* something, the speaker is *doing* something: *performing an action*. Using (187a), the speaker gets married; using (187b) she apologizes; using (187c) she names the ship; using (187d) she makes a bet. The result: insofar as the speaker isn't describing, there's no need for a fact described; and hence no need to posit an inner act—whatever that might be.

So much for Austin's philosophical motivation. The importance of his work for present purposes is that it provides a final illustration of the Use Theory of Meaning. As you've seen and will continue to see, language is used in any number of ways. A short list: people ask questions and give orders in language, they get engaged and married in language, they make bets and promises in language, they congratulate and berate, warn and entice, apologize and curse, rank and classify, argue and hypothesize, appoint and baptize, and so on—all in language. (See Vendler 1972 and Wittgenstein 1953 for much more.) Given this variety, one's theory of meaning must be able to apply to many different kinds of language. A semantics which handles only descriptive language will not do.

If a sentence doesn't describe anything—isn't capable of being true or false—then its meaning cannot be exhausted by its truth conditions. This is familiar from the discussion of interrogatives in Chapter Five, and it applies here as well. Given this, what can the meaning of **performatives** like (187a-e) be? Here's a partial answer (though I'm not sure it was Austin's answer): the meaning of a performative expression is captured by the **speech act** it is customarily used to perform. So, 'I promise to be there tomorrow' is used to make a promise.

A different point about conditions of use: as I've said, Austin maintained that the characteristic feature of performatives is that performatives are not descriptive, and hence not truth-evaluable. In which case, they can never be false. Nevertheless, he says, though never false, they "suffer from certain disabilities of their own. They can fail to come off in special ways" (107). Describing the language, then, requires describing not only the various kinds of speech acts and the devices for performing them: it also requires describing what conditions must be in place—the **felicity conditions**—for bringing off this kind of action. So, a complete theory of meaning, as an Austinian conceives it, will (a) pair expressions with action types, and (b) give the conditions under which uttering an expression of the appropriate type results in the action's actual performance. In short: what is required of a theory of meaning, according to a Use Theorist of the Austinian stripe, is *not* a specification of an expression's denotation, its sense, or its associated idea-in-the-mind. Rather, says the Austinian, a theorist of meaning must fill in the following **speech act schema** for each and every expression of the language:

(188) *The Speech Act Schema*: A speaker S performs a linguistic action of type A if and only if (iff)
(a) S utters an expression E, where E is a device for doing A
(b) The conditions C—the felicity conditions—obtain.

The job of the meaning theorist becomes finding, for every E in the language, the corresponding action A and felicity conditions C. *This* is what a theory of meaning looks like, from Austin's perspective. (Notice, by the way, that this speech act schema applies to declarative sentences as well: to things which *are* true and false.)

You have encountered expression types continuously. And I trust you have some idea of what an action type is. Hence, E and A in the schema should pose no problem. But the notion of a felicity condition—i.e. what is meant by C—may not hit you at first. Here are some samples, to give you the idea. First kind of felicity condition: if the action is actually going to be performed, the conventional procedures must exist in the culture. For example, in North America you can't get divorced by saying, 'I divorce you' three times. That's because, around here anyway, that convention doesn't hold. Second kind of felicity condition: to actually succeed in performing the action, the circumstances must be appropriate. For example, if I say 'I appoint him consul', the indicated object better not be dead, or a hunk of cheese; furthermore, as the speaker, I'd better be in a position to appoint someone consul. Otherwise, though I may utter the words, I don't actually make a consular appointment. Third kind of felicity condition: the speaker must have the requisite beliefs and intentions. This might be called the *sincerity requirement*. That is, if I say 'I congratulate you' when I am displeased, or don't think that you deserve the credit, I'm being insincere. (Imagine that!) In this case, although I may still perform the action, there is something amiss. My utterance is "unhappy". Fourth kind of felicity condition: the utterance shouldn't be said under duress. (Saying 'I confess' under threat won't result in a confession actually being made.) Fifth kind of felicity condition: the utterance should be performed "seriously". That is, not in a play, not as a joke, etc. Actors rehearsing their lines don't make promises; nor do singers, story tellers, and so on. There are other kinds of felicity conditions. But this should give you the idea of how to understand 'the conditions C' in (188).

An Example: Promising

John Searle was one of Austin's students. He attempted to carry forward Austin's project—roughly, the project of filling in the speech act schema, and thus giving a use-based theory of meaning. He did this by carefully examining one kind of performance: making promises. Looking at this detailed example will highlight the essential features of speech act theory.

Here is Searle's project: "I shall ask what conditions are necessary and sufficient for the act of promising to have been performed in the utterance of a given sentence" (1965, 120). As he says, making explicit comparison to the rules of a game, "The method here is analogous to discovering the rules of chess by asking oneself what are the necessary and sufficient conditions under which one can be said to have correctly moved a knight or castled or checkmated a player, etc." (120-121).

That's the project; here's the attempt. According to Searle 1965, given that speaker S utters a sentence t in the presence of a hearer H, S (sincerely) promises that p to H if and only if:

(a) Normal conditions obtain. (S and H share a language; the utterance is not made under duress, or in a play; and so on.)

158

(b) *S* expresses that *p* in the utterance of *t*. (This takes care of the propositional content of the promise; Searle can therefore abstract away from this side of speech acts.)

(c) In expressing that *p*, *S* predicates a future act *A* of *S*. (This distinguishes a promise from an avowal. One cannot promise *to have done something.*[62])

(d) The hearer *H* would prefer *S*'s doing *A* to *S*'s not doing *A*. What's more, *S* believes *H* would prefer his doing *A*. (This condition distinguishes literal promising from threatening.)

(e) It is not obvious to both *S* and *H* that *S* will do *A* in the normal course of events.

(f) *S* intends to do *A*. (This is a condition for a sincere promise. Obviously one can make an insincere promise too. However, Searle wants to mark the distinction.)

(g) *S* intends that the utterance of sentence *t* will place him or her under an obligation to do *A*. (As Searle says, this is the essential feature of promises.)

(h) *S* intends that the utterance of *t* will produce in *H* a belief that *S* intends to do *A*; and that *S* intends to be placed under the obligation of doing *A*. What's more, *S* intends to induce this belief in *H* by getting *H* to see that *S* intends to induce it.

These are supposed to be the necessary and sufficient conditions for promising. If you satisfy them, you promise. If you leave even one out, you fail to promise. Let's put aside the question of whether Searle's analysis of promising is accurate or adequate. The important lesson is what Searle is attempting, and what's involved. He is describing a linguistic act in detail—including its felicity conditions. He is, in effect, making a first stab at filling in the speech act schema, repeated here, for the case of promising:

(188) *The Speech Act Schema*: A speaker *S* makes a promise iff
(a) *S* utters an expression *E*, where *E* is a device for promising
(b) The conditions *C*—the felicity conditions—obtain.

This is what a theorist of meaning *does*, if he adopts the use perspective. What the above illustrates is how complex this can be.

You now have before you three illustrations of how the Use Theory of Meaning works: indexicals, descriptions and speech acts. This should leave you with a reasonable understanding of what's meant by the claim that meaning is use.[63] I end this chapter with a puzzle that arises if one takes this slogan perfectly seriously.

5. Quine and Meaning Nihilism

"Language is a social art". So begins Quine's (1960, ix) land-mark *Word and Object*. This slogan incorporates two important claims: that language is social, and that language is performance. In a later chapter I'll discuss the importance of the social character of language. At this point I want to consider a possible consequence which the emphasis on linguistic *action* may have: the conse-quence that *there are no meaning facts*. (The claim that there's no such thing as meaning seems a fitting finale to the third of three chapters which address the central question of what meaning is, and where it comes from!) Needing a label, I'll call this doctrine **meaning nihilism**. As I read Quine, there are two intimately relat-ed arguments for this conclusion.

Argument one builds on a result introduced when dis-cussing the knowledge perspective: that, in the situation of radical translation, the linguist can arrive at no uniquely correct transla-tion manual. This, Quine insists, is not a matter of the psychologi-cal or epistemological limitations of working linguists. The reason one can't find "the right" translation manual is that meaning, in the intuitive sense presupposed throughout this book, is **indetermi-nate**. Which is just another way of saying that there are no mean-ing facts. This, Quine supposes, is actually pretty obvious—if you think about it. He writes: "one has only to reflect on the nature of the possible data and methods to appreciate the indeterminacy" (1960, 72). Past philosophers (and linguists) have been blind to this obvious fact because they adopted "an uncritical mentalistic theory of ideas". Once one recognizes that language is social *behaviour*, rather than something inside the head, it becomes clear that no amount of verbal behaviour—social or individual—determines a unique theory of meaning. In which case, meaning in the traditional sense doesn't really exist. In short: for Quine—who rejects linguistic knowledge—all there can be to language is linguistic behaviour, and meaning facts (as philosophers usually conceive of them) "are not determinate functions of linguistic behaviour" (Quine 1960, 69) and "exceed anything implicit in any native's dispositions to speech behaviour" (1960, 70). In which case, despite uncritical intuitions to the contrary, there really aren't any meaning facts.

As I say, this is one argument for meaning nihilism. There's another. (Or, maybe more accurately, there's another way of stating

160

the same argument.) It goes like this (the term 'stimulus meaning' will be explained shortly):

Premise One: If **stimulus meaning** doesn't capture meaning in the intuitive sense, then nothing can.
Premise Two: Stimulus meaning doesn't capture meaning in the intuitive sense.

The conclusion, obviously, is that nothing can capture the intuitive sense of meaning. Which, evidently, is another way of affirming meaning nihilism. The argument is a simple one, once the premises are understood. Let me explain them.

Stimulus Meaning

What is stimulus meaning? I'm going to be simplifying here: Quine's own treatment of these matters is intricate and complex. Still, I hope the central idea will come through. Call the *affirmative* stimulus meaning of a sentence S the *class of stimulations that would prompt assent to S*. I stress: the *class* of stimulations, not *the* stimulation—this because many stimulations will work. So, for example, the stimulation of seeing a rabbit would prompt assent to 'Rabbit'. But so would the stimulation of seeing a toy rabbit, hearing rabbity noises, perceiving a rabbit hologram, and so on. These, insofar as they elicit assent to 'Rabbit', are all part of that term's affirmative stimulus meaning. Next step. Call the *negative* stimulus meaning of S all those stimuli which would prompt dissent. So, a patently empty field is part of the negative stimulus meaning of 'Rabbit'. Given this, the stimulus meaning of S will be the *ordered pair* of these two classes: the affirmative stimulus meaning and the negative stimulus meaning.

To make up an example: suppose $stim_1$, $stim_2$, and $stim_3$ would all produce assent to 'Anbup', and nothing else would. Suppose further that $stim_4$ and $stim_5$ would produce dissent to 'Anbup', but nothing else would. In that case, the affirmative stimulus meaning, negative stimulus meaning, and stimulus meaning of 'Anbup' are as follows:

(189)
(a) Affirmative stimulus meaning ('Anbup')=$\{stim_1, stim_2, stim_3\}$
(b) Negative stimulus meaning ('Anbup')=$\{stim_4, stim_5\}$
(c) Stimulus meaning ('Anbup')=<$\{stim_1, stim_2, stim_3\}, \{stim_4, stim_5\}$>

Okay then. Having said what stimulus meaning is, I now turn to the various ways in which stimulus meaning diverges from "real" meaning: meaning as ordinarily understood. (This in support of Premise Two.) Here's the general shape of the argument. Stimulus meaning captures the speaker's dispositions to assent and dissent in response to various stimulations. "Real" meaning captures, loosely, the situations in which the expression applies. However, as you'll see, stimulations which prompt assent can correspond to situations in which the expression *does not* intuitively apply; just as stimulations which *do not* prompt assent can correspond to situations in which the expression *does* intuitively apply. In which case, assent/dissent patterns are not indicative of when the expression applies. Which is a round-about way of saying that stimulus meaning does not capture meaning in the intuitive sense.

First class of cases: a sentence which prompts assent in situations where, intuitively, the sentence's "real" meaning does not apply. Consider Kate, a person who, common-sensically speaking, means by 'Rabbit' what ordinary English speakers do. Kate lives in an area with rabbit flies—little parasites which are usually a few feet from their rabbit host. Given this, imagine a scene which includes a rabbit fly. Imagine further that, in this situation, Kate would assent to 'Rabbit'. (Presumably because, as one would say, Kate believes that rabbit flies indicate that rabbits are nearby.) But suppose further that, despite the presence of the rabbit fly, there is no host rabbit. In this case, surely, the English word 'Rabbit' *even in Kate's mouth* doesn't apply. This is a case of a stimulation which prompts assent, even though the expression *does not* intuitively apply.

The diagnosis, put in ordinary terms, is this: a subject's assent/dissent patterns for a sentence S are determined by what she takes S to mean *and by what she believes*. And stimulus meaning is blind to this distinction; it conflates what, from the perspective of "real" meaning, are two very different things: the speaker's knowledge of language, and her knowledge of the world—her intrusive collateral information, as Quine would say. Stimulus meaning cannot, therefore, capture "real meaning".[64]

Second class of cases. Quine, in a slightly different context, describes stimulations which do not prompt assent in situations where the expression *does* intuitively apply. He writes:

> consider the Himalayan explorer who has learned to apply 'Everest'
> to a distant mountain seen from Tibet and 'Gaurisanker' to one seen

from Nepal. As occasion sentences[65] these words have mutually exclusive stimulus meanings for him until his explorations reveal, to the surprise of all concerned, that the peaks are identical (Quine 1960, 49).

That is, before discovering that 'Everest' and 'Gaurisanker' refer to the same mountain, the stimulus of an exceedingly tall summit seen from Nepal would *not* prompt assent to 'Everest'. Nevertheless, in the intuitive sense, 'Everest' applies. So, failure of assent does not indicate failure of application. In which case, stimulus meaning does not capture meaning in the intuitive sense.

Again, the diagnosis is roughly the same. What a speaker assents to, or dissents from, depends on lots of things—including collateral beliefs and desires which go far beyond the meaning of the sentence being queried. Indeed, a speaker might assent even where the expression fails to apply because he wants to be polite, or because, on the contrary, he wants to deceive, or because he's simply mistaken about the facts, or because of religious teachings, or...well, for who knows what reasons. Given this, it's no surprise that assent and dissent patterns are orthogonal to whether the sentence actually applies. And no surprise that stimulus meaning doesn't capture "real" meaning.

At the risk of dead horse whipping, I introduce one final case. It has an important enough place in the canon of philosophical examples that it's well worth a few paragraphs. The foregoing have been cases of *sentence* meaning not corresponding to stimulus meaning. ('Rabbit' and 'Everest' are to count as one-word sentences. That something is a one-word sentence is indicated by the use of capital letters: 'Red' and 'Rabbit' are sentences, whereas 'red' and 'rabbit' are words.) It also appears that, even if stimulus meaning and "real" meaning could be equated for *sentences*, that would be all. In particular, there's no way to correlate *word* meaning with stimulus meaning.

First obvious-but-not-compelling reason: words don't prompt assent/dissent, only sentences do. So there can be no such thing as "the class of stimulations which would prompt assent/dissent" for a word. (Again, one-word sentences count as sentences.) In which case, words don't even *have* stimulus meanings. Hence one can't possibly identify their "real" meaning with their (non-existent) stimulus meaning!

Being familiar with Frege, you might say: "The stimulus meaning of a word can be what the word contributes to the stimulus meaning of sentences in which it appears". Clever you. That's exactly what one ought to say. But saying this won't get you word meaning (in the classical sense), because of the second less-obvious-but-more-compelling reason why you can't equate word meaning with stimulus meaning: the stimulus meaning of a whole sentence does not determine the meaning of its lexical parts. Put otherwise: a single stimulus meaning can be built out of intuitively non-synonymous word meanings. In which case, there's no clear sense to be made of 'that which the word contributes' to the stimulus meaning: there's no such unique thing.

An example will undoubtedly help. Please concede, for the sake of argument, that the stimulus meaning of the hitherto untranslated sentence (190a) is identical to that of the English sentence (190b).

(190)
(a) Ech utpal gavagai
(b) There's a rabbit nearby

Hypothesis, to be eventually rejected: the meaning of the word 'gavagai' is the unique whatever-it-is which 'gavagai' contributes to the stimulus meaning of (190a). Now, suppose that past experience has led you to conclude that 'gavagai' corresponds not to 'there', 'a' or 'nearby', but rather to 'rabbit'. Given the stimulus meaning of the English (190b), you might conclude that 'gavagai' contributes RABBIT. And this would indeed be consistent with the stimulus meaning of the whole. But it isn't *determined* by the stimulus meaning of the whole. If 'gavagai' meant instead TEMPORAL RABBIT STAGE, the sentence 'Ech utpal gavagai' would prompt assent and dissent for precisely the same stimulations. Similarly if 'gavagai' contributed UNDETACHED RABBIT PARTS or PORTION OF RABBIT-STUFF or RABBITHOOD: in each case, the stimulus meaning of (190a) would remain constant and equivalent to (190b). The reason?

> Point to a rabbit and you have pointed to a stage of a rabbit, to an integral part of a rabbit, to the rabbit fusion, and to where rabbithood is manifested (Quine 1960, 52-53).

The thrust of the example: the stimulus meaning of *sentences* does not determine unique meanings for the embedded *words*. Because of this, one cannot equate word meaning with what the word contributes to the stimulus meaning of sentences in which it appears: there is no such entity as *the* unique thing which the word contributes. The *immediate* conclusion: even if stimulus meaning and "real" meaning could be equated for sentences, you can't construct *word* meaning out of stimulus meaning. Quine puts the *overall* conclusion succinctly: "We have now seen that the stimulus meaning as defined falls short in various ways of one's intuitive demands on "meaning"" (1960, 39).

Stimulus Meaning or No Meaning

Recall the line of argument. First premise: if stimulus meaning doesn't capture meaning in the intuitive sense, then nothing can. Second premise: as a matter of fact, stimulus meaning *doesn't* capture "real" meaning. In which case, there's really no such thing as meaning—as classically conceived. In the foregoing I have traced arguments for the second premise: that stimulus meaning doesn't capture "real" meaning. But what of the first premise?

It seems to me that it is supported by the assumption, explicit in Quine's slogan that language is a social *art*, that language simply *is* linguistic behaviour. In my terms: Premise One derives from adopting the use perspective *exclusively*. Language, for Quine, is "the complex of present dispositions to verbal behaviour" (1960, 27). In which case, meaning—if it exists—must arise out of verbal behaviour. (As he says, "words mean only as their use in sentences is conditioned to sensory stimuli, verbal or otherwise" (Quine 1960, 17).) This, in effect, limits meaning to stimulus meaning: if linguistic behaviour is all there is to language, then there cannot be linguistic facts—in particular, meaning facts—which extend beyond what linguistic behaviour determines. In a nutshell: all that linguistic behaviour determines, says Quine, is stimulus meaning. So, if "real" meaning is supposed to be more than stimulus meaning, it's actually a fiction.[66] I suspect Quine's argument is valid: that is, *if* language is nothing more than behaviour, then meaning in the familiar sense probably cannot be salvaged. (This bodes ill for the use theory of meaning.) But whether one should *agree* that language is exhausted by behaviour is, of course, a different matter. It's clear what I think: language is used all right. But it's also a system of symbols—a system which we *know*.

One final remark. Up until now, I've presented the Use Theory more or less uncritically. (Although, if Quine's critique works, the theory is in serious trouble!) I end with a general worry.

165

In my view, it makes the Use Theory far less plausible as a whole. The worry is this: in Part One, you saw that a semantics for a language must be compositional and recursive—otherwise, it cannot account for the unlimited number of meaningful expressions in a language. So, the meaning of whole expressions must be explicable in terms of the meaning of its parts, and how those parts combine and re-combine. The direct reference theory, and the mediated reference theories, each have very articulated stories about how this works. Not so the Use Theory. This is no accident. Ask yourself: how does the use of 'Every particle accelerator costs several millions of dollars' depend upon the use of 'particle', 'dollar', and so on? Worse: what *is* the use of 'every', 'several', 'million' and so on? These issues are left *completely* open. As such, the Use Theory—especially Wittgenstein and Strawson's versions of it—looks not so much false, as largely empty. At least as it stands.

Suggested Readings

The Use Theory of Meaning is most powerfully defended in Wittgenstein's work. See especially Wittgenstein 1953, 1958, 1974. For an introductory commentary, see Kenny 1973, Ch.8. Detailed discussion can also be found in Dummett 1979. On indexicals, consult Bar-Hillel 1954, Kaplan 1978, 1979 and Perry 1979. For a general introduction, see Martin 1987. Strawson's views, as presented in "On Referring", receive attention in Donnellan 1966. Russell 1957 contains a forceful reply to Strawson's original article.

The classic texts in speech act theory are Austin 1961, 1962 and Searle 1965, 1968, 1969, 1975. Bach and Harnish 1979 and Vendler 1972 contain valuable and detailed extensions. For more on language-as-action, see Lewis 1969, 1975, 1979 and Stalnaker 1972.

As for meaning nihilism, and the associated doctrine of the indeterminacy of translation, see Quine 1951, 1953b, 1959, 1960, 1972 as the primary source. Fans of the thesis include Davidson 1973, Dennett 1978, and Stich 1972. Those who have questioned its force include Chomsky 1969, Chomsky and Katz 1974, Evans 1975, and Fodor 1981b.

Chapter Ten:

Non-Literal Uses

In introducing and spelling out the Use Theory of Meaning, I have been treating literal uses of language. I now want to consider three non-literal uses of language: **conversational implicatures**, metaphor and Donnellan's **referential use** of descriptions. My discussion will, I hope, further fill out the claim that language is something we use.

1. Conversational Implicature

Possibly the most important, and most studied, variety of non-literal uses are **implicatures**. To introduce the idea, I'll follow Grice in starting with an example. Case one: A and B are talking about a mutual friend C. A says (191a); B replies with (191b):

(191)
(a) How is C getting on with his new job?
(b) Oh quite well, I think; he likes his colleagues, and he hasn't been to prison yet

What is B implying or suggesting? Maybe that C is dishonest, or that the new job involves illegal activities. Okay, but what did B *say*? What did he strictly and literally assert? Well, that C hasn't been to prison yet. Such cases led Grice to distinguish between what a speaker said, and what that speaker implicated. Simplifying somewhat: what is *said* is (roughly) the literal meaning of the utterance in the context. By contrast, what is implicated is what the speaker means—above and beyond the literal meaning.

That's what implicatures are. But where do they come from? How do speakers, in speaking, manage to create implicatures? How can they mean more than they say? Grice thinks that implicatures are "essentially connected with certain general features of discourse" (1975, 151). Grice identifies one feature of discourse in particular that gives rise to implicatures:

> Our talk exchanges do not normally consist of a succession of disconnected remarks, and would not be rational if they did. They are characteristically, to some degree at least, cooperative efforts. (151)

How do people maintain these cooperative efforts? Obviously, each person tries to cooperate. But what exactly do they try to do? According to Grice, they obey the **Cooperative Principle:**

> Make your conversational contribution such as is required, at the stage at which it occurs, by the accepted purpose or direction of the talk exchange in which you are engaged (151-152).

It's because speakers generally observe the cooperative principle that implicatures can arise.

The general principle is: cooperate. Applied to communicative efforts, this comes out as:[67]

(192) *The Cooperative Principle for Communication*
(a) Say what's required
(b) Say it when and how it's required.

This principle implies four sub-principles, which Grice calls **categories**.

(193) *Categories*
(a) *Quantity*: Say as much as is required, and don't say more.
(b) *Quality*: Try to say what's true and avoid saying what you believe to be false. And don't say that for which you lack evidence.
(c) *Relation*: Be relevant.
(d) *Manner*: Be perspicuous: avoid obscurity, ambiguity and unnecessary prolixity; and, be orderly.

The first two categories are, albeit roughly, applications of (192a): that speakers say what is required. The latter two categories, on the other hand, are (again, roughly) applications of (192b): that, in saying what is required, speakers do so when and how it is required. I summarize this with a table:

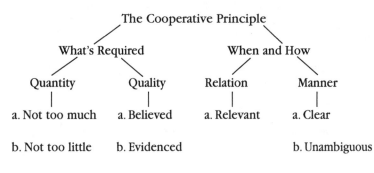

The Cooperative Principle

What's Required   When and How

Quantity   Quality   Relation   Manner

a. Not too much   a. Believed   a. Relevant   a. Clear

b. Not too little   b. Evidenced   b. Unambiguous

                                                    c. Brief

                                                    d. Orderly

I said: Grice thinks that implicatures—the speaker's meaning which extends beyond utterance meaning—are essentially connected to the cooperative principle. I've also just said what the principle is, and what some of its implications are. But just *how* does all of this give rise to implicatures? Look at example (191) again, from the hearer's perspective. The hearer (A) has just asked B how C is getting along in his new job. The speaker (B) utters (191b), repeated here:

(191b) Oh quite well, I think; he likes his colleagues, and he hasn't been to prison yet

B thereby *says* that C hasn't been to prison yet. But he *implicates* something further; namely, that C is dishonest. How does this work? The hearer, according to Grice, reasons as follows:

Premise 1: B is observing the cooperative principle.
Premise 2: If by sentence (191b), B meant only that C had not been to jail yet, then B would not be observing the cooperative principle.
Conclusion: B did not mean only that C had not been to jail yet by uttering sentence (191b).

This is the first step: discovering that the speaker's meaning is not exhausted by what is said. The next step is to find out what "the extra" is. Before turning to that, however, notice how the cooperative principle comes in: it is a *premise* that B is following it. This premise is warranted *if B really is communicating*: if communicating, B wants to achieve certain goals, and to achieve those goals, he must observe the cooperative principle. Doing otherwise wouldn't be rational. Hence, Premise 1 can be safely assumed. So, B cannot mean only that C hasn't been to prison yet.

Now for Step Two. The hearer knows there's something extra that B is communicating, but what is it? Here, the hearer must be creative. She asks herself:

(194) What could B have meant, consistent with B's observing the cooperative principle?

Frankly, no one knows how hearers come up with possible answers to (194). It's similar to asking how scientists arrive at scientific theories. So, I will leave out the "how", and just grant that the hearer somehow comes up with Premises 3 and 4:

Premise 3: If B meant that C was dishonest, B would be observing the cooperative principle.
Premise 4: There's no other thing which B could have meant, while observing the cooperative principle.

Once these premises are arrived at, it's easy to infer that B meant that C is dishonest. It follows from Premise 1 together with Premise 3 and Premise 4. So the hearer concludes that B meant that C is dishonest.

That's how implicatures are calculated. That is where they come from: from apparent violations of some part of the cooperative principle. In sum: sometimes what a *speaker* means outstrips the meaning of her *words*. The speaker says something, but may implicate other information at the same time. So, very roughly, a speaker's meaning = what is said + what is implicated. You know where 'what is said' comes from: it's the meaning of the expression, filled in according to the context. And you now know where implicatures come from: hearers count on people to mean what is required, when and how it is required. When what is said fails to meet these conditions, one looks around for other things that were meant. These are the implicatures.

2. Metaphor

I am in the process of discussing non-literal uses of language, in an effort to fill out the claim that language is something we use. I turn now to a particularly controversial and difficult case: metaphor. Here's what is wanted.

(195) *Questions about Metaphor*
(a) How are metaphors made?
(b) How are they understood?
(c) Why use metaphor at all?
(d) How is metaphor different from literal speech?

My game plan is to consider a number of responses to these questions. Any adequate view of metaphor must answer all of them, and plausibly. As you'll see, most answers don't stand up. Indeed, this discussion is very largely negative—saying why certain proposals *don't* work.

I begin with the Context Proposal.

(196) *The Context Proposal*: Metaphor is meaning in context

This view has one thing going for it: it's not exactly *false*, because metaphors do arise in context. But that doesn't distinguish metaphor from other non-literal speech. Irony and sarcasm both require context for understanding. When I say 'Great', whether I should be interpreted as meaning THAT'S AWFUL or THAT'S TERRIFIC clearly depends on context. (For example: if I say 'Great' about a surprise quiz for which I'm unprepared, I'm probably speaking sarcastically. If I say it upon receiving an A on said surprise quiz, then I undoubtedly mean it literally.) So, sarcasm is "meaning in context" too. But sarcasm isn't metaphor.

Worse, this definition of metaphor doesn't distinguish it from *literal* speech: context matters in literal speech because of **indexicality** and **ambiguity**. Indexical terms, you'll recall, are pointing words—examples include 'she' and 'that' in (197). Ambiguous sentences are given in (198).

(197) *Indexicals*
(a) She is a lawyer
(b) That is really cute

(198) *Ambiguity*
(a) Mary wrote a letter to the editor
(b) There's a pen on the floor

Notice: what an utterer of (197a) is *strictly and literally saying* depends (in part) upon which person the speaker means by 'she'. But that's a matter of context: what things are in the surrounding environment, which of them are human females, what the speaker is pointing at (if anything), and so on. Similarly for (197b) and the word 'that'. In the same way, the *literal* meaning of an utterance of (198a) depends upon which sense was intended. Is the utterer stating simply that Mary wrote to the editor—say, to invite him to dinner? Or is he affirming that Mary sent a letter to be published in the Letters to the Editor section? That depends, in ways I won't consider here, upon the context. Ditto for (198b): the literal meaning of an utterance of this sentence depends on what the speaker is talking about—a pen for writing, or a pen for pigs. So, even literal speech is "meaning in context"; in which case, the context proposal doesn't answer (195d). Metaphor, then, must be something more than the context proposal allows.

An initially more plausible—and more widely espoused— view is the Dual Meaning Proposal.

(199) *The Dual Meaning Proposal*: Metaphorical sentences have two meanings, a literal meaning and a metaphorical one.

According to this view, metaphorical sentences are equivocal. They have a restricted ("literal") sense and an extended ("metaphorical") sense. For instance, a proponent of this hypothesis would say that (200) has two meanings.

(200) That's cool

Read literally, this sentence is true of low-temperature objects. Read metaphorically, it's true of hip, fashionable things. This may well be the common sense view of metaphor. But it isn't a very good theory. Or so Searle (1979a) and Davidson (1978) have argued. Here are some reasons.

First objection: if metaphorical sentences were merely ambiguous, there would be nothing special about them. For example: if 'is an infant' is true of moralizing authors on its metaphorical reading then (201) is *straightforwardly true* on this metaphorical

172

reading. (Though it's false on the other, "literal", reading. Tolstoy wasn't a newborn at sixty.)

(201) Even at sixty, Tolstoy was an infant

This makes (201) look too much like (202), a case of true ambiguity.

(202) Even at sixty, Tolstoy had shiny locks

Sentence (202) really does have two readings. One in which 'locks' = 'security device' and another in which 'locks' = 'ringlets'. But this isn't metaphor. It's merely and simply a case of dual meanings. Intuitively, there's a difference. And the idea that metaphor is just secondary sentence meaning does not capture it. (Remember: two of the questions I began with were, (c) why use metaphor at all? and (d) how is metaphor different from literal speech? This Dual Meaning Proposal seems not to provide answers.)

Second objection: if metaphorical sentences had two meanings, and were just a species of ambiguity, there would be no difference between dead metaphors and live metaphors. Thus (203a-b)—dead metaphors both—really are ambiguous.

(203)
(a) Kicked the bucket
[Literal meaning: GAVE THE PAIL A KICK; metaphorical meaning: DIED]
(b) Mouth
[Literal meaning: BUCCAL CAVITY; metaphorical meaning: OPENING]

Said now, 'Phil kicked the bucket' doesn't "resonate" as a literary device. Nor does 'the mouth of the river'. But imagine how these would have sounded *before* bottles and rivers had mouths; and before bucket-kicking became fatal. There's a clear intuitive difference. Admittedly, what that difference amounts to isn't clear, but it's certainly there. But—here's the rub—there ought to be no difference whatsoever if metaphorical sentences generally have two meanings, a literal meaning and a metaphorical one. Since dead metaphor and live metaphor aren't the same thing, the Dual Meaning offers a flawed account of metaphor.

Third objection: an account of metaphor should allow the

ordinary meaning to remain even after the metaphorical character of the utterance is recognized. The Dual Meanings proposal fails on this count. Recall (198a-b) and (202). These are ambiguities.

(198)
(a) Mary wrote a letter to the editor
(b) There's a pen on the floor

(202) Even at sixty, Tolstoy had shiny locks

Typically, once you know which sense of the sentence the speaker intends, there's no "hangover" from the other. (An exception is systematically ambiguous poetry, like John Donne's "The Good-Morrow".) But things are different in the case of live metaphor: in live metaphor, it's important *not* to lose sight of the literal meaning. So metaphor isn't the same as ambiguity.

In the end, I suspect metaphorical meaning isn't a property of *sentences* at all. Metaphor is a matter of how sentences are *used*. Indeed, it seems to me that sentences can only have literal meanings. If that's right, then one ought not explain metaphor as *sentences* having two meanings. So the Dual Meaning Proposal won't work. Time to move on, then, to the next candidate: the Simile Proposal.

(204) *The Simile Proposal*: "All metaphor is really literal simile with the 'like' or 'as' deleted and the respect of the similarity left unspecified" (Searle 1979a, 417).

It's not clear how to understand this proposal. But, however one understands it, there are problems.

Suppose it's read as saying that sentences which express metaphors are, on their metaphorical reading, synonymous with sentences that express similes. This won't work because of the obvious fact that, while sentences which express similes are manifestly true, metaphorical readings of sentences aren't manifestly true. Take (205a-b) as examples. The proposal would seem to be that they are synonymous, at least on the metaphorical reading of (205b).

(205)
(a) Juliet is like the sun
(b) Juliet is the sun

Now: it's undoubtedly true that Juliet is like the sun. Indeed, it's *vacuously* true. That's because everything is like everything else in *some* respects. (E.g. Albert Schweitzer is like Attila the Hun in that both are famous humans, neither went to Carleton University, both were very dedicated to their chosen path, etc.) But, though Juliet is obviously *like* the sun, it's not at all true that she's obviously *identical to* the sun. That is, though (205a) is *patently* true, (205b) isn't—even on its metaphorical reading. So they cannot share a single meaning. (Besides, notice that we're once again talking about the metaphorical readings of *sentences*. And you just saw that metaphor likely isn't a matter of ambiguous sentences.)

Well then, suppose the Simile Proposal is read as saying that any metaphor can be *paraphrased* with a simile—but that the paraphrase captures what *the speaker* meant in using the sentence metaphorically. Returning to our examples above: it's not that sentence (205a) and sentence (205b) are synonymous. Nor are there literal and metaphorical senses of sentence (205b). Instead—goes the story—in using 'Juliet is the sun' metaphorically, what *Romeo* meant was that Juliet is like the sun. And, in general, whenever a speaker uses a sentence metaphorically, the metaphorical content of the speaker's meaning can be completely and accurately paraphrased by a simile.

This is better. But it still won't do. First of all, metaphors are (often) difficult to capture. They are hard to interpret, and hard to paraphrase. But if getting the metaphor were as easy as inserting 'like' into the sentence used, then metaphor should be mindlessly easy; paraphrase should be a breeze. It's not. Which calls the Simile Proposal into question.

A possible reply. The proposal is that any metaphor can be captured by a simile/paraphrase, and that the paraphrase spells out what the *speaker* meant in using the sentence metaphorically. In cashing out this suggestion, I imagined that when understanding a metaphorical use of a sentence of the form $\ulcorner A$ is $B \urcorner$, the hearer constructs a paraphrase of the form $\ulcorner A$ is like $B \urcorner$. The objection is that this doesn't adequately describe the process of metaphor comprehension, because it makes it look easier than it in fact is. All right then, let's suppose instead that the hearer constructs the simile paraphrase by using (206):

(206) *A* is like *B* in respect *R*

This makes metaphor comprehension look appropriately difficult, because you have to figure out what respect R is. To return to the Romeo and Juliet example: the hearer can go mechanically from (205b) to (207).

(205b) Juliet is the sun

(207) Juliet is like the sun in respect R

But filling in (207) will not be simple at all, since the hearer must determine what R is here. So constructing and understanding metaphor is correctly predicted to require a certain skill.

This "fix-up" answers the objection raised. But it creates a new difficulty of its own. Searle (1979a) raises the following concern. Let's suppose that some guy—call him Richard—is fierce, nasty and prone to violence. A friend is telling Vikram stories about Richard, all of which illustrate these character flaws. Vikram eventually agrees: 'Yep, Richard is a gorilla. No doubt about it'. What, according to the Simile Proposal, goes on in this exchange? The hypothesis, I presume, is that in using (208a) metaphorically, what Vikram says is captured by the simile paraphrase in (208b).

(208)
(a) Richard is a gorilla
(b) Richard is like a gorilla in being fierce, nasty and prone to violence

Notice: if this is right, then what Vikram (the speaker) means must—at the very least—have the same truth conditions as (208b). But—and here's the worry—what Vikram metaphorically communicates with (208a) can be true enough, even though the corresponding simile is *false*. Indeed, as a matter of fact, (208b) *is* false in the circumstances described, because gorillas—despite their reputation—are actually passive, sweet and gentle creatures. Nevertheless, what the speaker conveys is true. So what the speaker means, in speaking (208a) metaphorically, is not captured by the simile. Richard is undoubtedly like a gorilla in many ways. But the speaker, in the case described, isn't communicating information about *how Richard resembles gorillas*. He is communicating information about Richard. He is conveying, in part, that Richard is fierce, nasty and violent—traits which, as a matter of fact, *differentiate* Richard from gorillas! So metaphor isn't just a matter of simile or comparison.

Despite the foregoing criticisms, Searle thinks there is something significantly right about the Simile Proposal. What's correct and important is the insight that similarity often plays a central role in the comprehension of metaphor. The mistake, according to Searle, was thinking that, in making a metaphor, the speaker *claims* a similarity. Instead, noticing the similarity is often an important step in understanding the metaphorical speaker. Here's a comparison. Suppose someone says, 'There's a bulb under the table'. To fully understand, you'd need to know what kind of bulb: a light bulb or a tulip bulb? A natural enough way to find out would be to *look* under the table. That's a reasonable **strategy of comprehension**. But the strategy of comprehension employed in understanding this utterance isn't part of its *meaning*: LOOK UNDER THE TABLE is no part of the meaning of this utterance of 'There's a bulb under the table'. In the same way, searching for similarities is a useful strategy for comprehending (205b). But the similarities between Juliet and the sun needn't be part of what Romeo meant. Searle puts it well: "Similarity...has to do with the production and understanding of metaphor, not with its meaning" (1979a, 414). He adds: "Similarity functions as a comprehension strategy, not as a component of meaning" (Searle 1979a, 415).

This leads us to Searle's positive view:

(209) *Searle's Proposal*: When a speaker says $\ulcorner X$ is $P \urcorner$ metaphorically, she communicates that $\ulcorner X$ is $R \urcorner$.

This clearly differentiates metaphor from literal speech. In literal speech, when a speaker says $\ulcorner X$ is $P \urcorner$ she communicates that X is P. But how are metaphors made and understood? Searle goes into quite a lot of detail, which needn't concern us. The basic framework, however, is worth sketching. There are three steps:

> 1. Discover that $\ulcorner X$ is $P \urcorner$ is not meant literally—because $\ulcorner X$ is $P \urcorner$ is clearly false, or trivially true, or nonsense, or what have you.
> 2. Compute all possible values of R. (Searle lays out principles for doing this. I'll skip them.)
> 3. Restrict the values of R (i.e. find out what the "really meant" values are).

In short: you start with $\ulcorner X$ is $P \urcorner$ and end up with $\ulcorner X$ is $R \urcorner$—*not* $\ulcorner X$ is like P in respects $R \urcorner$. In searching for R you will in all likelihood consider ways in which X is like P. So similarity plays a role. But this is part of the strategy of comprehension, not (necessarily) part of the meaning of the utterance.

One problem with this proposal is that it doesn't really answer the third question about metaphor: why use metaphor at all? Donald Davidson would register a related complaint. Davidson thinks it's a mistake to treat metaphor as "primarily a vehicle for conveying ideas" (1978, 431). Not only doesn't the *sentence* have a second meaning, according to Davidson, but the metaphor-maker doesn't either. A sentence, used metaphorically, may nudge us into seeing certain things; it may cause us to have certain thoughts. But, Davidson insists, one shouldn't confuse these effects with meanings of the metaphor. Nudging isn't stating.

This point can be illustrated by comparing the case of a photograph. A photograph may cause you to have certain thoughts. But these effects aren't part of the meaning of the photograph, since photographs don't encode thoughts at all. Davidson writes,

> How many facts or propositions are conveyed by a photograph. None, an infinity, or one great unstatable fact? Bad question. A picture is not worth a thousand words, or any other number. Words are the wrong currency to exchange for a picture (1978, 440).

According to Searle, when speaking metaphorically, the utterer communicates something of the form $\ulcorner X$ is $R\urcorner$. For Davidson, trying to put the meaning of a metaphorical utterance into the form $\ulcorner X$ is $R\urcorner$ is akin to looking for a statement or statements equivalent to a picture. And this is precisely why spelling out the metaphorical meaning of an utterance is so difficult. And what makes metaphor different and important.

3. Referential-Attributive

A final example of non-literal language use: Keith Donnellan (1966) contrasts what he terms the **referential** and **attributive** use of definite descriptions, and argues that neither Russell nor Strawson recognize both. He writes:

> A speaker who uses a definite description attributively in an assertion states something about whoever or whatever is the so-and-so. A speaker who uses a definite description referentially in an assertion, on the other hand, uses the description to enable his audience to pick out whom or what he is talking about and states something about that person or thing (Donnellan 1966, 237).

The easiest way to introduce this distinction is to start with examples. I'll go over two: sentences (210a) and (210b).

(210)
(a) Smith's murderer is insane
(b) Who is the man drinking the martini?

One could use the first sentence in two distinct ways. Here is an example of the *attributive* use. Smith has been brutally murdered. Smith was a great guy. Only a crazed lunatic would murder him, and with such brutality. Someone, surveying the murder scene in puzzlement, says (210a), meaning thereby:

(211) Whoever murdered Smith is insane

Here, on the other hand, is an example of the *referential* use. Jones has been charged with Smith's murder. He behaves in a bizarre fashion in court. Someone sums up Jones' antics by saying (210a), 'Smith's murderer is insane', meaning thereby:

(212) Jones is insane

Notice: in the first situation, the speaker refers to *whomever* fits the description. In the second situation, the speaker refers to the guy he has in mind—regardless of whether he fits the description: here, 'Smith's murderer' can be used referentially to talk about Jones *even if Jones didn't kill Smith*.

Indeed, Donnellan says, the difference between the two uses can be brought out by "considering the consequences of the assumption that Smith had no murderer" (1966, 237). On the attributive use, Donnellan says, if Smith wasn't murdered, the utterance of (210a) is neither true nor false, since the speaker wouldn't have attributed insanity to anyone: no one fits the description 'the murderer of Smith'. With respect to the referential use, on the other hand, "where the definite description is simply a means of identifying the person we want to talk about, it is quite possible for the correct identification to be made even though no one fits the description we used" (Donnellan 1966, 237-238). So, even if no one murdered Smith, the utterance of (210a) is still true if the use is referential, and Jones is insane. Donnellan (1966, 238) draws the general lesson:

...there are two uses of sentences of the form, "the ϕ is Ψ." In the first, if nothing is the ϕ then nothing has been said to be Ψ. In the second, the fact that nothing is the ϕ does not have this consequence.[68]

Donnellan stresses that the referential-attributive distinction also shows up in non-assertive speech. That's where the second example comes in:

(210b) Who is the man drinking the martini?

The description 'the man drinking the martini' can be used attributively in the following situation. The chairperson of the local Teetotallers Union is informed that a man is drinking a martini. He cannot see the man himself, and he wants to find out who the alcohol-imbibing scoundrel is—so he asks (210b). As Donnellan says:

> In asking the question the chairman does not have some particular person in mind about whom he asks the question; if no one is drinking a martini...no person can be singled out as the person about whom the question was asked (238).

The very same description can, however, be used referentially as well. Here's an example. Suppose everyone is looking at a guy who is drinking from a martini glass. Christine wants to know who the guy is, so she says: 'Who is the man drinking the martini?' Notice: Christine can successfully refer to the man in question *even if he's not drinking a martini*; even if, for example, he's actually drinking ginger ale in a martini glass. Nevertheless, Christine's query is about *that guy over there*, since—used referentially—'the guy drinking a martini' is simply a tool for identifying the person being talked about.[69]

Donnellan himself might not see it this way, but one can take the referential use to be another illustration of a non-literal use: in this case, a non-literal use of a definite description. What the description token *literally* refers to, in the context, is the unique object—if any—which satisfies it. This is, roughly, the attributive use. What the description token *non-literally* refers to is what the speaker refers to. Again: this is, roughly, the referential use.

The parallel with conversational implicature and metaphor should be obvious. In the former two, one distinguishes speaker's meaning from literal meaning. Whereas, in the referential-attributive case, one distinguishes speaker's *reference* from literal reference.

Suggested Readings

Grice's (1975) "Logic and Conversation" is the ground-breaking paper on conversational implicature. An early and insightful commentary is Sadock 1978. Sperber and Wilson (1986, 1987) systematize Grice's ideas, showing how all his categories (quality, quantity, manner and relation) can be reduced to relevance.

There is a very large literature on metaphor. Among contemporary accounts, Max Black's (1962) paper "Metaphor" is something of a landmark. (See also Black 1979.) My central source is John Searle's (1979a) paper, also called "Metaphor". As is typical for Searle, the writing is mostly clear and accessible. Donald Davidson's (1978) "What metaphors mean" is a classic but difficult paper. The referential-attributive distinction is lucidly discussed in Kripke 1977 and Searle 1979b. Both offer alternative accounts of the phenomenon. Davis 1991 is a useful anthology for pursuing all of these topics.

Chapter Eleven:

Language and Community

Language is a system of symbols which we know and use. Taking the system perspective, meaning is simply a relation between abstract symbols on the one hand, and non-symbols on the other. Language knowers, and language users, need play no essential part.

When looking at language from the knowledge perspective, by contrast, it is natural to focus on the language knower, and to identify the meaning of an expression E with what such a knower mentally grasps, in knowing the meaning of E. In which case, meanings might as well be ideas. Similarly, when taking the use perspective, it makes sense to fixate on the language user, and to think of meaning/grasping as amounting to appropriate use: that is, an agent grasps the meaning of E if and only if she can use E appropriately. Which suggests that meaning simply is use.

In this chapter, I will continue to explore the use perspective, and the associated use theory of meaning. In particular, I want to introduce the social aspect of language, an element omitted above. The importance of this element, for the use perspective, can be nicely brought out by the following puzzle.

1. Non-Literal Use and the Need for Conventions

As you saw in the last chapter, uses can be either literal or non-literal. This may raise a doubt in your mind: if meaning is use, how can there be non-literal uses? That is, supposing meaning and use are the same, how can there be uses which deviate from meaning? A related problem: the foregoing discussion of non-literal uses suggests that, given the right circumstances, an expression can be used in any old way. Here's one of my favourite cases, introduced earlier. A professor can use sentence (213) in a letter of reference to suggest that the student in question is incompetent.

(213) Mr. X has very neat handwriting

Or, consider an example introduced by John Searle (1965, 120). An American soldier might speak the sentence (214) with the intention of convincing some Italians that he is actually a *German* soldier. (Praying they'll recognize the sound of the German language, without actually understanding it.)

(214) Kennst du das Land, wo   die Zitronen   blühen?
      Know you the Land, where the lemon-trees bloom?
      Do you know the land where the lemon trees bloom?

The thing is, if expressions can be used in such bizarre ways, how can meaning come from use? It would seem that (213) should mean, in part, that Mr. X is an incompetent student, since it can be used this way; and that (214) should mean, among other things, I AM GERMAN. But this is absurd.

These worries about the Use Theory of Meaning miss a central fact. It's not just individuals, but whole communities which use languages. And community use, unlike individual use, is largely regular. Here's another way of putting the point: there are *conventions* of language use. And these conventions remain in force even when language is used *unconventionally* (read *non-literally*). So, the use theorist will say, meaning is *conventional* use. Hence, returning to the troubling examples, the meaning of (213) is the use to which it is *conventionally* put; namely, asserting that Mr. X has neat handwriting. The meaning of (213) is emphatically *not* every purpose which it may, on occasion, serve. Ditto for (214) and every other natural language symbol.

Of course, having said this, the use theorist owes an account of what conventional use amounts to. There's a temptation to merely say that conventional use is how the linguistic community uses the symbol. But this is too vague. David Lewis (1969, 1975) offers a more insightful analysis. He writes:

> Conventions are regularities in action...which are arbitrary but perpetuate themselves because they serve some sort of common interest (Lewis 1975, 490.).

An obvious example: driving on the right side of the road is a convention. It's a regularity in action, and it serves the common purpose of preventing smash-ups. The regularity perpetuates itself because, given that everyone else drives on the right hand side of the road, it's a good idea for you to do the same. But the regularity is arbitrary in the sense that there is an equally viable alternative regularity; namely, driving on the left hand side of the road. And that alternative regularity would perpetuate itself, once established.[70]

Conventional usage, then, is usage which is regular, arbitrary and self-perpetuating. Insofar as non-literal uses are irregular, non-arbitrary and not perpetuated—which is inevitably the case—they are not conventional. Hence, they do not affect meaning. (The introduction of convention nicely brings out two other important features of the use perspective on language. Use theorists typically maintain that language, beyond being an activity, is a social and rational activity. The regularities are in *community* behaviour, hence social. And they are perpetuated by common interest, hence rational.)

2. The Private Language Argument

Some philosophers would argue that the fact that languages are used by communities is not simply contingent. Instead, some will say, language is *essentially* communal. One proponent of this view is Wittgenstein. And he provides a strikingly original argument for it: the so-called **private language argument**.

First important fact: linguistic rules are not like natural laws. They are more like laws in the legal sense. And one of the marks of a legal rule is that you can fail to follow it: a rule which cannot be broken isn't really a rule at all. This is where Wittgenstein's private language argument takes off. He asks his reader to join him in a thought experiment. I reconstruct it as follows. Suppose Leroy, a creative and sensitive poet, wants to keep a diary of his feelings and sensations. Being anxious to conceal his inner life from others, Leroy (who is creative, remember) invents a secret code for use in his diary—that way, even if someone finds the diary and attempts to read it, they won't understand what he has written. Focus now on a particular sensation which Leroy has. I'll call it *S*. Leroy experiences *S*, and writes in his diary:

(215) Fiona at 3:12 p.m., July 20th

He resolves to write 'Fiona' in his diary each time he feels a sensation of the same kind as *S*.

But now comes the puzzle: no one can correct Leroy's use of 'Fiona'. There is, in this case, no distinction between seeming right to Leroy and actually being right. Which means Leroy's "rule" can't appropriately be called a rule at all. I repeat: a rule is the sort of thing which *can* be violated. As Wittgenstein puts it:

> But in the present case I have no criterion of correctness. One would like to say: whatever is going to seem right to me is right. And that only means that here we can't talk about 'right' (1953, 92).

The general lesson, drawn from this example, is that there cannot be *private* rules.

What distinguishes right from wrong in the ordinary case is the community. It is the community which "supplies the needed contrast between merely seeming to be correct and actually being correct" (Martin 1987, 47). In which case, there can be no rules without a community—and no language without common convention. Hence language isn't just *contingently* communal, it's necessarily communal.

Kripke on the Private Language Argument

Saul Kripke provides an interesting commentary on the Private Language Argument.[71] He suggests that "the 'private language argument' as applied to sensations is only a special case of much more general considerations" (Kripke 1982, 475). The more general consideration is that:

> it is not possible to obey a rule 'privately': otherwise thinking one was

obeying a rule would be the same as obeying it (Wittgenstein 1953, 81).

Kripke thinks that this finding is harder to accept with sensations. Surely, it might be said, in the realm of inner sensation rules *must* be private. One wants to say:"Since the sensations are available only to me, only *I* can name them". That is why Wittgenstein spends extra time on this special case. Or so Kripke maintains:

> Although Wittgenstein has already discussed these basic considerations in considerable generality [earlier in the *Philosophical Investigations*], the structure of Wittgenstein's work is such that the special cases of mathematics and psychology are not simply discussed by citing a general 'result' already established, but by going over these special cases in detail, in the light of the previous treatment of the general case (1982, 476).

Kripke begins his exposition of the Private Language Argument by noting some truisms. The symbols '+' and 'plus', he says, are used to denote a well-known mathematical function; namely, addition. Furthermore, he notes, typical agents can find the value of this function for many arguments. This ability, it may be supposed, is owing to the agent's "grasp of a rule". Of course, because human lives are finite there will always be, for each agent, sums which that agent has never calculated. Nevertheless, the rule for '+' and 'plus', which the agent grasps, applies to these uncalculated values as well. That's the set up. Now, allow me to re-introduce Leroy. Suppose Leroy, being a poet with no taste for mathematics, has never applied the rule for '+' to numbers as large as 57. In which case, he's never performed the operation in (216).

(216) 68 + 57

He does so now, arriving at the answer '125'.

Next step: imagine that Scott, a "bizarre skeptic" as Kripke (1982, 477) calls him, questions Leroy's certainty about his answer. Scott argues as follows:

Premise 1: You, Leroy, have never explicitly given yourself the instruction to arrive at '125' when given '68 + 57'.
Premise 2:All your past applications of '+' are finite in number, and involve numbers less than 57.
Conclusion:All of your self-instructions and past applications of '+' are consistent with the following rule—the rule for 'quus':

(217) *The Quus Function*

$x \oplus y = x + y$ if $x, y < 57$

$x \oplus y = 5$ otherwise

The skeptic then suggests to Leroy: although you don't realize it, by the word 'plus' you have always meant the function that I have named 'quus'; therefore, you're wrong to reply '125'. What you ought to answer is '5'.[72] Notice that *nothing* Leroy has thought or done refutes the skeptic. Kripke puts it nicely:

> The basic point is this. Ordinarily, I suppose that, in computing '68 + 57' as I do, I do not simply make an unjustified leap in the dark. I follow directions I previously gave myself that uniquely determine that in this new instance I should say '125'. What are these directions? By hypothesis, I never explicitly told myself that I should say '125' in this very instance. Nor can I say that I should simply 'do the same thing I always did,' if this means 'compute according to the rule exhibited by my previous examples.' That rule could just as well have been the rule for quaddition (the quus function) as for addition (Kripke 1982, 478).

The result that *nothing* determines that by 'plus' Leroy meant addition, and that he is not justified in replying '125', is "insane and intolerable" (Kripke 1982, 480). Kripke thinks that Wittgenstein offers a way out of this result. But a side effect of the "way out" is that there cannot be any private languages: the "solution" to the puzzle will not admit such a language. Here is Wittgenstein's "solution". There is no fact about a speaker, *considered in isolation*, which determines whether he meant plus or quus by '+', in the past. To think of someone as following a rule requires "taking him into our community and applying our criteria for rule following to him" (Kripke 1982, 485). It's not *Leroy's* intentions, or *Leroy's* past behaviour that determines what he ought to say, when given (216). What determines the correct reply in this case is what Leroy's fellow speakers say. Of course, if this is right, then the very idea of a private rule is incoherent: rules can only exist in communities. So once again, it's not merely a contingent fact that language is community-based.[73]

3. Davidson on the Limits of Convention

In the last two sections I stressed how important convention is to language. Convention, I said, allows one to talk coherently of non-literal uses, while endorsing the Use Theory of Meaning. And, more importantly still, if Wittgenstein is right, a language without public conventions would not be a language at all, for, without conventions, the necessary contrast between correct use and incorrect use would be lost. I end this chapter by considering the *limits* of convention, as discussed by Donald Davidson.

First, a background question: what determines the meaning of an utterance? There are two basic views on this question. According to **convention theorists**, utterance meaning is determined entirely by the conventions governing the use of the expression; according to **intention theorists**, utterance meaning derives entirely from the speaker's intentions. An example. A convention theorist will say that the meaning of a token of (218) is determined by linguistic conventions—including the conventions for how indexicals acquire their reference in context.

(218) That's a beautiful tree

An intention theorist, on the other hand, maintains that the meaning of any token of (218) is determined by the speaker's intentions; in particular, which thing *the speaker* meant by 'that'.[74]

So much for background. Now to the issue at hand. Donald Davidson is a confirmed intention theorist. Michael Dummett is an influential convention theorist.[75] The two have engaged in an important debate about the contribution of convention to linguistic communication. I cannot review the entire controversy here. Instead, I'll focus on Davidson's claim— against Dummett—that convention contributes (at best) very little to the determination of **illocutionary force**. That should give you a feel for what the issues are.

In Chapter Five, I presented some of the ideas in Davidson 1979. One issue I didn't take up was the relationship between *moods* on the one hand, and *actions* on the other. In particular, the issue of whether, and to what degree, the mood of the sentence type determines the kind of action performed. If you take a convention-based approach, you will suppose that mood-plus-context completely determines illocutionary force (i.e. the kind of action performed). If you take an intention-based approach, on the other hand, you will suppose that it is the speaker's intentions which determine illocutionary force. Whatever Davidson's positive view, he thinks the convention-based approach cannot be correct.

Davidson considers and rejects several proposals about how syntactic moods are related to speech act kinds. Taking declarative utterances[76] as his example, he dismisses first what I'll call 'the Simple Proposal':

(219) *The Simple Proposal*: The class of declarative utterances is identical to the class of assertions.

According to this proposal, every utterance of a declarative is an assertion, and every assertion is an utterance of a declarative. The objection to this Simple Proposal should be obvious: there are many utterances of declaratives which are not in fact assertions—for example, they may be uttered on stage, in a joke, in a song, and so on. In short, being an utterance of a declarative sentence is not a sufficient condition for being an assertion. The Simple Proposal has to go.

Davidson therefore turns to a more sophisticated hypothesis, which he attributes to Dummett (1973): the Convention Proposal.

(220) *The Convention Proposal*: Where conventionally specified conditions C obtain, the class of declarative utterances is identical to the class of assertions.

That is, the idea is to replace the identity in (221a) with that in (221b):

(221)
(a) $\{x: x$ is a declarative utterance$\} = \{x: x$ is an assertion$\}$
(b) $\{x: x$ is a declarative utterance produced under conventional specified conditions $C\} = \{x: x$ is an assertion$\}$

On this line, producing a declarative is a necessary condition for making an assertion, but it's not a sufficient condition. For a declarative may be uttered without the conventionally specified conditions for assertion obtaining. In which case, no assertion is made.

Now the issue between intention and convention is joined: Dummett is here offering a convention-based account of assertion in particular, and of the moods in general. His rationale? He takes the only two options to be:

(222)

(a) Performing a speech act *A* consists in having intentions *I*

(b) Performing a speech act *A* consists in participating in conventional practice *P*

Dummett rejects (222a) for anti-mentalist reasons: he denies that the kinds of exceedingly complex intentions required by a Grice-inspired intention-based analysis can be reasonably attributed to individuals. That leaves only (222b). And what is the "conventional practice", in the case of making an assertion? Using certain linguistic forms (in particular, declarative sentences) in certain conventionally determined situations. Hence the Convention Proposal. Davidson, in contrast, will argue against this proposal.

First objection to the Convention Proposal: it's flatly obvious that you can make an assertion in lots of ways. For instance, I might assert that Joan is wearing her purple hat by saying 'Did you notice that Joan is wearing her purple hat?' Reply to the first objection: Dummett denies that such "obvious cases" are really counterexamples. He (1993, 209) distinguishes—rightly I think—between "what the speaker actually says and the point of his saying what he did". On the basis of this distinction, he dismisses the usual and obvious counterexamples: they conflate what was asserted with what the speaker wanted to achieve. Applying this reply to the earlier example: in saying 'Did you notice that Joan is wearing her purple hat?', I may wish to induce a belief. But, Dummett insists, I don't strictly and literally assert anything.

Rebuttal, against Dummett: using a declarative sentence in conventionally specified conditions is nevertheless *not* a necessary condition for asserting. You can *assert*—not just communicate, but assert—in lots of ways; in particular, you can assert by producing unembedded words and phrases.[77] Thus any of the following words and phrases can be used on their own to make assertions:

(223)

(a) The butler. No question. [Said by a detective to his aid]

(b) From Spain. [Said while looking at a recently arrived letter]

(c) Water. Vodka. Gin. [As the speaker indicates three different glasses]

These are not declarative sentence utterings because—obviously—words and phrases are not declarative sentences. So, equally obviously, they are not assertoric sentence utterings *under conventionally specified conditions*. Nevertheless, they're assertions. This case is importantly different from the usual counterexamples in that, in using unembedded words and phrases, speakers actually *assert* propositions; they do not merely communicate them. (For instance, the speaker may *lie*, and not merely mislead, by using unembedded words and phrases.)[78]

The foregoing is largely an empirical objection: Dummett's convention-based proposal simply doesn't fit the facts of language use. Davidson's most powerful argument against the Convention Proposal, however, is that uttering a declarative, even in "conventionally specified circumstances", *cannot* be sufficient for making an assertion. His argument for this conclusion is what I'll call the 'Super Sign Argument'. It goes like this:

(224) *The Super Sign Argument — Premises*
Assumption: The Convention Proposal is true.
Premise 1: Whatever is conventional about assertion can be put into words.
Premise 2: If the Convention Proposal is true, and if whatever is conventional can be put into words, then a Super Assertion Sign is possible.
Premise 3: A Super Assertion Sign is *not* possible.

The argument is easy to follow, once you know what the premises mean. Allow me to explain.

Premise 1 is an application of a dictum which Davidson (1982, 269) attributes to Frege: any conventional feature of language can be made explicit with a symbol. I've never been quite sure what this means, but this will do for present purposes: for any "conventionally specified circumstances" it ought to be possible to agree on a symbol whose use *makes* these circumstances obtain.

Premise 2 says that *if* this is possible, then assuming the Convention Proposal is correct, there could be a super assertion sign. A **super assertion sign** is a symbol whose use *guarantees* that an assertion is made. For example, one might invent the word 'supersert' and stipulate that any sentence which follows it is inevitably asserted. Then, the thought would be, anyone using sentence (225)—although we should be careful here: not anyone *mentioning* this sentence—would of necessity be asserting that Floyd is foolish.

(225) Supersert: Floyd is foolish

The rationale for Premise 2 is this: according to the Convention Proposal, saying a declarative in conventionally specified conditions C is sufficient for making an assertion. Now, given Premise 1, one could introduce a symbol whose use *guaranteed* that conditions C obtain. (Returning to the example: this would be the job of 'super-sert'.) In which case, producing this symbol, together with a declarative, would then be a sufficient condition for making an assertion. So, if the Convention Proposal is true, and if Premise 1 is true, there could exist a Super Assertion Sign.

Now for Premise 3. It says that, as a matter of fact, there *couldn't* be a super assertion sign—not even a made-up one, like 'supersert'—since no one could successfully introduce such a sign. Here's why, according to Davidson:

> It is easy to see that merely speaking a sentence [with the super asser-tion sign] cannot be counted on to result in an assertion; every joker, storyteller, and actor will immediately take advantage of the strength-ened mood to simulate assertion (Davidson 1979, 113. See also Davidson 1982).

In short, even if you attempted to create a super assertion sign, you wouldn't achieve your goal—because people would immediately use your sign in jest, or on the stage, or whatever, *without thereby making assertions*. Davidson adds:

> What this argument illustrates is a basic trait of language, what may be called the autonomy of linguistic meaning. Once a feature of lan-guage has been given conventional expression, it can be used to serve many extra-linguistic ends; symbolic representation necessarily breaks any close tie with extra-linguistic purpose. Applied to the pre-sent case, this means that there cannot be a form of speech which, solely by dint of its conventional meaning, can be used only for a given purpose, such as making an assertion or asking a question (Davidson 1979, 113-114).

This is what is meant by Premise 3. Given all this, you can now see how the Super Sign argument—repeated below—works its magic.

(226) *The Super Sign Argument—Conclusions*
Assumption: The Convention Proposal is true.
Premise 1: Whatever is conventional about assertion can be put into words.
Premise 2: If the Convention Proposal is true, and if whatever is

conventional can be put into words, then a Super Assertion Sign is possible.

Premise 3: A Super Assertion Sign is *not* possible.

Conclusion 1: A Super Assertion Sign is both possible and not possible.

Conclusion 2: The Assumption—i.e. that the Convention Proposal is true—must be false. [By *reductio ad absurdum*, using Conclusion 1]

If the Super Sign argument works, it shows that using a declarative sentence, even in "conventionally specified conditions", cannot be sufficient for making an assertion. And, I argued, this is not a necessary condition for assertion either. Davidson puts the conclusion nicely: "grammatical mood and illocutionary force, no matter how closely related, cannot be related simply by convention" (Davidson 1982, 270). This conclusion can be applied much more generally, of course. The result: the role of convention in determining utterance meaning is importantly limited. On the other hand, as you saw in the first two sections, the conventional aspect of meaning appears not to be wholly dispensable. Hence, language use appears to be partly, but not entirely, conventional (i.e. social and communal).

Suggested Readings

David Lewis' seminal work on convention appeared first in Lewis 1969. His (1975) paper "Languages and Language" contains a useful—and fairly brief—exposition. Michael Dummett (1973 and elsewhere) has also repeatedly stressed the importance of convention to language.

Understanding Wittgenstein's private language argument isn't easy. There are as many versions of it as there are Wittgenstein interpreters. The original source is Wittgenstein's (1953) book *Philosophical Investigations*. Helpful commentaries on it include Hacker 1990, Kenny 1973, Ch.10 and Strawson 1954. Kripke's reading of Wittgenstein can be found in Kripke 1982. It is reprinted, in part, in Martinich 1990. A collection of papers on the private language argument can be found in Jones 1971.

For more on convention and intention see Davidson 1982, 1986, Donnellan 1968, Kaplan 1978, 1979, McGinn 1981, MacKay 1968, Strawson 1964 and Wettstein 1984.

Chapter Twelve:

Conclusion

By way of conclusion, allow me to summarize. I hope this summary will make clear some of the ways in which the various philosophical issues about language, introduced in this book, fit together.

Theories of Meaning

Semantics has been a central focus of this book. As you saw, there are at least three kinds of "things" that can get paired with syntactic structures: external objects, ideas, and uses. In each case, there are numerous sub-options.

External objects may be either directly or indirectly linked with symbols. Taking the link to be direct, the semantics for *names* is quite simple: they denote individuals. However, even within this simplest extensional option, semantics gets complicated when one considers other kinds of expressions: verbs, common nouns and other predicative expressions, logical connectives, declarative sentences, and so on. On the other hand, introducing functions kept the semantics *fairly* tractable, since the only things introduced were individuals, truth values, and functions on these. So, for example, as a first pass I suggested that sentences denote truth values, predicates denote functions from individuals to truth values, and sentential connectives denote functions from two truth values to one truth value. Turning to quantifier phrases (like 'someone' and 'nobody'), it seemed clear that these were *not* name-like: they appear not to denote individuals. Instead, it emerged that quantifier phrases refer to complex functions: functions from a propositional function (i.e. a function of type *Ind→TV*) to a truth value. Hence 'Nobody smokes', for example, does not express a statement about some peculiar object NOBODY. Instead, it expresses a statement about SMOKES: namely, the statement that this function never outputs true. (Russell, you'll recall, makes a similar claim about definite descriptions: they too are quantifier-like.)

Where the link between the symbol and its referent is *indirect*, semantics get still more complex. First, because there are at least two further sub-options: reference may be mediated by Fregean senses, or it may be mediated by functions from possible worlds to extensions. Second, because various kinds of "thing" are now required at *each* semantic level. For instance, within Frege's system, names designated individuals, but expressed individual concepts; and sentences designated truth values, but expressed propositions. Nevertheless, despite the added complexity, both mediated reference alternatives look more promising than the Russell-style direct reference approach because of opaque contexts—e.g. modal contexts and psychological contexts—in which substitution of co-referential terms in the very same construction can result in (apparently) non-synonymous expressions. Similarly, the introduction of a mediator between expression and reference helped to solve Frege's puzzle: the problem of how ⌜a=b⌝ can be informative.

Having discussed the variants on the Thing Theory, I turned to the Idea Theory of Meaning. Taking ideas, rather than external objects, as meanings leaves several options open, of course. Ideas may be construed as mental images (à la Hume), as ordinary propositional attitude states (à la Grice), or as not-so-ordinary expressions in mentalese (à la Fodor). (The viability of the last depending, as you saw, on the prospects for the computational-representational theory of mind.) Finally, I introduced the Use Theory of Meaning. Here too, there are numerous options: uses can be taken to be speech acts (Austin/Searle), language-games (Wittgenstein), 'general directions' (Strawson), or something else again. In each case, though, it's important to stress that it's *community use* which determines meaning, not individual use.

The general lesson? There are many different ways of doing semantics—and several ways of doing syntax. Indeed, as I indicated, there are even ways of specifying linguistic meaning *without* introducing "things" to serve as meanings. For example, Davidson's truth-theoretic semantics gives the truth conditions (and hence, purportedly, the meaning) of sentences by pairing sentences with *other sentences*. Here, meanings aren't external objects, mental entities *or* uses; indeed, meanings aren't objects at all.

The System Perspective

I began the book by introducing the system perspective. As I said: one way to think of language is as a kind of quasi-mathematical *system*—something like a logical calculus, or an algebra. Language, considered as a system, has at least three parts: syntax, phonology and semantics.

A syntax for a language—whether descriptive or prescriptive, though I am really concerned with the former—*cannot* take the form of a list of well-formed sentences, since no finite list would work. This strongly suggests that the syntax of any natural language must be both compositional and recursive: it must contain a finite number of minimal parts, and a finite number of rules for combining these parts (that's the compositional bit). Moreover, the output of the rules must themselves be able to serve as input (that's the recursive bit). Such a syntax will provide an infinite output.

As I explained: these rules may fit into one of two different castes. They may be construction-specific devices for combining the primitives together into ever larger units, or they may take the form of very general "super rules"—principles and parameters. Either way, the syntax must be complemented by phonological rules: rules for assigning sound patterns to the structures which the syntax creates. (I didn't discuss these.) And the syntactic rules must also be conjoined with a semantics, to cover the meaning aspect of linguistic symbols.

The Knowledge Perspective

After introducing the system of symbols, I turned to our knowledge of it: what we know, and how we come to know it. Regarding what we know: it's clear that knowing a language involves knowing at least its syntax, phonology and semantics. That is, speakers know how to pair syntactic structures (simple and complex) with both sound patterns and meanings. This knowledge permits them, in principle, to understand an unlimited number of sentences. Hence—as I stressed—what is known cannot be a list.

Regarding how we come to have knowledge of language: the rules, if one can call them such, turn out to be pretty complex. This has led many linguists to suppose that a good portion of our linguistic knowledge is innate. This hypothesis is also held to explain the existence of linguistic universals. And, it is said, innate knowledge of language explains how children are able to project a rule from a small (and certainly finite) sample of evidence.

Despite their promise, these conclusions—that we know linguistic rules, and that much of our linguistic knowledge is innate—are quite controversial. By way of illustrating the controversies, I considered two problems that arise when one attributes knowledge of language: problems about rule following, and problems about radical translation. The central issue about rule following comes to this: why suppose that linguistic behaviour is rule-guided—hence a matter of knowledge? Why not say, instead, that linguistic behaviour, like the behaviour of rocks, is *merely* regular? Especially given that the kinds of rules that linguists appeal to are quite peculiar: they're not official, they're not consciously available to the speaker, and they're not normative. A related worry: lots of different rule systems could, in principle, be specified—each of which would account equally well for all observable linguistic behaviour. Why suppose, then, that there's a single right answer to the question 'Which rules are being followed?' And if there *isn't* a single right answer to this question, why suppose that linguistic rules are known at all—let alone known innately? This was Quine's puzzle of radical translation.

The Use Perspective

Okay then: language can be seen as a quasi-mathematical system—a syntactic and semantic system. It can also be seen, somewhat less abstractly, as something which human beings know. (Though this perspective raises important worries.) Still less abstractly, one can look at language as a complex form of action. Something we *do*.

Language exists to be employed by individuals: that's why natural languages contain indexicals, and why they contain performatives. And, in use, language necessarily extends beyond the confines of sound/structure/meaning relationships—as established in the system, and known by the speaker. As you saw, an individual speaker may use a sentence to communicate things which that sentence does not mean: in metaphor, in implicature, and elsewhere; similarly, she may use an expression to refer to things which the expression itself does not refer to, as in Donnellan's referential use.

This raised an important worry: how can meaning amount to use, when use is so unconstrained? The reply was not far to find: it is not just individuals who use language. Whereas the knowledge perspective is largely individualistic—it is, after all, individuals who know languages—the use perspective encompasses both individuals *and* communities of speakers. Language, seen from this communal use perspective, is not only external—a kind of behaviour—it is also *social*. (Like a game, or a dance.) Meaning, then, is conventional use.

Those are the three philosophical perspectives on language mentioned in the title. The fact is, philosophers of language often favour one of them, to the exclusion of the others. Frege and Russell emphasized the system perspective; Chomsky and Fodor emphasize the knowledge perspective; Austin, Quine and Wittgenstein emphasized the use perspective. However, one *can* put all three perspectives together. The result would be something like this: individuals know languages—i.e. systems of symbols. Because individuals know languages, they can use them to do many things. (Though how they use the system is not wholly determined by the nature of the system itself.) But individuals form communities. Hence communities—not just *I* but *we*—use language. This is what the theme comes to: that language is a system of symbols which we know and use.

Notes

1. Laura Martin writes: "There seems no reason to posit more than two distinct *roots* that can properly be said to refer to snow itself (and not, for example, to drifts, ice, storms, or moisture) in any Inuit language. In West Greenlandic, these roots are *qanik* 'snow in the air; snowflake' and *aput* 'snow (on the ground)'" (Martin 1986, 422). For a general debunking, see Pullum's (1989) paper "The great Eskimo vocabulary hoax".

2. Or, to use an example suggested to me by Andrew Botterell: Consider a super-market sign which says 'Express Cash: 8 items or less'. This can be read as eight item *tokens* or eight item *types*. On the first reading, you couldn't use the aisle in question to purchase nine loaves of bread—that's more than eight tokens. On the second reading, you could buy as many loaf-tokens as you liked, but you couldn't buy bread, milk, coffee, apples, anchovies, pickles, popcorn, cheese *and* hot dogs. That would be more than eight item types.

3. The answer to this question varies enormously, by the way: some say English contains 100,000 words, while others say it's 300,000. The first estimate seems conservative; the latter, rather liberal. The difference in figures has (in part) to do with how one counts. For instance, how should one define 'word'? Are 'eat', 'eats' and 'eating' three different English words or just one word? What about 'goose' and 'geese'? And what is English anyway? For instance, are very antiquated words part of contemporary English? What about words borrowed from other tongues? Or Australian slang? You get the idea.

4. You probably noticed that these rules, as they stand, allow one to "build" things which aren't really English NPs. They allow, for instance, the combination of 'a' with 'apple'; but 'A apple' isn't well-formed in English. (One says '*An* apple' instead.) Though these rules are descriptively inadequate, I hope they nevertheless serve as illustrations—the purpose for which they are intended.

5. **C-command** is a prototypical structural relation in syntax. Its exact nature doesn't really matter for the purposes at hand. But for the curious, here's a rough definition: a point (or "node") X in a syntactic tree is said to c-command another node Y if and only if X isn't on top of Y and Y isn't on top of X and the first branching node

directly above X is also above Y. So, B c-commands C, D, E and F in the tree below because B isn't on top of them in the tree, nor are they on top of B; and the first branching node above B is A, and A is above C, D, E and F.

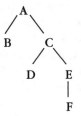

6. Better: there's no grammatical subject *on the surface*. Many linguists would say that this sentence *does* have a subject—the subject is **pro**, short for 'pronoun'. The element pro is just like other pronouns, except that it *isn't pronounced*. It's a "silent word", if you will, rather than a silent letter.

7. Actually, this is a tremendous simplification. But the general idea is right. For an introduction to syntax in a principles and parameters mode, see Haegeman 1991. The most important primary source for this approach is Chomsky 1981.

8. Here's my own view, for what it's worth. Studying I-language is unquestionably a reasonable enterprise. But there are good reasons for exploring the E-language and the common sense conception as well. Remember what I said, in the Introduction, about the interest of language. Given the divergent interests in language, there's little reason to suppose that exactly one approach will satisfy all. For instance, the relation between language and thought may well be best explored using the I-language conception. But language and culture, and possibly language as a guide to philosophy, will likely demand the common sense conception. Ditto for language and action, insofar as the actions in question are social, governed by norms, purposive, etc. What about the E-language conception? Well, one might well employ it in studies which lie somewhere between natural science and the humanities, such as teaching languages to foreign language speakers. Surely the best grammar for this purpose would *not* be a description of the native speaker's I-language! In short, there is room for multiple conceptions, because there are multiple topics and interests.

9. Notice too: well beyond Shakespeare's time there was very little in the way of widely accepted standards for spelling, pronuncia-

tion, etc. Indeed, even within a single play, Shakespeare was inconsistent in his spelling. He is even said to have used a dozen different spellings of his own name! But Elizabethan England didn't suffer too much as a result of this linguistic variation. England defeated the Spanish armada, and began the conquest of the Americas, without regimented standards of linguistic correctness.

10. To illustrate this point, suppose a crazed dictionary writer decided he didn't like the sound of the word 'telephone'. So, in his dictionary, he substitutes the word 'zoar' for 'telephone', and notes that the sound 'telephone' is meaningless in English. Does the publication of his dictionary make it the case that 'zoar' means TELEPHONE? Of course not. His dictionary is *mistaken* because it fails to capture the way English speakers talk. One ought, then, say the same about the rule which says that sentences which begin with 'and' are incorrect: this simply misstates the facts. (Here's a rule of thumb, to test claims that certain forms of speech are ungrammatical. If everybody uses the expression—including the pundits, English teachers, manual writers, etc. who denounce it—then it's perfectly grammatical, and ought to be generated by one's syntax.)

11. Not everyone agrees that a compositional semantics is required. See Schiffer 1987 for discussion.

12. Meaninglessness, in the case of a proper name, arises when an expression doesn't refer to anything. 'Trauts Mada', for instance, has no meaning—in English anyway. And that's precisely because it doesn't refer to anything. It has no denotation.

13. Actually, there is a puzzle here. If you believe this proposal, the parts of 'Andy smokes' and 'Andy the function from smokers to the TRUE' are synonymous—'Andy' denotes ANDY in each, and both 'smokes' and 'the function from smokers to the TRUE' denote THE FUNCTION FROM SMOKERS TO THE TRUE. Moreover, the (purportedly) synonymous parts of these sentences are arranged in the same way. Nevertheless, the whole sentences 'Andy smokes' and 'Andy the function from smokers to the TRUE' aren't synonymous. (The second isn't even meaningful.) Whence this difference in meaning? That's the puzzle. Proposed solutions would take me too far afield. If you're intrigued, see Frege 1892b. By the way: Frege 1884, 1891 each offer a clear, general, and philosophically rich discussion of functions, and of what they "buy us".

14. It will change because, assuming there are only two truth val-

ues—i.e. TRUE and FALSE—this proposal entails that there are only two possible meanings for sentences. A sentence can either mean TRUE or it can mean FALSE. But that's absurd. It's obvious that not all true sentences are synonymous, nor are all false sentences synonymous. For a useful discussion, see Barwise and Perry 1985.

15. Order isn't really an issue in this case, since 'smokes Andy' isn't well-formed.

16. It's not just sentences that can be connected by 'and'. Predicates can be, too. For example, the sentence 'Snow is white and cold' is built up by conjoining 'white' with 'cold'. 'And', in this context, cannot refer to a function from two truth values to one. There aren't two sentences being combined. What, then, is the semantic type of this so-called **predicate conjunction**? Well, it takes two predicates and makes a single one. The semantic type of predicates is $Ind{\rightarrow}TV$. So, predicate conjunction takes two of these to one: $<<Ind{\rightarrow}TV>,<Ind{\rightarrow}TV>>{\rightarrow}<Ind{\rightarrow}TV>$. Notice that, despite its complexity, this semantic type is built from the "basic elements". (As an exercise, find the semantic type of 'and' in the expression 'John and Phil live in Ottawa'.)

17. This point can also be made in terms of **predicate satisfaction**. A predicate—notice, a bit of language—is said to be **satisfied** if and only if it applies to something. Thus 'owns a horse' and 'has met Queen Elizabeth II' are both satisfied predicates, because there are horse owners and people have met Queen Elizabeth II. But 'owns a unicorn' and 'has met Canada's President' aren't satisfied by anything, since there are no unicorns, and Canada doesn't have a President. The meaning of 'something' can then be given as follows: a sentence formed by concatenating 'something' with any *satisfied* predicate is true. A sentence formed by concateating 'something' with any *unsatisfied* predicate is false. For more on satisfaction, see Tarski 1944. I pause to note an important distinction between the object, if any, which satisfies a predicate (and thus makes the corresponding existential generalization true) and the object to which the **existential quantifier** refers. 'Someone is Queen of England in 1995' is true. And there is, in some sense, a single individual that satisfies 'is Queen of England in 1995'. But she isn't the referent of the quantifier phrase 'someone'. The referent of 'someone' is a complex function—a function from propositional functions to a truth value. It is not an individual.

18. Actually, Russell purposely blurs the distinction between sen-

tences and propositions in this work. He writes that, "in dealing with propositions, we are dealing in the first instance with symbols" (Russell 1919, 213). In my exposition, however, I respect the distinction between symbols and their meanings.

19. An interesting side note: one of the revolutionary things about Russell's proposal is that it introduces the notion of "misleading grammar". Russell writes:

> Misled by grammar, the great majority of those logicians who have dealt with this question have dealt with it on mistaken lines. They have regarded grammatical form as a surer guide in analysis than, in fact, it is. And they have not known what differences in grammatical form are important. "I met Jones" and "I met a man" would count traditionally as propositions of the same form, but in actual fact they are of quite different forms: the first names an actual person, Jones; while the second involves a propositional function, and becomes, when made explicit: "The function 'I met x and x is human' is sometimes true (1919, 213).

The idea of misleading surface grammar is a potent one. It undergirds the many famous attempts to solve (or dissolve) philosophical puzzles by close analysis of language.

20. Using logical symbolism, this may be re-written as:

$(\exists x)(x$ is P.M. of Canada$)$ & $(\forall x)(\forall y)[(x$ is P.M. of Canada & y is P.M. of Canada$)$ $\supset$ $x=y]$ & $(\forall z)(z$ is P.M. of Canada $\supset$ z is tall$)$

As Russell points out, the first two conjuncts together can be paraphrased in English as 'There is exactly one P.M. of Canada'.

21. Russell talks about propositional functions being "sometimes true" or "always true". This may seem odd for two reasons. One is: this way of speaking suggests that they are true at some moment in time, or at all moments in time. This is not intended. Russell really means "true in all cases". The other thing that may seem strange is the idea that propositional *functions* can be true. Ordinarily one thinks of propositions, rather than propositional functions, as being true. I think this second peculiarity is equally harmless, though. One should simply read (i) as short hand for (ii):

(i) The propositional function F is sometimes true
(ii) There exists at least one argument a in the domain of F which

yields a true proposition when input into F.

22. The direct reference theory does run up against a problem with proper names. Notice: on this view, the meaning of a name *just is* its bearer—i.e. the individual designated by the name. So there ought to be no difference of meaning between (i) and (ii):

(i) Scott is Scott
(ii) Scott is Sir Walter

Russell (1919) says two things about this example, and others of the same kind. First: (i) and (ii) *do* express the very same proposition, when 'Scott' and 'Sir Walter' are really used as names. Second: sometimes sentence (ii) is used to mean 'The person named 'Scott' is the person named 'Sir Walter''. In short, identity statements are sometimes statements about language in disguise—i.e. they are sometimes statements about people's names, rather than statements about people. Only then are they non-trivial. I'll return to this in the next chapter.

23. As Kenny (1995) demonstrates in his (very fine and very accessible) introduction, Frege's views evolved considerably throughout his philosophical career. I have taken elements from his various periods and married them into an assemblage of "Fregean insights". In this sense, among others, the discussion which follows is ahistorical.

24. Similarly, the principle of compositionality and the principle of extensionality together entail that (i) and (ii) are synonymous.

(i) Mark Twain = Mark Twain
(ii) Samuel Clemens = Mark Twain

The meaning of each of the parts is the same—namely, the guy, equals, and the guy again. And the parts are ordered in the same way. And yet, these two sentences don't appear synonymous at all. Frege considers this another reason for rejecting the principle of extensionality. I return to this at length below.

25. I use 'meaning' here to translate 'Sinn', despite the controversies over how to render Frege's German. ('Bedeutung', rather than 'Sinn', is sometimes translated as 'meaning'.) Though in some ways less true to Frege's intent, I consider this usage more natural for those not previously familiar with Frege's writings. Another point:

there's far from universal agreement about Frege's views on the relationship between expression, sense and reference. This being a general overview, and not an intellectual history, I introduce only one reading of Frege. Some find one consequence of my reading odd: that an object *o* has the senses it does, independently of whether human beings ever *actually* perceive *o* under said senses. If this is an odd consequence, it's one I can live with.

26. Frege's argument for this claim? "For it cannot well be denied that mankind possesses a common treasure of thoughts which is transmitted from generation to generation" (1892a, 192). A rather controversial basis for his conclusion.

27. This should make you wonder: if sense is the way the object is given, how can there be senses without any corresponding object given? This is a very good question, with no easy answer. See Dummett 1973 for extended discussion.

28. Frege explicitly accepts an apparently odd consequence of his theory: that every true sentence refers to the same thing (viz. the TRUE) and every true proposition is just a different way of "looking at" the TRUE. Similarly, he allows that every false sentence refers to the same thing (viz. the FALSE), and every false proposition is just a different way of "looking at" the FALSE. In the end, this "apparently odd consequence" may only amount to a novel (and hence peculiar) way of talking. For, as Frege stresses, what matters in evaluating a sentence is never merely its truth-value. Knowledge consists in recognizing both the nominatum *and the sense* of a sentence. Unrelated point: Frege calls the senses of sentences 'Gedanke', sometimes translated as Thoughts. But this term can suggest something mentalistic to the modern reader, and this is emphatically *not* what Frege intended. Thoughts "do not refer to the subjective activity of thinking but rather to its objective content which is capable of being the common property of many" (Frege 1892a, 201-202). To avoid misleading connotations, I use 'proposition' instead of 'Thought'.

29. This may seem perverse. But compare: sets contain objects as members. So, by analogy, Chomsky can be a part of a proposition in the same way Russell, Frege and Wittgenstein can be members of the set {Russell, Frege, Wittgenstein}. And notice: if there is such a set as this, then Russell must exist. Similarly, if the name 'Noam Chomsky' contributes the guy Chomsky to the proposition expressed by 'Noam Chomsky is over 50', then Chomsky must

exist. (This comparison was suggested to me by Lenny Clapp.)

30. Actually, this table, like the others before it, is ahistorical. The present table reflects the way modern logicians and semanticists have developed Frege's ideas.

31. Several contemporary philosophers would suggest that, despite initial appearances, *both* sentence (100a) *and* sentence (100b) are true. See Salmon 1986 for more.

32. As will emerge below, direct discourse is a sentential parallel to (104a) and (104b). Both involve actual quotation of expressions. Indirect discourse, on the other hand, is a sentential parallel to 'It's common knowledge that ___ is an author'.

33. Here's an alternative definition of 'opaque context'. An opaque context is one such that the following argument form isn't valid:

Premise 1: $E_1 = E_2$
Premise 2: $C \frown E_1$ is true
Conclusion: $C \frown E_2$ is true

Note too: some philosophers apply the term 'opaque' only to contexts that take singular terms, not sentences. My usage is the broader one.

34. Notice what Russell would say about this example: he'd insist that 'the number of basic physical forces' is a description. Hence, it has no referent. Hence it is *not* co-referential with 'four'.

35. What names and sentences *express* in opaque contexts—i.e. what they have as their *sense* in such contexts—is controversial. One option, at least for non-quotational cases, is that names and sentences express a sense of their ordinary sense. Thus, in opaque contexts, names express the sense of an individual concept while sentences express a sense of a proposition. Another option is that, in opaque contexts, expressions have their usual sense *as both sense and reference*. Equally a matter of debate is what predicates denote, and express, in opaque contexts.

36. Notice that Russell (1919) falls prey to a version of the Puzzle. He ends up saying that identity statements, when informative, are about language.

37. As Martin (1987, 151) stresses, "To say that something is impossible is not to say that it is merely unbelievable". The world can have a feature without you realizing it. For instance, you may not know who the President of Uruguay is. Similarly, the world can have a *modal* feature, without you recognizing it. Certain impossibilities may seem possible to you, and certain possibilities may strike you as impossible. In a slogan: even in the modal domain, **ontology** (very roughly: what there is) must be distinguished from **epistemology** (very roughly: how you discover what there is).

38. Whether, and to what extent, possible worlds talk carries nasty ontological consequences is a matter of debate. David Lewis (1973, 478) insists that possible worlds talk has powerful "ontological bite". He writes:

> I believe that there are possible worlds other than the one we happen to inhabit. If an argument is wanted, it is this. It is uncontroversially true that things could have been different in countless ways. But what does this mean? Ordinary language permits the paraphrase: there are many ways things could have been besides the way they actually are. On the face of it, this sentence is an existential quantification. It says that there exist many entities of a certain description, to wit 'ways things could have been'. I believe that things could have been different in countless ways; I believe permissible paraphrases of what I believe; taking the paraphrase at its face value, I therefore believe in the existence of entities that might be called 'ways things could have been'. I prefer to call them 'possible worlds'.

Lewis' cavalier enthusiasm for possible worlds isn't, however, universally shared. Some philosophers find possible worlds language obscure and deny that ordinary talk is ontologically charged in this way. Others—Stalnaker (1976, 472), for example—consider possible worlds language to be a convenient technical short hand, whose use is justified by its utility in theorizing. I leave the topic to one side. For discussion, see the various papers in Loux 1979.

39. Obviously the referent of 'The P.M. of Canada' will also vary from time to time. I ignore this relativization to times throughout.

40. Just as 'J.F.K. was the brother of Bobby' and 'Chrétien is the Prime Minister of Canada' express relations—the ones in (i) and (ii).

(i) Was-Brother-Of(J.F.K.)(Bobby)
(ii) Is-Prime-Minister-Of(Chrétien)(Canada)

41. This idea, of a shared meaning between declaratives and other moods, is widespread in contemporary philosophical writings. Nor is it exactly new. For example, Wittgenstein (1953, 11) writes:

> Imagine a picture representing a boxer in a particular stance. Now, this picture can be used to tell someone how he should stand, should hold himself; or how he should not hold himself; or how a particular man did stand in such-and-such a place; and so on. One might (using the language of chemistry) call this picture a proposition-radical.

42. Hume distinguishes between **impressions**—which are more vivid, forceful and lively—and **copies of impressions**. As an example of an original impression he gives "the perceptions of the mind when a man feels the pain of excessive heat" (Hume 1748, 9). A copy would be, "when he afterwards recalls to his memory this sensation or anticipates it by his imagination". It's the latter, the copies of impressions, which Hume calls **ideas** and which I will call *images*. Importantly, notes Hume, one's stock of images is not exhausted by **simple ideas**—direct copies of impressions, got from merely recollecting actual sense experiences. Rather, **compound ideas** can also be formed, by "compounding, transposing, augmenting or diminishing the materials afforded us by the senses and experience" (Hume 1748, 11). This, one might suppose, is how people come to have mental images that do not correspond to anything real. Such images are compounds. Hume gives the example of a golden mountain. One can imagine such a thing by joining together two ideas—MOUNTAIN and GOLD—each got through impressions.

43. A word on what the idea theory need not entail. It needn't be the view—criticized in Mill 1867, 12-13—that words name ideas. That view would seem to require that, in saying 'John is late', I am talking about some idea or other. This consequence is unhappy, since, as a matter of fact, I'm clearly talking about *the man John*. And, barring crude phenomenalism, John isn't an idea. To avoid Mill's criticism, the idea theory can be taken as saying that words are associated with ideas, and that words get their meaning from an associated idea, though not by naming or referring to the associated idea. (Compare Frege on sense and reference.)

44. I owe this example to Tim Kenyon.

45. You might say: "Well, even if mental images aren't actually simi-

lar to what they represent, they might *look* similar". (Compare the portrait of Queen Victoria. It isn't exactly like the Queen—e.g. the portrait isn't actually fleshy or dowdy. But, you might say, it looks like her.) But *to whom* might images and their denotations look similar? To a little man "inside the head", a **homunculus**? You can, I hope, see the problem. There's another familiar difficulty that is worth noting, though space doesn't permit an adequate discussion. It's the **problem of misrepresentation**. Suppose Rene looks down the road and imagines he sees a horse-drawn buggy. He thinks: 'That buggy is barely moving'. Suppose that, unknown to Rene, it's not a buggy at all but a large rock. Rene's just-described thought is, it seems, about a rock. But if representation is a matter of similarity, how does Rene's buggy-image manage to (falsely) represent a rock? Cummins (1989, Ch.3) discusses these problems at length.

46. According to John Haugeland (1985), Thomas Hobbes (1588-1679) was the first philosopher to consider the possibility that mental representations might be quasi-linguistic.

47. It's tempting to some to mistake the quite controversial claim that there is a language of thought (LOT) for the flat-footed claim that there are propositional attitude states. But, as will shortly emerge, the language of thought hypothesis is merely one *theory* about the nature of the attitudes. For the moment, note that some philosophers—e.g. Dennett and (possibly) Stalnaker (1984)—affirm that there are believers, while denying that there are sentence-like representations inside the believer's head. That there are intentional states can be taken for granted. What such states *are* is very much a matter of dispute. (Compare: that there are stars was never really an issue. What the stars were, on the other hand—flaming balls, holes in a celestial canopy, angels—was up for grabs for a rather long time.) See Cummins (1989) and Fodor (1987a) for more on what LOT entails, above and beyond **intentional realism** (the view that there really are intentional states).

48. You might think that the language of thought proposal is ridiculous on the face of it, since there couldn't literally be sentences in the head: the brain isn't some kind of blackboard. But notice that symbols are importantly **media-independent**. You can token the very same word in sand, in skywriter's smoke, in ink, in paint, or using a row of pebbles. Stranger still, a word can appear on a cassette tape, a vinyl record, or a compact disc. Even in a computer's memory. (Indeed, as will emerge, the computer is precisely the

comparison Fodor et al have in mind.) So, if expressions can be tokened in these media, there's no reason in principle why they can't be tokened in brain-stuff. (See Dennett 1975, 504 for the deeper complexities of this problem.)

49. Why not say: "Thought takes place in language, all right, but the language is the one which the individual speaks". On this view, my language of thought would be English. This is not without its attractions, as Harman (1973, 1975) notes. But there are problems as well. As I've noted before: animals and infants think, but they don't speak any natural language. Besides, learning one's first language would seem to be a kind of thinking. So not all thinking can take place in one's first language. Furthermore, who hasn't had the experience of "looking for the right word" to express an idea? What sense does this make if the idea is inseparable from that word? See Pinker 1994 for more.

50. You might say that this story about decision-making is terribly oversimplified. Indeed it is. But complicating it would merely *improve* the case for Fodor and Harman's conclusion: that, in decision making, there's a great deal of highly complex representing going on.

51. In the same paper, Dennett also introduces a noteworthy objection to the language of thought story. He maintains that different individuals can all share a belief (e.g. the belief that some Frenchman was killed in London) without tokening *the very same formula*. Indeed, individuals of different species, futuristic computers, and extra-terrestrials may be capable of sharing human beliefs. But it's implausible that they share a language of thought with humankind. So, *pace* Fodor, believing cannot be a matter of tokening mentalese sentences.

52. Before deserting Dennett, let me leave you with a question, one whose answer isn't obvious, at least to me. If Dennett is right, what becomes of the theory of meaning? For instance, what, on Dennett's view, makes certain structures/sounds meaningful? And what is it for them to have the meaning they do, rather than some other or none at all? Dennett has clear *negative* views about this: it's not a matter of being paired with an internal formula. But what would his positive view be?

53. It is for this reason, among others, that Chomsky dislikes this term: it wrongly suggests that it's a *hypothesis*, up-for-grabs if you

will, that human beings are innately different from other species. Whatever the (de-)merits of the label, it is now widely employed. So I too will use it.

54. The next obvious question is: given this, what exactly does the innate endowment look like? Recently, Chomsky has been pushing a novel picture—one already encountered in Chapter Two. Here's the metaphor: the newborn has a board of switches before her. Some are permanently up, others are already down, and still others have yet to be set. The infant's task is to "set" the variable switches—the parameters—in response to environmental triggers.

55. Warning! Quine exegesis is a risky business at the best of times. So it's important to read discussions of his views with a sceptical eye. This is particularly true in my case since, to be frank, I am not very sympathetic to the Quinean perspective. Note too that, whereas Quine focuses on radical *translation*, I generalize to radical *rule attribution*.

56. This sort of consideration eventually leads Quine to **holism** about linguistic meaning. Roughly speaking, holism is "the doctrine that only whole languages or whole theories or whole belief systems *really* have meanings, so that the meanings of smaller units—words, sentences, hypotheses, predictions, discourses, dialogues, texts, thoughts, and the like—are merely derivative" (Fodor and LePore 1992, x). The inference apparently goes as follows. **Verificationism**—a view which Quine explicitly accepts—says that the meaning of a sentence is determined by its method of confirmation. But, Quine argues, confirmation is holistic: no sentence is supported in isolation. So meaning is holistic: it's not sentences, but only whole languages, which really have meaning. Quine (1986, 155-156) writes:

> The statement of verificationism relevant to this purpose is that "evidence for the truth of a sentence is identical with the meaning of the sentence"; and I submit that if sentences in general had meanings, their meanings would be just that. It is only holism itself that tells us that in general they do not have them.

57. This example is taken from Stich 1983.

58. Some say this highlights Quine's lack of imagination. On a related note, numerous authors have argued that Quine arbitrarily limits the data under consideration to speech behaviour. See especially

Chomsky 1980, Chomsky and Katz 1974, Fodor 1981b and Stich 1972.

59. He attributes this mistake to his own earlier work, by the way. In particular, he draws attention to Wittgenstein 1922:

> It is interesting to compare the multiplicity of the tools in language and the ways they are used, the multiplicity of kinds of word and sentence, with what logicians have said about the structure of language. (Including the author of the *Tractatus Logico-Philosophicus*.) (Wittgenstein 1953, 12)

60. Actually, there is a way around this result. One can say that descriptions are not names, but that they nevertheless *do* stand for something. For instance, the meaning of ⌜The F⌝ is that function which takes a propositional function to TRUE if and only if there is exactly one F and every F yields TRUE for the input propositional function. See Neale 1990 for more.

61. It's true that saying 'I promise to be there tomorrow' may *imply* the truth of certain propositions. But they aren't what is being *asserted*. According to Austin, nothing is being asserted. He writes:

> However, although these utterances do not themselves report facts and are not themselves true or false, saying these does very often imply that certain things are true and not false, in some sense at least of that rather woolly word *"imply"*. For example, when I say "I do take this woman to be my lawful wedded wife", or some other formula in the marriage ceremony, I do imply that I'm not already married, with wife living, sane, undivorced, and the rest of it. But still it is very important to realize that to imply that something or other is true, is not at all the same as saying something which is itself true (Austin 1961, 107).

62. Searle thinks that 'I promise I didn't do that' involves a non-literal use of 'promise'.

63. It's worth noting that Grice, whom I treated as an idea theorist, also had a close affinity with the use theorists. In particular, putting it very roughly, Grice (1957, 76) took conventional meaning to arise from what speakers typically mean by expressions—i.e. how they typically *use* said expressions. That Grice could be both a use theorist and an idea theorist shouldn't really surprise: the perspectives I've introduced needn't be at odds with one another.

64. At best, stimulus meaning captures meaning (as intuitively understood) only when no background assumptions play a part in causing assent/dissent. These cases do occur. Quine calls them 'observation sentences' and gives 'Red' as a possible example. He writes: "It is for observation sentences in some such sense that the notion of stimulus meaning constitutes a reasonable notion of meaning" (1960, 44). He also concedes that stimulus meaning may effectively capture the meaning (in the classical sense) of certain logical terms—in particular, the truth functional connectives, though not the quantifiers (see 1960, 60). But these exceptions, if such they be, are cold comfort in the face of meaning nihilism for everything else.

65. Quine defines **occasion sentences** as those which "command assent or dissent only if queried after an appropriate prompting stimulation" (1960, 35-36). Examples include 'Red', 'His face is dirty' and 'Rabbit'. Occasion sentences contrast with **standing sentences**. These may prompt assent/dissent even without a prompting stimulation. (Sentences of mathematics are obvious examples.)

66. Quine has a closely related argument, from language acquisition, which leads to the same conclusion. He writes:

> In acquiring [language] we have to depend entirely on intersubjectively available cues as to what to say and when. Hence there is no justification for collating linguistic meanings, unless in terms of men's dispositions to respond overtly to socially observable stimulations. An effect of recognizing this limitation is that the enterprise of translation is found to be involved in a certain systematic indeterminacy. (1960, ix)

Of course this argument may lose some of its force if much of linguistic knowledge is innate.

67. Grice fully recognizes that his cooperative principle for conversation is an application of the principles that govern rational cooperative action generally: following these rules is the reasonable thing to do. Grice says,

> I would like to be able to think of the standard type of conversational practice not merely as something that all or most do in fact follow but as something it is reasonable for us to follow, that we should not abandon. (1975, 153)

This explains certain facts. First, speakers don't have to be taught these maxims. Second, the maxims look to be universal. Third, speakers expect their interlocutors to abide by the principles—because speakers take their audience to be rational.

68. Donnellan compares his view with that of Strawson 1950. First point: Donnellan says that, according to Strawson, if someone asserts that the φ is Ψ, he has not made a true or false statement if there is no φ. Second point: Donnellan attributes to Strawson the view that, if there is no φ, then the speaker has failed to refer to anything in saying that the φ is Ψ. Donnellan says that this second claim is just false, because the speaker may be using 'the φ' referentially. As for the first claim, it may be right *for the attributive use*, but it is certainly wrong about *the referential use*. You can see why. If 'the φ' is being used "to point", as it were, then a statement (true or false) may be made *about the thing pointed to*, even if neither it nor anything else happens to be φ.

69. A helpful comparison: used referentially, a definite description picks out *whatever the speaker wishes to discuss*—the thing which the speaker intends. This looks just like the "pointing function" of indexicals. In a sense, then, when used referentially (210a) and (i) are very similar. As are (210b) and (ii).

(i) *That guy* is insane
(ii) Who is *that*?

70. To see what's *not* conventional about this practice, consider the humour in the following suggestion. The Rhino Party of Ontario once proposed (tongue firmly in cheek) to celebrate Ontario's British heritage by making it a left-hand drive province. Not favouring radical and rapid change, the Party further suggested that the new rules be implemented gradually, over a five year period—beginning with trucks and busses!

71. An exegetical note: Kripke's discussion is best taken as "arguments which occurred to Kripke while reading Wittgenstein". It is very doubtful whether Kripke has accurately captured Wittgenstein's thinking on these topics. Nor does he claim to.

72. Importantly, the skeptic is not a total skeptic about meaning (at least at this point). To even state his objection, Scott must agree, at least provisionally, that Leroy's present word 'plus' and his *present* symbol '+' refer to the function that everyone's familiar with. Scott must further agree, again at least provisionally, that his *present* word

'quus' and his symbol '⊕' refer to that weird function in (217). What the skeptic is raising doubts about is whether Leroy is presently conforming to his *previous* linguistic intentions. If the word 'plus', as Leroy employed it *previously*, denoted the quus function—rather than the plus function—then Leroy's past use was such that, when given (216), he should reply '5'. For that is what quus determines for this case.

73. Kripke draws a parallel between what he calls "Wittgenstein's new form of skepticism" and Hume's classical skepticism. Both thinkers, he says, develop a sceptical paradox, based on questioning a certain move from past to future. Hume famously wondered how one could justifiably infer causation on the basis of one event following another; or, how one can make reliable inferences from past events to future events. Wittgenstein, as Kripke is reading him, wonders how an agent justifies saying that she is still using a rule as she had always used it. Both give sceptical solutions to their puzzles. Hume said: there is no causation, there is only correlation of events. He said further that nothing justifies the inference from past to future. People simply make it. According to Kripke: "[Wittgenstein's] solution to his own sceptical problem begins by agreeing with the sceptics that there is no 'superlative fact' (§192) about my mind that constitutes my meaning addition by "plus" and determines in advance what I should do to accord with this meaning" (1982, 481). However, says Kripke, Wittgenstein denies that meaning one thing rather than another requires such a fact.

74. There's a third alternative which I ignore—though it's *prima facie* the most plausible of the three. A **mixed theorist** says that sometimes utterance meaning is determined conventionally, and sometimes it's determined by speaker's intentions. For example, a mixed theorist might say that the reference of *indexicals* is determined purely conventionally—i.e. the conventions say what the reference will be, given the context; it's not open for the speaker to refer to whatever she wishes—but maintain that *metaphorical* meaning depends largely upon speaker's intentions.

75. Keith Donnellan is another intention theorist. See the exchange between him (Donnellan 1968) and MacKay (1968). Other convention theorists include Austin, Searle, and—possibly—Wittgenstein.

76. An utterance may be classified in at least two ways: in terms of what syntactic and semantic type it is a token of, and in terms of the speech act it was used to perform. In what follows, 'declarative',

'interrogative' and 'imperative' classify utterances in terms of syntax; while 'assertion', 'asking' and 'order' classify them in terms of speech act performed. The issue, then, may be put this way: what is the relationship between declarative utterances (i.e. utterances of declarative sentence types) and assertions (i.e. the act of making a statement)? Switching to the other moods: how are interrogative utterances related to askings, and imperative utterances related to orders?

77. This paragraph adapts ideas from Stainton (in press). See also Stainton 1994, 1995.

78. There is a natural and obvious reply to this objection: the ellipsis defence. One might suppose—in fact Dummett (1973:298) *does* suppose—that these apparent word and phrase utterances are really "just elliptical sentences". As a matter of empirical fact, however, the items produced are not elliptical sentences—at least not in any sense which would help Dummett. For the overwhelming evidence, see Barton 1990, Brame 1979, Napoli 1982, and Yanofsky 1978. Davidson mentions two other problems with Dummett's line. First, there's no reason to believe that the conventions appealed to actually exist (Davidson 1979, 114). Second, when one cannot tell whether a speaker is making an assertion, or playing a game, or asking a question, it's typically *not* because something conventional is missing. Rather, what's often missing in such cases is knowledge of the speaker's *intentions*.

References

[Note: Where page references in the text correspond to a reprinted version, the location of the reprint is given as well.]

Alston, William P. 1964. *Philosophy of Language*. Englewood Cliffs: Prentice-Hall.

Aqvist, Lennart. 1975. A *New Approach to the Logical Theory of Interrogatives*. Tubingen: Gunter Narr Verlag.

Austin, John L. 1961. Performative Utterances. In *Philosophical Papers*. Edited by J.O. Urmson and G.J. Warnock. Oxford: Oxford University Press. Reprinted in Martinich 1990.

——. 1962. *How to Do Things with Words*. Edited by J.O. Urmson and M. Sbisa. Cambridge: Harvard University Press.

Bach, Emmon. 1989. *Informal Lectures on Formal Semantics*. Albany: State University of New York Press.

Bach, Kent and Robert M. Harnish. 1979. *Linguistic Communication and Speech Acts*. Cambridge: The MIT Press. Reprinted in part in Davis 1991.

Bar-Hillel, Yehoshua. 1954. Indexical Expressions. *Mind* 63: 359-379.

Barton, Ellen. 1990. *Nonsentential Constituents*. Philadelphia: John Benjamins Publishing Company.

Barwise, Jon and John Perry. 1975. Semantic Innocence and Uncompromising Situations. In *The Foundations of Analytic Philosophy*, edited by P. French, T.E. Uehling and H.K. Wettstein. Midwest Studies in Philosophy, vol. 6. Minneapolis: University of Minnesota Press. Reprinted in Martinich 1990.

Bechtel, William. 1988. Connectionism and the Philosophy of Mind. *The Southern Journal of Philosophy* 26 (Supplement):17-41. Reprinted in Lycan 1990.

Belnap, Nuel D. and Thomas B. Steel Jr. 1976. *The Logic of Questions and Answers*. New Haven: Yale University Press.

Bennett, Jonathan. 1971. *Locke, Berkeley, Hume: Central Themes*. Oxford: Clarendon Press.

Berkeley, George. 1710. A *Treatise Concerning the Principles of Human Knowledge*. Edited by T.E. Jessop. London: Nelson.

Black, Max. 1962. Metaphor. In *Models and Metaphors*. Ithaca: Cornell University Press.

——. 1973. Meaning and Intention: An Examination of Grice's Views. *New Literary History* 4:257-279.

——. 1979. More about Metaphor. In *Metaphor and Thought*, edited by A. Ortony. Cambridge: Cambridge University Press.

Blackburn, Simon. 1984. *Spreading the Word*. Oxford: Oxford University Press.

Block, Ned, ed. 1981. *Readings in Philosophy of Psychology*. Vol. 2. Cambridge: Harvard University Press.

Bloomfield, Leonard. 1926. A Set of Postulates for the Science of Language. *Language* 2:153-164.

Brame, Michael K. 1979. A Note on COMP S Grammar vs. Sentence Grammar. *Linguistic Analysis* 5:383-386.

Bromberger, Sylvain. 1966. Questions. *The Journal of Philosophy* 63:597-606.

Carnap, Rudolf. 1947. *Meaning and Necessity*. Chicago: University of Chicago Press.

Cartwright, Richard. 1987. On the Origins of Russell's Theory of Descriptions. In *Philosophical Essays*. Cambridge: The MIT Press.

Chierchia, Gennaro and Sally McConnell-Ginet. 1990. *Meaning and Grammar. An Introduction to Semantics*. Cambridge: The MIT Press.

Chomsky, Noam. 1957. *Syntactic Structures*. The Hague: Mouton.

——. 1962. Explanatory Models in Linguistics. In *Logic, Methodology and Philosophy of Science*, edited by E. Nagel, P. Suppes and A. Tarski. Stanford: Stanford University Press.

——. 1965. *Aspects of the Theory of Syntax*. Cambridge: The MIT Press.

——. 1969. Quine's Empirical Assumptions. In *Words and Objections: Essays on the Work of W.V. Quine*, edited by D. Davidson and J. Hintikka. Dordrecht: Reidel.

——. 1975. On Cognitive Capacity. In *Reflections on Language*. New York: Pantheon. Reprinted in Block 1981.

——. 1980. *Rules and Representations*. New York: Columbia University Press.

——. 1981. *Lectures on Government and Binding*. Dordrecht: Foris.

——. 1986. *Knowledge of Language*. New York: Praeger.

——. 1988. *Language and Problems of Knowledge: The Managua Lectures*. Cambridge: The MIT Press.

——. 1990. Language and the Problem of Knowledge. In *The Philosophy of Language*, edited by A.P. Martinich. Oxford: Oxford University Press.

——. 1993a. A Minimalist Program for Linguistic Theory. In *The View from Building 20: Essays in Linguistics in Honor of Sylvain*

Bromberger, edited by K. Hale and S.J. Keyser. Cambridge: The MIT Press.

——. 1993b. *Language and Thought.* Wakefield, RI: Moyer Bell.

——. 1995. Bare Phrase Structure. In *Government and Binding and the Minimalist Program*, edited by G. Webelhuth. Oxford: Blackwell.

Chomsky, Noam and Jerrold J. Katz. 1974. What the Linguist is Talking About. *Journal of Philosophy* 71:347-367.

Church, Alonzo. 1951. The Need for Abstract Entities. *American Academy of Arts and Sciences Proceedings* 80:100-113. Reprinted as "Intentional Semantics" in Martinich 1990.

Churchland, Patricia S. and Paul M. Churchland. 1983. Stalking the Wild Epistemic Engine. *Nous* 17:5-18. Reprinted in Lycan 1990.

Churchland, Patricia S. and Terrence J. Sejnowski. 1989. Neural Representation and Neural Computation. In *Neural Connections, Mental Computations*, edited by L. Nadel and others. Cambridge: The MIT Press. Reprinted in Lycan 1990.

Churchland, Paul. 1988. *Matter and Consciousness*. Revised Edition. Cambridge: The MIT Press.

Clark, Andy. 1989. *Microcognition: Philosophy, Cognitive Science, and Parallel Distributed Processing*. Cambridge: The MIT Press.

Cummins, Robert. 1989. *Meaning and Mental Representation*. Cambridge: The MIT Press.

Davidson, Donald. 1967. Truth and Meaning. *Synthese* 17:304-323. Reprinted in Davidson 1984.

——. 1968. On Saying That. *Synthese* 19:130-146. Reprinted in Martinich 1990.

——. 1973. Radical Interpretation. *Dialectica* 27:313-328. Reprinted in Davidson 1984.

——. 1975. Thought and Talk. In *Mind and Language: Wolfson College Lectures 1974*, edited by S. Guttenplan. Oxford: Oxford University Press. Reprinted in Davidson 1984.
——. 1978. What Metaphors Mean. *Critical Inquiry* 5:31-47. Reprinted in Martinich 1990.

——. 1979. Moods and Performances. In *Meaning and Use*, edited by A. Margalit. Dordrecht: D. Reidel. Reprinted in Davidson 1984.

——. 1982. Communication and Convention. In *Dialogue: An Interdisciplinary Approach*, edited by M. Dascal. Amsterdam: John Benjamins. Reprinted in Davidson 1984.

——. 1984. *Inquiries into Truth and Interpretation*. Oxford: Oxford University Press.

——. 1986. A Nice Derangement of Epitaphs. In *Truth and Interpretation: Perspectives on the Philosophy of Donald Davidson*, edited by E. LePore. New York: Basil Blackwell.

Davis, Steven. 1976. *Philosophy and Language*. Indianapolis: The Bobbs-Merrill Company, Inc.

——. ed. 1991. *Pragmatics*. Oxford: Oxford University Press.

Dennett, Daniel C. 1975. Brain Writing and Mind Reading. In *Language, Mind and Knowledge*, edited by K. Gunderson. Minnesota Studies in the Philosophy of Science, vol. 7. Minneapolis: University of Minnesota Press. Reprinted in Rosenthal 1991.

——. 1977. A Cure for the Common Code? Reprinted in Dennett 1978.

——. 1978. *Brainstorms*. Cambridge, MA: Bradford Books.

——. 1981.Three Kinds of Intentional Psychology. In *Reduction, Time and Reality*, edited by R. Healy. Cambridge: Cambridge University Press. Reprinted in Garfield 1990.

——. 1987. *The Intentional Stance*. Cambridge: The MIT Press.

Devitt, Michael and Kim Sterelny. 1987. *Language and Reality: An Introduction to the Philosophy of Language*. Cambridge: The MIT Press.

Donnellan, Keith. 1966. Reference and Definite Descriptions. *Philosophical Review* 75:281-304. Reprinted in Martinich 1990.

——. 1968. Putting Humpty Dumpty Together Again. *Philosophical Review* 77:203-215.

Dowty, David R., Robert E. Wall and Stanley Peters. 1981. *Introduction to Montague Semantics*. Dordrecht: Reidel.

Dummett, Michael. 1973. *Frege: Philosophy of Language*. London: Duckworth.

——. 1976. What Is a Theory of Meaning? (II). In *Truth and Meaning: Essays in Semantics*, edited by Gareth Evans and John McDowell. Oxford: Oxford University Press.

——. 1978. Frege's Distinction between Sense and Reference. In *Truth and Other Enigmas*. London: Duckworth. Reprinted in Moore 1993.

——. 1979.What Does the Appeal to Use do for the Theory of Meaning? In *Meaning and Use*, edited by A. Margalit. Dordrecht: Reidel. Reprinted in Moore 1993.

——. 1981. *The Interpretation of Frege's Philosophy*. London: Duckworth.

——. 1991. *The Logical Basis of Metaphysics*. Cambridge: Harvard University Press.

——. 1993. Mood, Force and Convention. In *The Seas of Language*. Oxford: Oxford University Press.

——. 1994. *Origins of Analytical Philosophy*. Cambridge: Harvard University Press.

Evans, Gareth. 1975. Identity and Predication. *Journal of Philosophy* 72:343-363.

——. 1982. *Varieties of Reference*. Edited by John McDowell. Oxford: Oxford University Press.

Evans, Gareth and John McDowell. eds. 1976. *Truth and Meaning: Essays in Semantics*. Oxford: Oxford University Press.

Evnine, Simon. 1991. *Donald Davidson*. Stanford: Stanford University Press.

Field, Hartry. 1972. Tarski's Theory of Truth. *Journal of Philosophy* 69:347-375. Reprinted in Garfield and Kiteley 1991.

——. 1978. Mental Representations. *Erkenntnis* 13:9-61. Reprinted in Block 1981.

Fodor, Jerry A. 1975. *The Language of Thought*. Cambridge: Harvard University Press.

——. 1978. Propositional Attitudes. *The Monist* 61:501-523. Reprinted in Fodor 1981.

——. 1980. Methodological Solipsism Considered as a Research Strategy in Cognitive Psychology. *The Behavioral and Brain Sciences* 3:63-72. Reprinted in Fodor 1981.

——. 1981a. *Representations*. Cambridge: The MIT Press.

——. 1981b. Some Notes on What Linguistics is About. In Block 1981.

——. 1985. Fodor's Guide to Mental Representations. *Mind* 94:76-100.

——. 1987a. Why there still has to be a language of thought. In *Psychosemantics*. Cambridge: The MIT Press.

——. 1987b. Modules, Frames, Fridgeons, Sleeping Dogs, and the Music of the Spheres. In *The Robot's Dilemma: The Frame Problem in Artificial Intelligence*, edited by Z. Pylyshyn. Norwood, NJ: Ablex Publishers. Reprinted in Garfield 1990.

——. 1990. A *Theory of Content and Other Essays*. Cambridge: The MIT Press.

——. 1994. *The Elm and the Expert: Mentalese and Its Semantics*. Cambridge: The MIT Press.

Fodor, Jerry A. and Ernest LePore. 1992. *Holism: A Shopper's Guide*. Oxford: Blackwell.

Fodor, Jerry A. and Zenon Pylyshyn. 1988. Connectionism and Cognitive Architecture: A Critical Analysis. *Cognition* 28:3-71.

Foster, John. 1976. Meaning and Truth Theory. In *Truth and Meaning: Essays in Semantics*, edited by Gareth Evans and John McDowell. Oxford: Oxford University Press.

Frege, Gottlob. 1879. *Conceptual Notation*. Translated by T.W. Bynum. Oxford: Clarendon.

——. 1884. *Foundations of Arithmetic.* Translated by J.L. Austin. Oxford: Blackwell.

——. 1891. Function and Concept. In *Collected Papers on Mathematics, Logic and Philosophy*, edited by Brian McGuinness. Oxford: Basil Blackwell.

——. 1892a. On Sense and Reference. In *Translations from the Philosophical Writings of Gottlob Frege*, edited by P. Geach and M. Black. Oxford: Basil Blackwell. Reprinted in Martinich 1990 as "On Sense and Nominatum".

——. 1892b. On Concept and Object. In *Collected Papers on Mathematics, Logic and Philosophy*, edited by Brian McGuinness. Oxford: Basil Blackwell.

Fromkin, Victoria and Robert Rodman. 1993. *An Introduction to Language*. Fifth edition. New York: Harcourt, Brace, Jovanovich.

Garfield, Jay, ed. 1990. *Foundations of Cognitive Science*. New York: Paragon.

Garfield, Jay and Murray Kiteley. eds. 1991. *Meaning and Truth: The Essential Readings in Modern Semantics*. New York: Paragon.

Geach, Peter. 1962. *Reference and Generality*. Ithaca: Cornell University Press.

Gibson, Roger F. 1982. *The Philosophy of W.V. Quine: An Expository Essay.* Tampa: University Press of Florida.

——. 1986. Translation, Physics, and Facts of the Matter. In *The Philosophy of W.V. Quine*, edited by L.E. Hahn and P.A. Schilpp. La Salle, Illinois: Open Court.

Grice, H. Paul. 1957. Meaning. *Philosophical Review* 66:377-388. Reprinted in Martinich 1990.

——. 1968. Utterer's Meaning, Sentence-Meaning and Word-Meaning. *Foundations of Language* 4:1-18. Reprinted in Davis 1991.

——. 1969. Utterer's Meaning and Intentions. *Philosophical Review* 78:147-177.

——. 1975. Logic and Conversation. In *Speech Acts*, edited by P. Cole and J.L. Morgan. Syntax and Semantics, vol. 3. New York: Academic Press. Reprinted in Martinich 1990.

——. 1989. *Studies in the Way of Words*. Cambridge: Harvard University Press.

Hacker, Peter M.S. 1990. *Wittgenstein: Meaning and Mind. A*n Analytical Commentary on the *Philosophical Investigations*, vol. 3. Oxford: Blackwell.

Hacking, Ian. 1975. *Why Does Language Matter to Philosophy?* Cambridge: Cambridge University Press.

Haegeman, Liliane. 1991. *Introduction to Government and Binding Theory.* Oxford: Blackwell.

Halliday, M.A.K. 1978. *Language as Social Semiotic.* London: Arnold.

——.1984. Language as code and language as behaviour. In *The Semiotics of Culture and Language.* Vol. 1, edited by Fawcett, R. and others. London: Frances Pinter.

Hamblin, Charles L. 1973. Questions in Montague English. *Foundations of Language* 10:41-53.

Harman, Gilbert. 1970. Language Learning. *Nous* 4:33-43. Reprinted in Block 1981.

——. 1973. *Thought.* Princeton: Princeton University Press.

——. 1975. Language, thought and communication. In *Language, Mind and Knowledge*, edited by K. Gunderson. Minnesota Studies in the Philosophy of Science, vol. 7. Minneapolis: University of Minnesota Press.

Harris, Randy Allan. 1993. *The Linguistics Wars.* Oxford: Oxford University Press.

Haugeland, John. 1979. Understanding Natural Language. *The Journal of Philosophy* 76: 619-632. Reprinted in Garfield 1990.

——. 1985. *Artificial Intelligence: The Very Idea.* Cambridge: The MIT Press

Hernández Iglesias, Manuel. 1990. *La semántica de Davidson: Una introducción crítica.* Madrid: Visor.

Higginbotham, James T. 1993. Interrogatives. In *The View from Building 20: Essays in Linguistics in Honor of Sylvain Bromberger*, edited by K. Hale and S. Keyser. Cambridge: The MIT Press.

Hintikka, Jaakko. 1974. Questions About Questions. In *Semantics and Philosophy*, edited by M. Munitz and P. Unger. New York: New York University Press.

——. 1976. *The Semantics of Questions and the Questions of Semantics.* Acta Philosophica Fennica, vol. 28. Amsterdam: North-Holland.

Hook, Sidney, ed. 1969. *Language and Philosophy: A Symposium.* New York: New York University Press.

Hume, David. 1748. *An Enquiry Concerning Human Understanding.* Edited by Eric Steinberg. Indianapolis, IN: Hackett.

Jackendoff, Ray S. 1977. *X-bar Syntax: A Study of Phrase Structure.* Cambridge: The MIT Press.

Jones, Owen R., ed. 1971. *The Private Language Argument.* London: Macmillan.

225

Kaplan, David. 1968. Quantifying In. *Synthese* 19:178-214. Reprinted in Martinich 1990.

——. 1972. What is Russell's Theory of Descriptions? In *Bertrand Russell*, edited by D.F. Pears. Garden City, NY: Anchor Books.

——. 1978. Dthat. In *Pragmatics*, edited by P. Cole. Syntax and Semantics, vol. 9. New York: Academic Press. Reprinted in Martinich 1990.

——. 1979. On the Logic of Demonstratives. *Journal of Philosophical Logic* 8:81-98. Reprinted in Davis 1991.

Kenny, Anthony. 1973. *Wittgenstein*. Cambridge: Harvard University Press.

——. 1995. *Frege*. London: Penguin.

Kripke, Saul. 1972. Naming and Necessity. In *Semantics of Natural Language*, edited by D. Davidson and G. Harman. Dordrecht: Reidel. Reprinted in Martinich 1990.

——. 1977. Speaker's Reference and Semantic Reference. In *Contemporary Perspectives in the Philosophy of Language*, edited by P.A. French, T.E. Uehling and H.K. Wettstein. Minneapolis: University of Minnesota Press. Reprinted in Martinich 1990.

——. 1979. A Puzzle About Belief. In *Meaning and Use*, edited by A. Margalit. Dordrecht: D. Reidel.

——. 1982. *On Rules and Private Language*. Cambridge: Harvard University Press. Reprinted in part in Martinich 1990.

Lasnik, Howard and Juan Uriagereka. 1988. A *Course in GB Syntax*. Cambridge: The MIT Press.

Lees, Robert B. 1960. *The Grammar of English Nominalizations*. Bloomington: Indiana University Press.

Lewis, David. 1969. *Convention: A Philosophical Study*. Cambridge: Harvard University Press.

——. 1970. General Semantics. In *Semantics of Natural Language*, edited by D. Davidson and G. Harman. Dordrecht: Reidel.

——. 1973. Possible Worlds. In *Counterfactuals*. Cambridge: Harvard University Press. Reprinted in Garfield and Kiteley.

——. 1975. Languages and Language. In *Language, Mind and Knowledge*, edited by K. Gunderson. Minnesota Studies in the Philosophy of Science, vol. 7. Minneapolis: University of Minnesota Press. Reprinted in Martinich 1990.

——. 1979. Scorekeeping in a Language Game. *Journal of Philosophical Logic* 8:339-359. Reprinted in Davis 1991.

Loux, Michael J. 1979. *The Possible and the Actual*. Ithaca, NY: Cornell University Press.

Lycan, William G. 1979. The Trouble With Possible Worlds. In *The Possible and the Actual*, edited by M. Loux. Ithaca, NY: Cornell University Press. Reprinted in Garfield and Kiteley 1991.

——. 1981. Towards a Homuncular Theory of Believing. *Cognition and Brain Theory* 4:139-59.

——. ed. 1990. *Mind and Cognition: A Reader*. Oxford: Blackwell.

MacKay, Alfred F. 1968. Mr. Donnellan and Humpty Dumpty on Referring. *Philosophical Review* 77:197-202.

Marantz, Alec. 1995. The Minimalist Program. In *Government and Binding and the Minimalist Program*, edited by G. Webelhuth. Oxford: Blackwell.

Marr, David. 1982. *Vision*. San Francisco: W.H. Freeman.

Martin, Laura. 1986. Eskimo words for snow: A case study in the genesis and decay of an anthropological example. *American Anthropologist* 88:418-23.

Martin, Robert M. 1987. *The Meaning of Language*. Cambridge: The MIT Press.

Martinich, A.P., ed. 1990. *The Philosophy of Language*. Second edition. Oxford: Oxford University Press.

McGinn, Colin. 1977. Semantics for Nonindicative Sentences. *Philosophical Studies* 32: 301-311.

——. 1981. The Mechanism of Reference. *Synthese* 49:157-186.

Mill, John Stuart. 1843. Of Names and Propositions. In *A System of Logic*. London: Longmans. Reprinted in Garfield and Kiteley 1991.

Montague, Richard. 1974. *Formal Philosophy: Selected Papers of Richard Montague*. Edited by R.H. Thomason. New Haven: Yale University Press.

Moore, A.W. ed. 1993. *Meaning and Reference*. Oxford: Oxford University Press.

Napoli, Donna Jo. 1982. Initial Material Deletion in English. *Glossa* 16:85-111.

Neale, Stephen. 1990. *Descriptions*. Cambridge: The MIT Press.

Partee, Barbara. 1975. Montague Grammar and Transformational Grammar. *Linguistic Inquiry* 6:203-300.

Perry, John. 1979. The Problem of the Essential Indexical. *Nous* 13:3-21. Reprinted in Garfield and Kiteley 1991.

Piatelli-Palmarini, Massimo, ed. 1980. *Language and Learning: The Debate between Jean Piaget and Noam Chomsky*. Cambridge: Harvard University Press.

Pinker, Steven. 1994. *The Language Instinct*. New York: William Morrow.

Pinker, Steven and Jacques Mehler. 1988. *Connections and Symbols*. Cambridge: The MIT Press.

Platts, Mark. 1979. *The Ways of Meaning*. London: Routledge and Kegan Paul.

Pullum, Geoffrey K. 1989. The great Eskimo vocabulary hoax. *Natural Language and Linguistic Theory* 2:275-81. Reprinted in *The Great Eskimo Vocabulary Hoax and Other Irreverent Essays on the Study of Language*. Chicago:The University of Chicago Press.

Putnam, Hilary. 1967.The "innateness hypothesis" and explanatory models in linguistics. *Synthese* 17:12-22. Reprinted in Block 1981.

——. 1973. Meaning and Reference. *Journal of Philosophy* 70: 699-711. Reprinted in Martinich 1990.

——. 1975.The Meaning of 'Meaning'. In *Language, Mind and Knowledge*, edited by K. Gunderson. Minnesota Studies in the Philosophy of Science, vol. 7. Minneapolis: University of Minnesota Press.

Pylyshyn, Zenon. 1980. Computation and cognition: issues in the foundations of cognitive science. *Behavioral and Brain Sciences* 3:111-169. Reprinted in Garfield 1990.

Quine, W.V.O. 1951.Two Dogmas of Empiricism. In *From a Logical Point of View*. Cambridge: Harvard University Press. Reprinted in Martinich 1990.

——. 1953a.Three Grades of Modal Involvement. *Proceedings of the XIth International Congress of Philosophy* 14:65-81. Reprinted in *The Ways of Paradox and Other Essays*. New York: Random House.

——. 1953b. The Problem of Meaning in Linguistics. In *From a Logical Point of View*. Cambridge: Harvard University Press.

——. 1956. Quantifiers and Propositional Attitudes. *The Journal of Philosophy* 53:177-187. Reprinted in Martinich 1990.

——. 1959. Meaning and Translation. In *On Translation*, edited by R.A. Brower. Oxford: Oxford University Press.

——. 1960. *Word and Object*. Cambridge:The MIT Press.

——. 1961. Reference and Modality. In *From a Logical Point of View*. Second Edition. Cambridge: Harvard University Press.

——. 1969. Epistemology Naturalized. In *Ontological Relativity and Other Essays*. New York: Columbia University Press.

——. 1972. Methodological reflections on current linguistic theory. In *Semantics of Natural Language*, edited by D. Davidson and G. Harmon. Dordrecht: Reidel.

——. 1986. Reply to Roger F. Gibson, Jr. In *The Philosophy of W.V. Quine*, edited by L.E. Hahn and P.A. Schilpp. La Salle, Illinois: Open Court.

Radford, Andrew. 1981. *Transformational Syntax: A Student's Guide to Chomsky's Extended Standard Theory*. Cambridge: Cambridge University Press.

——. 1988. *Transformational Grammar: A First Course*. Cambridge: Cambridge University Press.

Ramberg, Bjorn T. 1989. *Donald Davidson's Philosophy of Language: An Introduction*. Oxford: Blackwell.

Reichenbach, Hans. 1938. *Experience and Prediction*. Chicago: University of Chicago Press.

Rosenthal, David M., ed. 1991. *The Nature of Mind*. Oxford: Oxford University Press.

Rumelhart, David E. 1989. The Architecture of Mind: A Connectionist Approach. In *Foundations of Cognitive Science*, edited by M.I. Posner. Cambridge:The MIT Press.

Rumelhart, David E. and J. McClelland, eds. 1986. *Parallel Distributed Processing: Explorations in the Microstructure of Cognition*. Two volumes. Cambridge:The MIT Press.

Russell, Bertrand. 1905. On Denoting. *Mind* 14:479-493. Reprinted in Martinich 1990.

——. 1919. *Introduction to Mathematical Philosophy*. London: George Allen & Unwin. Reprinted in part in Martinich 1990 as "Descriptions".

——. 1957. Mr. Strawson on referring. *Mind* 66:385-389.

Sadock, Jerrold M. 1978. On Testing for Conversational Implicature. In *Pragmatics*, edited by P. Cole. Syntax and Semantics, vol. 9. New York:Academic Press. Reprinted in Davis 1991.

Salmon, Nathan. 1986. *Frege's Puzzle*. Cambridge:The MIT Press.

Schiffer, Stephen. 1972. *Meaning*. Oxford: Oxford University Press.

——. 1981. Truth and the Theory of Content. In *Meaning and Understanding*, edited by H. Parret and J. Bouraresse. Berlin: Walter de Gruyter.

——. 1987. *Remnants of Meaning*. Cambridge:The MIT Press.

Searle, John R. 1965.What is a speech act? In *Philosophy in America*, edited by M. Black. Ithaca: Cornell University Press. Reprinted in Martinich 1990.

——. 1968. Austin on Locutionary and Illocutionary Acts. *Philosophical Review* 77:405-424.

——. 1969. *Speech Acts*. Cambridge: Cambridge University Press.
——. ed. 1971. *The Philosophy of Language*. Oxford: Oxford University Press.

——. 1975. Indirect Speech Acts. In *Speech Acts*, edited by P. Cole and J.L. Morgan. Syntax and Semantics, vol. 3. New York:Academic Press. Reprinted in Martinich 1990.

——. 1979a. Metaphor. In *Metaphor and Thought*, edited by A. Ortony. Cambridge: Cambridge University Press. Reprinted in Martinich 1990.

——. 1979b. Referential and Attributive. *Monist* 62:190-208. Reprinted in Davis 1991.

Segal, Gabriel. 1991. In the mood for a semantic theory. *Proceedings of the Aristotelian Society* 91:103-118.

Sperber, Dan and Deirdre Wilson. 1986. *Relevance: Communication and Cognition*. Cambridge: Harvard University Press.

——. 1987. Précis of *Relevance: Communication and Cognition. Behavioral and Brain Sciences* 10:697-754.

Stainton, Robert J. 1994. Using non-sentences: An application of Relevance Theory. *Pragmatics and Cognition* 2:269-284.

——. 1995. Non-Sentential Assertions and Semantic Ellipsis. *Linguistics and Philosophy* 18:281-296.

——. In Press. What Assertion Is Not. *Philosophical Studies*.

Stalnaker, Robert. 1972. Pragmatics. In *Semantics of Natural Language*, edited by G. Harman and D. Davidson. Dordrecht: D. Reidel. Reprinted in Martinich 1990.

——. 1976. Propositions. In *Issues in the Philosophy of Language*, edited by A.F. McKay and D.D. Merrill. New Haven: Yale University Press. Reprinted in Garfield and Kiteley 1991.

——. 1984. *Inquiry*. Cambridge: The MIT Press.

——. Forthcoming. Reference and Necessity. In *Companion to the Philosophy of Language*, edited by C. Wright and R. Hale. Oxford: Blackwell.

Sterelny, Kim. 1990. *The Representational Theory of Mind*. Oxford: Blackwell.

Stevenson, Charles L. 1944. *Ethics and Language*. New Haven: Yale University Press.

Stich, Stephen P. 1972. Grammar, Psychology, and Indeterminacy. *Journal of Philosophy* 79:799-818.

——. ed. 1975. *Innate Ideas*. Berkeley: University of California Press.

——. 1983. *From Folk Psychology to Cognitive Science: The Case Against Belief*. Cambridge: The MIT Press.

Stich, Stephen P. and Ted A. Warfield. eds. 1994. *Mental Representation: A Reader*. Oxford: Blackwell.

Strawson, Peter F. 1950. On Referring. *Mind* 59:320-344. Reprinted in Martinich 1990.

——. 1954. Review of *Philosophical Investigations*. *Mind* 63:70-99.

——. 1964. Intention and Convention in Speech Acts. *The Philosophical Review* 73:439-460.
Tarski, Alfred. 1944. The Semantic Conception of Truth and the Foundations of Semantics. *Philosophy and Phenomenological Research* 4:341-375. Reprinted in Garfield and Kiteley 1991.

Tienson, John L. 1988. Introduction to Connectionism. *Southern Journal of Philosophy* 26 (Supplement):1-16. Reprinted in Garfield 1990.

Vendler, Zeno. 1972. *Res Cogitans*. Ithaca: Cornell University Press. Reprinted in part in Martinich 1990 as "On Saying Something" and "Thoughts".

Weisler, Steven. 1991. An Overview of Montague Semantics. In *Meaning and Truth: The Essential Readings in Modern Semantics*, edited by Jay Garfield and Murray Kiteley. New York: Paragon.

Wettstein, Howard K. 1984. How to Bridge the Gap Between Meaning and Reference. *Synthese* 58:63-84. Reprinted in Davis 1991.

Whorf, Benjamin Lee. 1956. *Language, Thought and Reality*. Edited by J.B. Carroll. Cambridge: The MIT Press.

Wittgenstein, Ludwig. 1922. *Tractatus Logico-Philosophicus*. Translated by C.K. Ogden. London: Routledge & Kegan Paul.

——. 1953. *Philosophical Investigations*. Translated by G.E.M. Anscombe. Oxford: Basil Blackwell.

——. 1958. *The Blue and Brown Books*. Oxford: Basil Blackwell.

——. 1974. *Philosophical Grammar*. Oxford: Basil Blackwell.

Yanofsky, Nancy. 1978. NP utterances. *Chicago Linguistics Society: Papers from the Regional Meeting* 14:491-502.

Ziff, Paul. 1967. On H.P. Grice's Account of Meaning. *Analysis* 28:1-8.

Index

function, propositional, SEE
    PROPOSITIONAL FUNCTION

Gaurisanker, 162-163
gavagai, 143-144, 164
Geach, Peter, 87
Gedanke, 207
generate, 16, 20, 23, 63, 91, 136
German soldier, 184
Gibson, Roger, 146
GOFAI, 120, 122, 125
'golden mountain, the', 57
'goose'/'geese', 201
gorilla, 176
graceful degredation, 122
'grass is green', 38-39
Grice, H. Paul, 100, 103-104, 106-
    112, 118, 127, 167-169, 181, 191,
    196
grunge, 3

Hacker, Peter, 194
Hacking, Ian, 9
Haegeman, Liliane, 28
hairs, 101
Halliday, M. A. K., 9
Hamblin, Charles, 96
handkerchief, 107-108
Harman, Gilbert, 9, 115
Harnish, M., 166
Harris, Randy Allen, 16
'__ has nine letters', 68-69
Haugeland, John, 120, 122
Hernández Iglesias, Manuel, 96
Hesperus, 66
Higginbotham, James, 96
Hintikka, Jaakko, 96
Hobbes, Thomas, 211
holism, 213
hopefully, 24
Hume, David, 100, 102, 109, 112,
    127, 134, 196

I-language, 20-23

'I met a man', 47-48, 55-58
Idea Theory of Meaning, 30, 99-103,
    106, 108, 111-112, 117-119, 126,
    149, 151, 153, 196
illocutionary force, 189, 194
imperative, 92-93, 95
implicature, 167-170, 180-181, 199
impressions, 100-101
"incorrect speech", 24-27
Ind, 37
Ind. Con, 67-68
indefinite descriptions, 47-48, 50-51,
    58
indeterminacy, 146, 160, 166
indexicals, 151, 153, 159, 166, 171,
    189, 198
indirect discourse, 69-72
indirect reference, 71-72, 74, 77, SEE
    ALSO MEDIATED REFERENCE
individual concept, 67-68, 71, 74,
    196
innateness, 18, 133-139, 146
instrumentalism in psychology, 128-
    129, 131
intension, 80-82, 87-88, 91, 100
intensional, 20, 23
intention theorists, 189-190
intentional causation, 116
intentional realism, 211
Intentional Stance, 120, 127-132
intentional states, 100, 108-109, 111-
    113, 118, 127, 158, 189-191
interrogative, 17, 92-96, 156
Inuit words for snow, 4, 201
'Is the door open?', 92
'It's a truth of arithmetic that __', 73

Jackendoff, Ray, 28
Joan (the purple hat), 191
'Jones is an athlete', 106-107
'Juliet is the sun', 174-177
Julius Caesar, 33

Kaplan, David, 60-61, 88, 166, 194